WINNING THE WAR WITH YOUR FLESH!

HEALING FOR MEN BATTLING
SELF-DESTRUCTIVE SEXUAL PATTERNS

EVERETT T. ROBINSON,
A BROTHER IN RECOVERY

outskirtspress

DENVER, COLORADO

Acknowledgements

I wish to thank publicly the many people who supported my writing this book. I am very grateful for the assistance I have received from each one of the following brothers and sisters in the Lord:

To Denise, my wife and the love of my life, who was the first one to read each Lesson, giving me honest feedback on clarity and, of course, my spelling.

I want to give many thanks to Ray Baribeau for your timeless energy in proof reading the first several drafts and giving great directional tips that were gratefully implemented.

I am also really blessed to have a daughter-in-law who paints and draws so well. Thanks Pam for doing the illustrations in the book, may God bless you for your kindness. Love you girl

Many thanks, blessings and prayers for: Anne, Bob, Greg, Ray, Rich, Bill ,Dave, Joshua, Lenny, Milton, David, Joel, Zac, Joe, Dieterik, Mark, Lance and Pastor Dave; all of whom were kind enough to write testimonies about the value of the recovery information being presented.

I am especially grateful for Dave Z., Josh S. and Rex R. for their personal support and prayer time with me during the development of this book. And thanks to Rich B. for his persistence and encouragement for me to write this book so he can go "help" his home state of Tennessee.

I am grateful to Pastor Melonie and Christ the King Community Church in Bellingham, WA. for their support in providing valuable resources for the Stand Firm class mentioned within.

My deep appreciation goes out to Pastor Derek for his encouragement and suggestions. His insights and conversations are, as always, uplifting.

I also would like to thank Pastor Grant for his "Stand Firm" preaching every week which greatly influenced my moving ahead with this book.

And all my gratitude and prayers for Raul and all the men in Band of Brothers for Christ located in Bellingham, WA. May the Lord Jesus always bless you.

I am also very thankful for Sara, Jennifer and all the other workers at Outskirts Press for their support, advice and energy in publishing this book.

Lastly, and most importantly, I am deeply and eternally grateful to Jesus Christ who made this all possible; without HIS loving sacrifice and constant intercession I'd still be outside in the dark whistling in the middle of the hurricane.

Famed cancer patient and bicyclist Lance Armstrong has been known to say, "I'm not a victim. I'm a survivor." I have great respect for people who have gone through the worst of what life can throw at a person, and simply survive. I have even greater admiration for those who can turn around and help others make it, with the wisdom they've gleaned. Everett Robinson is one of these rare individuals, a survivor and a survivalist of sexual addiction.

You hold in your hand a manual that charts a course away from sexual temptation, flirtation, titillation, obsession and destruction. It puts feet to the Lord's Prayer: "Lead us not into temptation, but deliver us from evil." May you be delivered to a life of sexual wholeness and health.

God bless you,

Dave Browning
Senior Pastor, Christ the King Community Church, International
Author of: *Deliberate Simplicity, Hybrid Church* and *What Leaders Do*

As I was starting to write this book I prayed and asked God,

"So what if only one man surrenders his life to worship and serve you after reading this book?"

The Lord replied, "One is enough!" I then prayed that you will be that man.

Jesus said in Luke 15:10

"In the same way, I tell you, there is rejoicing in the presence of the angels of God over one sinner who repents."

Foreword

My recovery journey started back in 1990. It was raining heavily as I was sitting in my car thinking of taking my life. I was in a deserted parking lot and was overwhelmed with guilt from the bad choices I had made. I had committed adultery not once but many times during the previous year and worst of all, I knew I would do it again if given the opportunity. I was out of control and destroying everything I loved.

I knew I loved my wife, I knew I loved my kids, and I knew I loved Jesus yet I still could not regain control of my compulsive acting out. I felt defeated, disconnected and disgusted with myself. I had lost all self-respect. As I sat in the car crying I told God I deserved to die and asked him what I should do…he said one thing, "The Truth will set you free."

I was shocked; no one knew what I had done. I was scared to tell my wife because she would leave and take the kids. I was afraid I would lose my job. I was even afraid of hurting the ones I was cheating with who did not want me to stop. I was dominated with fear yet when I cried out I heard "The Truth will set you free" and I felt very calm.

I asked God to go before me and I went home and told my wife. It was one of the toughest things I have ever done. As you can imagined it crushed her and we had several days of deep pain and confrontation. Then God told me to go and tell my Pastor. He listened very kindly, told me I was to stay in the church but he would have to discipline me (which he did) but he also told me something that amazed me. He said, "I have dealt with many men in our church cheating on their wives but you are the first one who ever came to me and confessed before they were caught." He told me God would have mercy on me for being honest.

During this event in my life my recovery began, I would like to say it all was great from then on but I relapsed several times and my addiction moved into new areas I never dreamed it would. God revealed to me that I was in a war for my soul and that there were deep weeds in the garden of my personality that needed to be pulled. Over the next ten years I went on an emotional roller coaster, spiritually up and then back down again. Yet God was faithful, he never gave up on me, my recovery became my purpose.

God had me go through many different experiences that led me back to sobriety, back to His side where I would be safe. The lessons you will find in this book all come from my inner healing. God said to me "Feed my sheep" so I wrote down everything he gave me to share with men who were starving for freedom from what was killing them. I truly hope you are hungry.

Contents

Introduction:
Men Desperately Dying in Darkness

The Light of Scripture: Romans 13:11-14

And do this, understanding the present time. The hour has come for you to wake up from your slumber, because our salvation is nearer now than when we first believed.

The night is nearly over; the day is almost here. So let us put aside the deeds of darkness and put on the armor of light.

Let us behave decently, as in the daytime, not in orgies and drunkenness, not in sexual immorality and debauchery, not in dissension and jealousy.

Rather, clothe yourselves with the Lord Jesus Christ, and do not think about how to gratify the desires of the sinful nature.

The Problem: **Providing help to men who are being destroyed by evil**

The Solution: **Write a book that will provide them with hope for their situation and healing for their problem.**

The Procedure: **Pray for wisdom, Pray for love, Pray for courage**

My Prayer

Dear Father in Heaven, I am so overwhelmed by this assignment. I feel inadequate to write a book that will be life-giving to many who desperately need it. Come Holy Spirit and write this book so I do not miss anything that needs to be written or write anything that does not need to be read. If this book is to reach men in the deepest part of their personalities…their souls…you must increase and I must decrease.

Dear reader, did you know that…

A world famous Golfer
A Candidate for Vice Presidency of the United States
A U.S. Senator
A Governor of one of the most powerful states in America
A Movie Star
An Elementary School Teacher
A High School Principal
A Rock and Roll Star
A President of the United States of America
A Political Leader of Italy
A Bishop in a Worldwide Religion
A Pastor of a very large Church
A Pastor of a very small Church
A Police Officer
A High School Teacher
A famous Anchor for a top News Station
A Public Defender
A Judge
A Pro Football Player
A Pro Basketball Player
A Father of Two
And the author of this book

Plus millions of men like them around the world were all taken prisoner by self-destructive behavior patterns often called sexual addiction (SA). We were caught acting out inappropriately, publicly disgraced, identified as being untrustworthy, and then rejected by family, friends and self? If you don't know about sexual addiction you have been asleep in a world of darkness; a world that intends to destroy as many people as it can. We are in a War and must battle in the trenches…but where are the trenches and how can you do battle and win this War? This workbook has been created to answer your questions.

Time to wake up!

Many of these famous individuals and millions of others never recovered because they would not put in the time it takes to get healed. Recovery is hard work that takes all of one's effort. Recovery must become a top priority if you are to obtain a changed lifestyle. But time and work will not bring healing and freedom if you also do not have POWER to overcome that which "owns" you. As you surrender your struggle to God he will provide you with this power.

This book contains information for all those who desperately need freedom from the emotional bondage that is chaining them to sexual acts which are compulsive, embarrassing, humiliating and life threatening. While this book focuses primarily on sexual addiction the root causes of self-destruction are the same regardless of what you are addicted to. So if SA is not your struggle but alcohol, drugs, eating, gambling, shopping or something else is…keep on reading. Just like Bill B. you too can find answers and power from the truth within this book if you apply it to your life like he did. In doing so he escaped the prison inside of him that led him to write the following:

Wasted Time

Written by Bill B. and sent to Everett during the first year of a five-year prison sentence.

The time that I've wasted is my biggest regret
Spent in these places I'll never forget,
Sitting, thinking of things that I've done
The crying, the laughing, the hurt and the fun.

Now it's just me; the shame and the guilt
Behind a wall of emptiness I alone have built,
I'm trapped in my body, just wanting to run
Back to my youth with its laughter and fun.

The chase is over, there's no place to hide
Everything is gone, including the pride,
With reality staring me right in the face
I'm scared, alone, and stuck in this place

Memories of the past flash through my head
The pain is obvious by the tears that I shed,
I ask myself, "Why…where did I go wrong?"
I guess I was weak when I should have been strong.

Life in the fast lane, on seeds I have sown
My feelings were lost, afraid to be shown,
As I look at my past it's so easy to see
The fear that I had; afraid to be me.

Now I wait for the day I'll get a new start
And the dreams I still hold in my heart,
I know I can make it, at least I must try
Cause I've so much to live for and I don't want to die.

An open apology to women

I would like to state here my admission of guilt and a request for forgiveness from all the women whom I wronged when I was acting out. I have made personal amends with many of you but for those whom I have not spoken with (and may never meet or hear from again) I am sincerely sorry for the pain I caused you.

There are no excuses for my bad choices. I can never make up for the damage I have done. I can and I will (as a sign of my remorse) move forward in helping other men learn how to not mistreat (use, abuse, victimize) women. Writing this book will never be enough to make up for the wrongs I committed against you, but if you can accept my apology I am sure it will help you with your inner healing. I pray that God will assist you with your pain and your recovery.

This book is written for men (and women)

My ministry and the message in this book are primarily for men but everything that is written in this book pertains to women as well. If you are a wife, mother, sister, daughter, or a friend of a man who needs to read this book you will find valuable answers to your questions about the addiction they have, why it drives you crazy and how it keeps millions of people in bondage today.

If you are a woman supporting a man who struggles with addiction, then understanding the "roots" of behavior patterns will help you become more effective. Many well-meaning women often unintentionally push their men deeper into addiction due to their lack of understanding of what the driving forces are behind it. I guarantee your perceptions will change because of what God will share with you. Here is a testimony from a Sister in the Lord who reviewed a rough draft of the book:

> *Recovery by definition means returning to a normal state of health, mind and strength. To me it means that and so much more. After four years of sharing, crying and rejoicing in the healing that recovery classes bring I can now confidently say out loud that "I Matter" and that I like who I am becoming.*

I am inspired by those, like my friend and teacher Everett, who reached out and helped me on my journey when I felt I was going through everything alone. I learned so much by reviewing the manuscript for this book. I only wished I had read it when I was younger then I would not have been so hard on myself and others.

I am blessed and encouraged by the tremendous support of those who heard my stories and understood. I am excited to move forward and celebrate my life knowing that God and recovery has saved it. Anne S.

And if you are struggling with sexual addiction (or any other addiction) you too can have freedom from that which abuses you every day. Just read and complete the activities. Jesus has more healing for you than you have pain. He has more love than you have hurt. And he will give you hope in place of your despair.

The Light of Scripture

While this is a book on recovery from sexual addiction (any addiction) it is also a discipleship program. Many men have made commitments over and over again to God only to find that they very quickly slide back into sexual acting out when faced with temptation. This is called "relapsing". Let me be very clear that while there are "No Excuses" for self-destructive behavior, there are many reasons why it occurs. One of the key reasons is a lack of understanding of just how important God's Word is in your recovery. I believe it is impossible to fully recover without accepting God's truths found in his Word. Therefore, it is with great honor for me to use God's Word, his Holy Scriptures, to bring Light to a dark problem.

I prayed that God would provide the verses and the places in the book he wanted me to use them. I am very well aware that I have left out many scriptures that are just as relevant as the ones I did use. All of God's Word is perfect and you need to read all of it to receive its full benefit. And I did not leave anything out due to any scripture (prophecy) being more important than another, for God says in:

2 Peter 1:19-21
"And we have the word of the prophets made more certain, and you will do well to pay attention to it, as to a light shining in a dark place, until the day dawns and the morning star rises in your hearts. Above all, you must understand that no prophecy of Scripture came about by the prophet's own interpretation. For prophecy never had its origin in the will of man, but men spoke from God as they were carried along by the Holy Spirit."

So at the beginning of each Section and Lesson of this book you will find what I call "The Light of Scripture". To solve dark problems that are fed by a world full of darkness you must have Spiritual Light to show you God's Truth. It is only by God's truth and light that you will find your way back home.

Psalm 119:105
"Your word is a lamp to my feet and a light for my path."

The Problem, Solution and Procedure

Each Lesson provides a very brief summary of the problem, solution and procedure being discussed in that Lesson. The problem is clarifying what is keeping you from succeeding in recovery. It targets a "road block" stopping you from moving forward in your journey towards health. The solution is the action you must take to remove the blockage that is keeping you stuck in your acting out. And lastly, but most importantly, the procedure is what you need to actually do to make sure the solution works. These three key elements are placed at the beginning of each Lesson to give you a "heads up" as to what is in that particular Lesson. Just reading them without the information provided in the Lesson will not do you much good so please see them as a beginning point rather than an end.

My prayer

Each Lesson will also begin with a section called, "My Prayer". I put my prayers in each Lesson because it clearly demonstrates that I am in need of God's forgiveness, love and power just like you. I am a recovering addict who is on a spiritual journey and am neither better nor worse than you are. I just happen to be a short ways down the road of recovery ahead of you. I'm privileged and honored to help you if you want freedom from sexual addiction, but it only happens when you do the hard work it will require. No one else can do it for you.

God saved me and cleaned me up for a purpose. And that purpose is to help others who are struggling with addictive lifestyles. I am totally committed to any person who wants freedom in Christ. Why he chose me, I am not sure but I am so indebted to God and so grateful for his mercy and grace that I have accepted the challenge. To do this He has given me the gift of teaching. But to undertake such an important mission I must pray as I write.

Recovery truths – What do you believe?

Other important parts in each Lesson are the recovery concepts that I have identified as, "Recovery Truths". Each truth is a summary statement of something you need to remember if your recovery is to be successful. Each statement provides you with a very specific focus on something you need to understand, accept and apply while working on your "stuff". Consider them "stepping stones" that take you through the Lesson and the book.

At the end of each RT you will be given two choices; <u>I Agree</u> or <u>I Disagree</u>. Obviously the "I agree" choice means you agree with the statement and the "I Disagree" means you don't think it is true in your life. These choices challenge you to not just passively read but to actively personalize the information as you move through the book. They are there to force you to ask yourself two important questions, "What do I believe?" and "Are my beliefs helping or hindering my recovery?"

But men don't learn by reading!

I don't know how many times I have been told that men won't read anything that is too complicated; that men cannot understand deep concepts. I also get the statement that "men hate being "preached to" by adding bible verses" to any message. And I have heard many times that "Dumbing it down" is the only way to go, which goes right along with the "Keep it simple stupid! (KISS)" formula for teaching. In summary, if it isn't drawn on Man Cave walls in crayon men just won't get it. While all of this is true of men who do not want to recover, I have found it totally false for those who seek freedom and healing. Thank goodness we don't use this same line of reasoning sharing God's Word.

I completely reject this view of men not being able to learn. Most of these comments come from people who have had very negative experiences with critical parents and teachers in school. They see knowledge as someone trying to control them to do something they do not want to do. And they project their negative feelings and experiences onto all men assuming that they too do not want to learn. Providing men with these kinds of excuses will not help them turn their lives around.

One of the things I have found in my recovery work is that most men are starved for information that is useful in reducing their failure and pain. They are tired of reading and hearing things that don't help them get past their hurt and moral breakdowns. But when they do hear something or see something that does tell them how to move beyond their suffering and sobriety struggle, they become very interested. Finding something, anything that will help them find freedom, is often very shocking to them as many of them have lost hope throughout the years.

It is also my experience that every man who does his recovery work daily gets healed while those who don't, stay the same, which means they are getting worst. Those men who want to change, "eat the information up" and ask for more while those who really want to keep on sliding into darkness throw it away or make fun of it. Recovery and addiction are both about making choices, some of those choices will heal us and some will kill us. Thank God, Jesus did not hesitate to teach the truth regardless of what men wanted.

In the end, your recovery will have very little to do with what you think and want; all the information in this book is designed to lead you to God's power...which is the only thing that helped me heal. Approach it with an open mind and you may find it is just what you have been looking for. Men who are destroying their lives must learn how to behave differently or they will die. And this kind of learning requires deep healing for deep pain.

Deep pain, Deep digging, Deeper healing

While going through the early stages of my recovery I saw three different Counselors over a period of two years. While all three were Godly, kind men, not one of them knew how to challenge me about my behavior. They all told me that I was "healed" because I had confessed and was forgiven. Unfortunately, I was still a prisoner to my addictive preferences and patterns.

I praise God for them but they did not help me find freedom in Christ. The "poison" within me was still in control and I relapsed many times after because none of them knew how to get to the poison that was controlling my thinking, feelings and behavior. They were too kind and gentle to confront me in the loving way I needed to be confronted. They did not have the knowledge, skills or understanding to realize what they were dealing with. In short, getting deep roots out often requires deep digging and this book equals one big shovel.

I had just finished teaching a recovery class and a man came up to me and said he was frightened by what I had said. He confessed to believing in God but told me God would never be as "mean" as I was when speaking in class. He said he was afraid of coming back to the next class. I smiled at him and said, "Well I am glad something I said hit your dark side…if you were unmoved by the teaching I would have been concerned you may never recover. As for coming back next week, I am not responsible for your healing, that is between you and God…maybe you should ask him what you should do." He was at the next class and many more after that. Of course, he no longer sat in the front row…grin.

The point is still well taken; I do not "sugar-coat" what God has given me to share with you. Many times while you are reading you will feel upset, angry and convicted by what I am writing. My only response to you is Praise God! Ask God to show you which dysfunctional root within your personality did the message just strike. It could very well be the one He is telling you He needs to pull out of you.

Identifying personal preferences and patterns

Like any other important activity in life, you will only get out what you put in. As you read be honest with yourself and God about those things in you that need removing. No one else can do this work for you. Sitting and thinking about it is not recovery…it is "spiritual stubbornness" that will lead to you failing over and over again. As you read, PRAY to God and ask him to open your mind to what He would have you learn in each Lesson.

God will meet you where you are at. Only you (with God's help) can identify what your personal patterns and private preferences are. God will remove them and put better patterns and preferences in their place but you must be willing to put in the "sweat" required to be restored. Most addicts want friends more than they want freedom. They want to be accepted as they are and not challenged to change into whom they were created to be. If that is your mind-set you will not like what you read in this book. I have been called to… as one of my brothers in recovery so beautifully put it… "Lay the wood to you." I want to point out that this brother finished the class and then signed up for it again, so I guess the "wood" didn't hurt him too bad. What are a few splinters among brothers anyway?

In recovery an effective Coach is seldom your friend, and, your friends seldom make good coaches. As a Spiritual Coach my job is to help men who are willing to free themselves from self-destructive thinking and behaving by "teaching, rebuking, correcting and training" them in God's truth. I do not think of myself as a good writer but the truths I will share with you can help you leave behind the pain you live with every day. My main goal in doing these things is to help men strengthen their spirits, while at the same time weaken their flesh. My spiritual orders are found in:

2 Timothy 3:16-17
All Scripture is God-breathed and is useful for teaching, rebuking, correcting and training in righteousness, so that the man of God may be thoroughly equipped for every good work.

All I can do is pray that you will listen to what God is saying to you. If he can save and restore me, He can definitely do the same for you.

Taking your inventory at the end of each Lesson

It is very important that, after reading each Lesson you personalize the information by writing down what you are struggling with; record your thoughts and feelings and objections on paper. It is essential for your healing that you write down what God shows you. By completing your inventory activities you are contracting with yourself to change what is destroying your life.

One of the major problems most addicts struggle with is thinking "I don't need to write it down, I know that already." Let me just say that your thinking is what got you into the trouble you are in and that same thinking will not get you out of it. For the purposes of recovery you must "dump", "drain", "vent", and "expel" the darkness that is in you. In short, "If it is not written down it won't get changed!" When write things out it brings your problems into the Light where you can see them for what they really are. As long as the darkness (addictive thoughts) stays inside of you it will own you, control you, and hurt you and your loved ones again.

The inventory activities have been developed for you to take your recovery journey to another level. Besides providing you with a space to journal your thoughts and feelings about topics in each Lesson, the inventory will also give you an opportunity to write out prayers asking God for help. Looking back on your record of these prayers at a later date will give you new perspectives of how far your recovery has gone. By completing these activities you can get a clearer picture of just what personal issues are causing you pain. They will also bring to light more character flaws that God wants to help you overcome; and it will give you specifics about how your flesh is sabotaging your life.

To succeed you must become a student of recovery; a person who wants to learn how to improve their life. No one who takes a class (any class) and refuses to take notes, read the textbook, participate in the learning activities or even attend the course ever succeeds in that class. Recovery is the most important learning experience you will ever have. Pass and you will receive your life back, fail and you will become sicker than you already are. There is no middle ground.

Testimonies from Brothers in Recovery

At the end of each Lesson in the book I will be adding testimonies (in no particular order) from men who have taken the Stand Firm class so you can "hear" just how important this information was in their finding freedom. These men all started off in recovery angry, scared and confused like many of you, but they decided it was time to start doing things differently than they had been doing.

I asked the men to talk about how the class concepts helped them improve their relationship with God, themselves and their families. As you read their words trust what they are telling you, it may be just the witness you are looking for. They would all tell you, "Jump on in, the Water of Life is fine!"

Here is the first one:

> *What I learned from the information contained in these pages was priceless for my recovery from sexually addictive behaviors. One paragraph can only scratch the surface of what I've learned!*
>
> *I learned what I can do when addictive thoughts, voices, and movies won't stop playing in my mind. Plus how many ways my flesh can sabotage my desire to stop relapsing, causing me to keep repeating my addictive behavior patterns. I learned how boundaries can protect me and others from my impulsive decisions.*
>
> *And I found out how my emotional needs and feelings contributed to my acting out. I also learned what makes and keeps people trapped in toxic relationships, a major cause of relapse for me and so many others.*

Sincerely, Bob C

Section One: Understanding the Problem, Accepting the Solution

Lesson 1 – What is Addiction?

The Light of Scripture: Romans 6:19, 23

I put this in human terms because you are weak in your natural selves. Just as you used to offer the parts of your body in slavery to impurity and to ever-increasing wickedness, so now offer them in slavery to righteousness leading to holiness.

For the wages of sin is death, but the gift of God is eternal life in Christ Jesus our Lord.

⌇

The Problem: **You are not in control of your "acting-in" which leads directly to your "acting-out".**

The Solution: **Learn how to control your biggest enemy before it destroys you.**

The Procedure: **Surrender your pride (fear) so you can learn what you don't know**

My Prayer

Dear Lord Jesus, your word is so clear, as I read it may I never forget it. Help me Father in Heaven to understand my limitations, character flaws and personality weaknesses. Please help me to accept your will for my life. I need you if I am to survive today. I thank you for the power to write about the truths that you will use to help those men who want freedom, healing and life in your Spirit. I thank you for each and every person who reads this book.

WINNING THE WAR WITH YOUR FLESH!

In 1803 a major event occurred that doubled the size of the United States. Thomas Jefferson, the US President bought the Louisiana Purchase from France. It included not only New Orleans and Louisiana but also what now amounts to most of 14 different states. It included 828,000 square miles which equaled just over 530 million acres, all for $ 15 million dollars. That was a steal of a deal as it worked out to be roughly 3 cents per acre.

So what's all that have to do with recovery? Hang on; be patient…I'm getting to it. Prior to the purchase St. Louis was the end of the line for westward expansion in the U.S. With the purchase complete St. Louis now became the starting point for many new adventurers heading west to find new land and wealth. During the next 50 years, large wagons called prairie schooners were built by the thousands and outfitted with food and many other supplies for people to venture out to settle the new territory.

Starting out most of these "settlers" saw the trip west as a big adventure, a grand opportunity to own land and fulfill their dreams of living life the way they wanted to. Leaving St. Louis their schooners were stuffed with all their valuables knowing they would not be coming back and that there would be few, if any, luxuries where they were going. They soon realized their mistake.

Traveling 20 miles a day the wagon trains moved slowly west; it was not a quick journey. It didn't take long to realize that many of their big items were too heavy for them to carry across the rough terrain. When wagons broke down there were no quick fixes, everything took time and involved very hard work and sacrifice. These early pioneers had to throw out many of the items that just weeks before were considered to be so essential to the journey.

Recovery is exactly the same process. It is a long journey that often requires great sacrifices from you. Many of your character flaws and habitual ways of thinking and behaving have great value to you now. They are all you have ever known and you do not want to "leave them behind". But it is exactly these parts of your personality that God wants to strip away; to get you to let go of them so He has made the recovery journey a "tough" one. Praise God!

Recovery Truth # 1   **I Agree _____ I Disagree _____**
You can't make the Journey of Recovery by yourself; you need help from others so pride and isolation are your first obstacles to overcome and leave behind.

"Breakdowns" for the pioneers actually became blessings from God because not only did it make them dump things that were not necessary, but it also forced them to work in "teams". When one wagon broke down the whole wagon train often stopped and everyone helped fix the "problem". Isolation and independence quickly turned into team work and interdependence.

As God stripped away everything that was detrimental to the pioneer's success he also confronted their pride, which told them they could do it alone. Recovery never works when you isolate, you need others who are going in the same direction as you are, to keep your recovery wagon moving forward. Recovery works the same way; you cannot do it alone, you must "team up" with other brothers who are traveling on the same journey. When you do you will find some of the most important ingredients you will need for your recovery; and that is co-operation, friendship and loyalty.

In fact, early in the journey, the people who learned to work together for the good of the group developed the strongest wagon trains or "communities". This molding together of work groups through hard work and challenges actually toughened them up for the real threats that lay ahead. Once they were past the point of no return obedience became mandatory, those who disobeyed were either punished or removed from the wagon train. "Self-Discipline" became the real vehicle that got them where they were going.

As the pioneers moved deeper into the new territory they had to face many life-ending threats. To stay alive they needed fresh water, food, shelter from violent storms; and most importantly, protection from enemies that would kill them. Attacks from hostiles were always a concern, but these came not only from the Native Americans whose land they were passing through but also from bands of outlaws and thieves who preyed on the settlers. Violent acts of nature also plagued them such as extreme thunder and lightning storms, swarms of locusts, heavy flooding, and snow and dust storms. The challenges were great and the personal price high. Many pioneers died. Not all who started the journey lived to tell the tale.

And so it is with recovery. Many men who start their journey never make it. I can think of several men I have worked with who are now back in prison, divorced and/or separated from their families, lost their jobs and careers, and who actually died from their choice to "go on alone" without help from others. Like many of the wagons going west, they got stuck in the "mud" and didn't have the "skills" to get out on their own.

They did not want to give up their most prize processions: their will, pride, fear, self-centeredness, lust, anger, need for revenge and plain old stubbornness. Hanging on to these "valuables" kept many pioneers from finding freedom, from finding a new life. Recovery is a war for your Soul and when you are in such a war there are only survivors and fatalities. Which one will you choose to be?

Recovery Truth # 2   I Agree _____ I Disagree _____
You are in a WAR for your physical health, worldly freedom, spiritual life and everything related to them!

So what is Addiction?

Addiction equals slavery: you are being controlled by something or someone who makes you do what you do not want to do and then punishes you for doing it by making you do it all over again. Addiction is like a "Pimp" you cannot escape and must work for every day. This Pimp is a cruel master that you must serve whenever he calls you. Your behavior under addiction's control is like a freight train that is taking you straight to destruction.

Make no mistake about it: Addiction "cripples, steals and destroys" everything you love and hold valuable and then it kills you. Many people lose jobs, relationships with loved ones, houses, cars, friends and their health due to patterns of self-destructive thinking, feeling and behavior. Let me say it very clearly in a different way, addiction is very expensive…it will spend all your time, your energy and your money destroying you.

Recovery Truth #3   **I Agree _____ I Disagree _____**
Acting In Leads to Acting Out.

This truth simply means that every time we act outwardly in the environment there is a corresponding action within us that drives us to behave that way. For example, before I go downstairs to get the apple that is in the refrigerator I must feel hungry enough and like apples enough to spend the amount of energy it takes to go get it. Addiction is no different; "Acting In" is the "hunger and preference to want it bad enough" (motivation if you will) while "Acting Out" is the "going and getting it".

Addiction is a series of self-destructive behaviors called "habitual patterns" that we repeat over and over again to acquire something that is destroying our lives. For instance, "mental masturbation' is the fantasying you do before you decide to sexually touch yourself while masturbation is the actual act itself. Here are some other examples for those who are sexually addicted:

"Acting In" would include compulsive thinking/feeling patterns such as:

- Lusting with your eyes (undressing women and/or men; children)
- Fantasizing sexually about women and/or men (mental masturbation)
- Visualizing about someone else while you are having sex with your spouse
- Planning, rehearsing deviant (immoral) sexual activities in your mind
- Plotting/Gathering information for sexual deviant encounters with others
- Feeling acceptance and approval while fantasizing sexual images
- Feeling like "I have earned the right", "I deserve this" before acting out
- Calculating how you will get the money needed for such activities
- Rationalizing (lying to self) all such behavior as normal and therefore, OK
- Remembering encounters, replaying sexual experiences in your mind

"Acting Out" would include compulsive behavior patterns such as:

- Flirting, seducing, baiting women/men into sexual conversations and actions
- Fornication/Prostitution/Adultery/Affairs with women and/or men
- Touching children inappropriately for sexual satisfaction
- Visiting married women when you know their husbands are gone

- Viewing Pornography on the internet, TV (soft porn)
- Watching adult (xxx) movies
- Reading adult books and magazines (soft porn)
- Phone sex/Sexually explicit video cam transmissions/Internet sex talks
- Saying/writing sexually explicit things to get attention
- Visiting/participating adult chat rooms
- Going to erotic massage parlors
- Masturbation in private and in public
- Letting yourself be touched sexually against your will
- Cruising in your car looking for opportunities, victims
- Peeping, looking in windows to see others undress, having sexual contact
- Speaking inappropriate sexual terms/stories/jokes around women
- Offering money for sexual "favors" or services
- Over riding a woman's will to sexually do what you want to do; rape, sexual assault

Recovery Truth #4   **I Agree ____ I Disagree ____**
You Will Reap What You Sow.

One of the most sobering experiences I had while in community college happened when I played on one of the college's basketball teams. On that team there was a young man who was as good a ball player as I was bad. He was very likable and easy going.

One weekend, while at a party where he was drinking, he was asked to go pick someone up. He left the party and driving through a neighborhood nearby he ran over a child riding his bike. He left the scene of the accident because he was scared but was found and arrested. He ended up going to prison for vehicular manslaughter.

All his education, friendships and hope for the future stopped immediately… what he thought would never happen to him happened. Even worse than all the time he lost in prison, was the guilt he will suffer for the rest of his life with the death of the child. He was a good man, kind and fun to be around. He was very well liked…but in an instant his life changed due to his choice to drink and drive.

All addicts understand there are severe consequences to acting out the way they do, they just think those consequences "will not happen to them". Drinkers all know many other alcoholics before them who suffered greatly for their obsessive drinking. Drug users understand the same thing…many others have overdosed but still think "that will not happen to me". Sexual addicts often say to others, "I'm not hurting anyone," or "it's my personal life so stay out of it."

One of the most powerful lies found inside an addict's heads is, "It will never happen to me." Once they believe this blinding lie they jump into addiction, always believing they can get out anytime they chose to, without any serious damage being done. Nothing is further from the truth…listen to what God's word tells us:

> **Galatians 6:7-8**
> *"Do not be deceived: God cannot be mocked. A man reaps what he sows. The one who sows to please his sinful nature, from that nature will reap destruction; the one who sows to please the Spirit, from the Spirit will reap eternal life."*

But I Don't Need God, I have Science and Band-Aids for all my "wounds"!

Many men I have worked with have fallen back on this misconception as a means of avoiding God's truth about sin and its consequences. To illustrate how inept man's wisdom can be in trying to "fix" sexual mistakes, read the following excerpt from a recent article. It clearly illustrates how mankind actually compounds the problem when they avoid the moral conversation and only stick to the science end of things.

"Gonorrhea Superbug: Scientists Find Strain Resistant to All Antibiotics

Researchers have discovered a strain of gonorrhea that is resistant to all antibiotics currently available to treat it. This new strain can transform a common and once easily treatable infection into a global threat to public health; the researchers said."

> "Gonorrhea is caused by the bacterium *Neisseria gonorrhea*, and is spread through sexual activity. It is one of the most common sexually transmitted diseases in the world. In the United States alone, there are an estimated 700,000 cases annually, according to the Centers for Disease Control and Prevention (CDC)." www.myhealthnewsdaily.com.

I am sure that all 700,000 G-victims in the U. S. thought "it will never happen to me" while they were acting-out. And this is only one consequence, there are many, many more as you will see listed below:

The cost of sexual addiction is overwhelming, consider the following:

Typical Consequences of Sexual Acting Out

- Abortion (51 million U.S. citizens killed since 1972)
- Widespread Sexually Transmitted Diseases (STD's)
- Death and extreme loss of health from STD's
- Physical harm, getting punched out/shot by wife, husband, or boyfriend
- Prison time where anything might happen
- Loss of respect, trust and safety from family and friends
- Loss of marriage, kids, friends and jobs
- Loss of self-respect and extreme guilt and stress from deep shame
- Loss of time and money you will never get back
- Increased fear of what is going to happen to you during the rest of your life
- Acceleration of your addiction taking you deeper into slavery

Recovery Truth #5   **I Agree _____ I Disagree _____**
Sexual Addiction is actually a World Wide War waged on individuals, family members, communities, and nations.

Here are a few facts that you may not know (Google "sexual addiction statistics" for many more)

1. Sex is the # 1 topic search on the Internet.
2. There are over 240 million pornographic pages online.
3. 42.7% of Internet users view pornography.
4. Every second - 28,258 internet users are viewing pornography.
5. Every 39 minutes: a new pornographic video is being created in the United States.
6. 2006 Worldwide Porn Revenues equaled $ 97.06 Billion.
   (That is more than Microsoft, Google, Amazon, EBay, Yahoo!, Apple, and EarthLink's revenues combined) and that was six years ago, what is it now?

Source: http://internet-filter-review.toptenreviews.com/internet-pornography-statistics.html

Additional world-wide statistics are:

- 43% of all internet users view pornographic material
- 35% of all internet downloads are pornographic
- "sex" and "porn" are among the top 5 search terms for kids under 18
- San Fernando Valley, Ca. produces 90% of all pornographic films and releases 20,000 adult movies per year.
- The highest rated countries in the world based on porn revenues are: China (28%), South Korea (27%) Japan (21%), the US (14%) and Australia (5%).

Source: http://www.zamaanonline.com/internet-pornography-statistics-2258

So how goes the "War" within the Church?

A book I highly recommend is <u>40 Days of Purity</u> by Pastor Jason Hubbard. On page 4 of his un-published book he quotes the following statistics:

- Pornography is the fastest growing addiction among men in America. The pornography industry grossed double that of all purchased music downloads.
- Porn sales have made more money than professional basketball, football, and baseball combined. Pornography is now America's favorite pastime.
- 51% of pastors say that looking at pornography on the Internet is their biggest temptation.
- 34% of church-going women say they intentionally go to pornography web sites.
- 70% of women involved in pornography are survivors of child abuse and incest.
- 12-17 year-olds are the largest viewers of Internet pornography in America.
- 1 out of 6 boys and 1 out of 3 girls have been molested before they turn 18.
- Nine out of every ten kids, ages 8-16, have viewed porn online.
- 3000 soft-porn images appear on MTV every week.
- 50% of born again Christians think it is ok to have premarital sex if you are in a committed relationship
- Over 100,000 websites offer illegal child pornography
- Every day 8,000 people in America contract a sexually transmitted disease.
- Pornography video rentals increase in hotels more than any other time when a Christian conference comes to town.

Another Christian source (and there are many to choose from) states:

- 7-10 lay leaders visit adult web sites once a week.
- 4 out of 10 Pastors do the same.
- 50% of Christian men are addicted to Porn.
- Chuck Swindoll calls Sexual Addiction "the number one problem in your church."
- Focus on the Family receives 10,000 calls, emails, and letters every day; the request for help with SA is the number one request they receive.
- Oprah has referred to SA as "American's #1 Addiction".

Source: http://www.freedombeginshere.org/?page=the-porn-crisis

I was discussing porn statistics with a Christian brother who said, "Statistics are only important to the person who makes them up." My reply to him was, "And to all the family members of someone who ends up becoming one!" If you take action by getting help you don't have to become another "statistic". Unless, of course, you like that old Egyptian river…Denial; then you will just have to learn about statistics the "hard way".

Sexual addiction is a world-wide plague; recent news revealed that extensive pornography was even found at Osama bin Laden's house. Explicit, hard-core videos were collected by the navy seals as they searched the house for "Intel". The article also stated that it was not unusual to find pornography in the possession of al-Qaida operatives. My point in adding this information is simply that all humans (such as those listed at the beginning of the introduction), regardless of belief, are capable of being poisoned by this addictive material and behavior; and all can die from it as seen from the Aids and other STD epidemics sweeping the world. Sexual addiction, like cancer, does not recognize gender, nationality, personal appearance, social status, or religious affiliation. It simply destroys you.

Even great institutions of higher education, where you would think people would be smart enough to understand the depth of the problem are often heavily infected with pornography. Many students not only watch it non-stop, but also pay for their education by making pornographic websites and movies. As institutions of "higher education" you would think they would also be centers for higher moral standards; but unfortunately, as illustrated by the recent events at Penn State (and many other well respected institutions), this is, sadly, not the case. Insensitivity to the suffering of the victims of sexual abuse is almost always driven by indifference to goodness and decency.

So where is there any hope for you and your situation?

Don't get discouraged by how big the problem is in the world or by the pain you are in, continue reading and you will find the hope you need to do the hard work required in recovery. Hope comes with the mercy that God gives you when you seek him.

Romans 15:4
For everything that was written in the past was written to teach us, so that through endurance and the encouragement of the Scriptures we might have hope.

A Testimony from a Brother in Recovery

Before I became a Christian in recovery, I was simply in recovery. We often talked, during 12 step meetings, about the 12 steps of recovery and the need for a "higher power" and our "selfishness", especially as it applied to relationships with others, which seemed to be a common thread for all of us. After 20 plus years in recovery, 10 of which I was a practicing Christian, I seemed to be at a stop in my recovery and could not progress. I was struggling with new addictions and temptations. Then, after taking a class with Everett, the veil was lifted and things began to come clear. Never, in all my years of recovery work, did anyone ever mention the "inner voice"... that negative, self-critical and criticizing voice that we all hear, but no one talks about.

What a shock and a revelation! All of a sudden I began to have a context for my recovery that made sense as I began to realize that when my inner voice stopped criticizing me, it was because it was criticizing someone else! This terminal uniqueness of having a negative, self-critical inner voice had held up certain critical parts of my recovery!

In my years as a Christian, I have often heard the term "my flesh", but was left to figure out what "my flesh" really was. Because I didn't know what that meant, fighting temptation was a losing battle and I simply felt like I had to accept that; there wasn't really anything I could do about it. It was going to drag me back into the muck and grime that I so wanted to climb out of whether that was what I wanted or not!

Everett showed me that yes, there was a specific place within us that sin dwells, and without knowing where that was, we could not only not fight our addictions, but never aspire to anything greater than that pig that enjoys rolling around in its pen. His concept of actually "plugging in" to a power greater than me gives me hope... I don't have to do it alone, because when we are plugged in... sin just doesn't have the same hold on us as it did. I am grateful that Everett was led and is being used by GOD as he is... it has made a huge difference in my life!

Greg W.

So What Can You Do to Get Healed?

1. Read with an open mind

Please complete the Inventory activities for Lesson 1 before reading Lesson 2.

Lesson 1 - Time to Take Your Inventory

What were you Thinking when you read Lesson 1?

How are you Feeling after reading Lesson 1?

How is what you are Thinking and Feeling now going to help you with your recovery?

What are you going to change in your behavior after reading Lesson 1?

What Bible verses from Lesson 1 are you committed to memorizing?

Lesson 1: Activity 1 – Taking Ownership

The following information can be used for personal goal setting and/or small group sharing if you have such a support group.

A. What are three areas on the sheet where you are currently "acting in" (thinking about doing wrong)?

1.

2.

3.

B. What are three areas where you are currently "acting out" (actually doing wrong)?

1.

2.

3.

C. Do you see any connections between the 3 "acting-in" behaviors and the 3 "acting-out" behaviors? If so, how so?

Lesson 2 –
There Are No Unwounded Christians;
We All Have Fallen Short

The Light of Scripture: Romans 7:15-20

I do not understand what I do. For what I want to do I do not do, but what I hate I do. And if I do what I do not want to do, I agree that the law is good. As it is, it is no longer I myself who does it, but it is sin living in me. I know that nothing good lives in me, that is, in my sinful nature.

For I have the desire to do what is good, but I cannot carry it out. For what I do is not the good that I want to do; no, the evil I do not want to do-this I keep on doing. Now if I do what I do not want to do, it is no longer I who does it, but it is sin living in me that does it.

‿

The Problem: **Lying & keeping secrets will kill you**

The Solution: **Admit the real depth of your problem today**

The Procedure: **Tell the truth to God and selected others you can trust; seek help today.**

My Prayer

Dear Lord Jesus, I praise your name and thank you for setting me free from my addictive thinking and actions. Even now as I serve you I still struggle with my flesh wanting me to sin everyday yet by your spirit I have the strength to seek your help instead. I ask for help today to write this Lesson so that it is clear enough to understand and powerful enough to move my brothers towards you. Thank you for helping me stay sober. What a blessing it is to know you.

Recovery Truth # 6   I Agree _____ I Disagree _____
If you're lying you're dying; living in lies leads to slavery, living in the truth leads to freedom. Choose your path carefully.

> **Proverbs 19:9**
> *A false witness will not go unpunished, and he who pours out lies will not go free.*

When I first confessed, everything in my body told me not to do it. A thousand thoughts came into my mind telling me how bad it would be if I said anything. And my mind also kept telling me that there was a way out without confessing. It told me to keep quiet and that I would be able to figure it all out by myself. But deep down in my spirit God told me otherwise. I actually finally understood I would always be a slave to what was controlling me. And that reality scared me far worse than the consequences of my acting-out did.

Men hate being controlled by anything, yet we give control of our lives up to many things: smoking, drinking, cheating, lying, eating, stealing, judgmentalness and killing to name a few of the more obvious ones. We can only be free when we live by the truth.

No more secrets

In recovery we have an old saying, "You are only as healthy as the number of secrets you have." This of course refers to those things you are doing that you hide from other people, especially your loved ones. The irony of it is that God sees everything you do and knows everything you think, so you really don't have any secrets he doesn't already know about. Thank God for that as it makes it easier to confess and seek his help so we can receive the inner healing that only comes from him. And as you will learn reading further in this book, He then gives us the Grace (power) to do what we cannot do in our own strength.

Recovery Truth # 7   I Agree _____ I Disagree _____
You are only as healthy as the number of secrets (sins) you have in your life.

> **Proverbs 28:13**
> *He who conceals his sins does not prosper, but whoever confesses and renounces them finds mercy.*

It is natural to want to hide your "dark" side. You want to do things in secret so others do not know what you are doing, because it is embarrassing. And often the reason you give for deceiving yourself is a lie itself, it is called rationalization. You tell yourself that "no one will get hurt" if they do not find out. Your wife and kids will not get hurt if they never know; not to mention your parents and brothers and sisters. And your friends, well they are all way better off thinking of you as not having any problems. Yet, in the end, when they do find out, they are hurt far worst because you were dishonest and kept it all a "secret". When someone keeps secrets from us we are the first to scream "foul".

God has mercy on those who seek him and confess theirs sins. Confessing is not just simply telling others what you did but expressing sincere remorse and a commitment to do whatever it takes to stop the negative behavior. Children often say they are "sorry" without really meaning it. Remember, saying, "I'm sorry" is shallow, but saying, "I was wrong when I did _____!" is a real confession. It takes a mature adult to admit why they are wrong and to promise to change for the better. Unfortunately, those who struggle with compulsiveness are more like children than mature adults. A big part of recovery is "growing up".

Recovery Truth # 8   **I Agree _____ I Disagree _____**
Recovery requires admitting our failures, fears and hurts to others you can trust!

>   **1 John 1:9**
>   *If we claim to be without sin, we deceive ourselves and the truth is not in us. If we confess our sins, he is faithful and just and will forgive us our sins and purify us from all unrighteousness.*

One fantasy you probably struggle with, is the idea that you can heal yourself without anyone ever knowing what you are doing. Of course, if you could (and you can't) then no one would ever find out just how awful you really are. This kind of self-delusion only leads you back to doing what God does not want you to do. And you go back easily enough because you believe you can "quit anytime you decide to". Nothing could be further from the truth.

Addiction is like quicksand, once you get in it, your efforts to get out actually force you to go deeper into it. Many addicts start off with good intentions but soon are sinking back into the same spiritual "quicksand" that God just got them out of. As the old saying goes, "The road to hell is paved with good intentions." Without God and other men's help you will only sink deeper into your "quicksand".

The struggles you are facing are timeless. Addictions go back to the beginning of civilization and have been around forever. Many people before you have "crashed and burned" because they thought they could quit without anyone's help. Almost every success story tells you otherwise. For example, the super success of many AA groups points to this fact. You need support from those who have been down the sobriety trail before you and lived to tell about it.

>   **Proverbs 27:17**
>   *As iron sharpens iron, so one man sharpens another.*

A great gift God has given you is "Brothers in the Lord" who understand the trials and tribulations of living apart from God's will. These brothers understand what you are going through because they were once in tough situations like you are. Maybe not exactly the same situation but there is enough common ground (pride, fear, anger, denial, secrets, acting out) that they can support your recovery.

Men are sharpened into iron when they meet in private with other men and confess their compulsive behaviors and personality weaknesses often called "character flaws". Healing begins by telling the truth to each other (confession) and by praying together for God's help. These men understand that they have no solutions for you, but know that God is merciful and able to restore you to health and sanity.

Years ago when I went to my first Christian 12-step group at my Church I was really taken back to find out that I would be in a group with 11 other men. The thought of no women being in the group terrified me. I could not think of a more boring thing to do than spend 2 hours once a week talking with men that I had never seen before. I actually went home and told my wife that I would not go back. Needless to say, after the beating stopped, I went the next week and every one after that.

This first small group of men set the tone for much of my recovery. Within weeks we had formed a bond that was everlasting…they became like brothers, friends and counselors. The key factors in the group working so well were: effective leadership, transparency, trust, respect, common goals and God's Spirit. Let's examine each key factor quickly:

- When small groups are led by men, who have no training in how to run a small group, they stay in conversation and never really "get down to it."
- Transparency is the skill of open yet appropriate self-disclosure. This type of conversation saves time and is the life's blood of the recovery work group.
- Trust is developed by having group guidelines that reinforce the concept, "What is said here stays here."
- Respect provides equal opportunity each week for men to share their "stuff" without advice or 20 questions occurring.
- "Common goals" simply means that everyone is committed not only to their own recovery but also to the recovery of every man that comes and shares.
- And lastly, healing cannot completely occur without prayer that brings God's power, love and a sound mind. Only the Creator can fix what is broken, so that it functions as it was created to do. Restoration is recovery.

Recovery Truth # 9   **I Agree _____ I Disagree _____**
There Are No Unwounded Christians: if you follow Jesus you will suffer, but if you don't follow Jesus, you will suffer more.

Many people believe that when we give our lives to Jesus everything that has been hurting us and all our bad habits will just cease to exist. Praise God it doesn't work that way! Now why in the world would I say that? Well God doesn't make mistakes so if he has decided we are to struggle becoming Christians I am sure, beyond a shadow of a doubt, that it is for our own good.

The main point here is that life is not going to be easy or full of freebees just because God comes into our lives. Every major character in the Bible faced adversity and had to rely on God to get through. Jesus, David, Ruth, Solomon, Moses, Mary, Paul, Peter, John and all the rest of the Saints listed in the Bible all had struggles in life. Tough times that made them want to quit and call it a day but the power of God brought them through when they called upon His name for help.

As Christians we still have to live in the same body, with the same sinful nature, in the same wicked world, being controlled by the same Evil that has been here from the beginning-Satan. So why become a Christian in the first place? Some of the main reasons are: to honor God who deserves all honor and glory; to worship Him, the only one who can and will deliver us from this world; to gain access to spiritual power, that gets us through the pain we feel in this life; and to let God shape you into the person that he created you to be in the first place, before the world morphed you into the addicted personality that you have become.

Recovery Truth # 10   I Agree _____ I Disagree _____
Pulling Weeds in Your Personality Garden is Hard Work…get ready for it

Unfortunately, there are "things" within you that hinder you from fully experiencing the freedom you can have from sexual compulsiveness. These things are "roots to the weeds living in your personality garden". God wants you to allow Him to pull each and every one of them so you can become who he created you to be. Many well intentioned Christians repeatedly fail due to not being spiritually, mentally, emotionally and socially "washed clean" of things that they have done (or had done to them) in their past.

Many people ask for God's forgiveness and walk free for a short period of time but soon the same old patterns of destructive thinking and behavior return with a vengeance. Relapse is very common in recovery, because we only cut off the top of the weed and fail to have God remove its full root. This book was written to help you remove the "roots" within you that are keeping you from finding total freedom in Jesus. It will help you identify what is sabotaging your walk with the Lord.

As one man in my class said, "I have been a Christian for 15 years and no one has ever told me what you are telling me, and it's in all the scriptures I have been reading for years!" God (not me) touched this brother in a new way and helped him to unload tons of inner garbage he had accumulated during his life. I just happened to be the messenger boy.

A Testimony from a Brother in Recovery

I am only one thought away from temptation. I am only one more thought away from relapse.

Temptation lurks everywhere and when I got lazy and sloppy with my time with Jesus one thought led to another and then I was scanning the Internet looking for free porn (I'm cheap). I told myself that it didn't hurt anybody and was only for entertainment and that I've been so busy lately that I deserved a break. Satan is so good at his lies that even though I know better, I had lost my "life line" to Jesus and kaboom, I fell.

All of the material in this book is valid, real and worthwhile. Don't give up on your recovery. I haven't. Only God through His son, Jesus, can heal my addictions and restore me to a clear thinking mind. I pray that we can both be over comers through the strength of faith and prayer.

Ray B.

So What Can You Do to Get Healed?
1. Read with an open mind
2. Complete your inventory honestly

Please complete the Workbook activities for Lesson 2 before reading Lesson 3.

Lesson 2 - Time to Take Your Inventory

What were you Thinking when you read Lesson 2?

How are you Feeling after reading Lesson 2?

How is what you are Thinking and Feeling now going to help you with your recovery?

What are you going to change in your behavior after reading Lesson 2?

What Bible verses from Lesson 2 are you committed to memorizing?

Lesson 2: Activity 1 - So How Enslaved to Sin Are You?

As a Spiritual Coach for men who have "sexual control issues" I find having each one complete a checklist of their acting out behaviors saves lots of time. Waiting for men to come out and just tell me how they are acting out is a slow process. Even if they share part of it the rest of it often stays hidden. By writing things down on paper every man has the opportunity to get a better perspective of just how self-destructive they have become.

This kind of "Spiritual Inventory" is your first step out of denial. When things stay in your head you will minimize them, telling yourself your situation isn't really as bad as it seems. This type of mental dishonesty fools only you, as others already see how dysfunctional you have become. And sooner or later something like getting arrested, going to jail, going to court and maybe even being divorced wakes you up from this delusional dream that keeps telling you "things aren't really as bad as they seem".

Avoiding the truth will always keep you a slave to sin. So completing a checklist not only saves time but also helps you clearly pinpoint exactly where you need to start focusing during recovery. The more time you save in recovery the sooner you can get healed.

Galatians 5:19-21

The acts of the sinful nature are obvious: sexual immorality, impurity and debauchery; idolatry and witchcraft; hatred, discord, jealousy, fits of rage, selfish ambition, dissensions, factions and envy; drunkenness, orgies, and the like. I warn you as I did before, that those who live like this will not inherit the kingdom of God.

The "acting out" behaviors listed in Galatians is just one of several places where God is very specific about which behaviors are unacceptable to him. In each of these Bible locations there are extensive lists of behaviors that lead to eternal damnation, which is separation from God for infinity (the rest of time).

As addicts we hate seeing these kinds of lists because we already think we are "no good" and "worthless" but to actually find out that we are worse off than we thought is more than we can handle. But in all recovery programs, to be healed, you must take an "inventory" of some kind. The good news is that you don't have to do this one alone because God and "SAM" are here to help you. Please complete the following inventory activity; there is good news at the end.

The Sexual Addiction Mirror (SAM)

All Addicts hate looking in any "mirror" that will reflect back the reality of who is standing before it. When we see our self up-close we often feel more shame and self-hatred. One of our strongest survival skills is denial, refusing to accept the truth about our actions and relationships. Avoiding all self-reflection books, programs or encounters is like avoiding the "Mirror".

Avoiding your reflection makes perfect sense in the twisted thinking world of an addict. But by not examining yourself closely you fail to see the many personality flaws that need healing. This often occurs because you don't believe these flaws can ever be fixed. Of course, by not trying to recover your real personality, to gain health, you guarantee failure in life.

To help you get out of this denial pattern I have created a quick self-report for you to fill out. It is called the Sexual Addiction Mirror or "SAM". Don't worry, unless you show others no one but you will ever see your ratings on the inventory. All I ask is that before you complete "SAM" that you pray and ask God how he would have you mark each item. When done rating each item please total your score as described below.

Frequency Rating Scale

Rate each item with the number that best indicates which statement is most truthful (accurate) about you. The term "Currently" means within the last year (1 year or less).

I have never thought about it.	0
I use to think about it but have never done it.	1
I currently think about it but not very often.	2
I currently think about it on a regular basis.	3
I currently think and talk about it.	4
I have done it but not in over a year.	5
I currently do it but not very often.	6
I currently do it on a regular basis.	7
I am totally consumed by it & do this every week.	8

The Sexual Addiction Mirror	Your Rating score
1. Dreaming about sexual relations with others.	
2. Remembering sexual encounters you had with others even though they happened long ago.	
3. Staring (looking frequently) at women's or men's sexual body areas when they are fully dressed.	
4. Getting sexually "turned on" thinking/reading about romantic interactions.	
5. Rereading intimate sexual interactions in books over and over.	
6. Getting turned on reading pornographic language.	
7. Stimulating yourself sexually after reading romantic or pornographic stories.	
8. Viewing pornographic videos, movies.	
9. Viewing pornographic web-pages on the Internet.	
10. Sexually stimulating yourself after viewing pornography.	
11. Sexually stimulating yourself while viewing pornography.	
12. Sexually stimulating yourself with objects.	
13. Having "phone sex", "sexting" with others.	
14. Having "cybersex" (video cam sex) with others.	
15. Visiting "strip", "pole dancing" clubs	
16. Watching others (peeping) through windows undress and/or having sex.	
17. Paying for erotic "adult" massage	
18. Exposing sexual parts of your body in public places.	
19. Participating in giving or receiving oral sex while in a parked or moving car.	
20. Having sexual contact outside your home with a non-professional sexual partner and you are not married.	
21. Having sexual contact outside your home with a non-professional sexual partner and you are married.	
22. Having sexual contact inside your home with a sexual professional (prostitute, etc.) and you are not married.	
23. Having sexual contact inside your home with a sexual professional (prostitute, etc.) and you are married.	
24. Letting others take pictures/movies of your sexual parts and/or of you committing sexual acts.	
25. Having sex with two or more people at the same time.	
26. Having sexual contact with someone of your gender.	

27. Giving/receiving anal sex.	
28. Taking money (or gifts) for sexual contact with others.	
29. Having sexual contact with animals.	
30. Having sex with children/teens.	
31. Having sex with family members	
32. Letting others tie you up (bondage) while having sex.	
33. Committing violent sex acts (rape, S&M.)	
34. Killing a sexual partner during or after sex	
35. Getting sexually excited reading this list.	
TOTAL SCORE:	

Interpretation of SAM scores

Once you have tallied up your item scores to get your total score use that number to identify a recovery scripture for you below:

Number Range	Recovery Interpretation Scripture
0-36 **Receive Mercy**	*But go and learn what this means: I desire mercy, not sacrifice. For I have not come to call the righteous, but sinners.* Matt. 9:
37-72 **Abstain from Sin**	*Dear friends, I urge you, as aliens and strangers in the word, to abstain from sinful desires which war against your soul.* 1 Peter 2:11
73-108 **Confess to Others and Pray**	*Therefore confess your sins to each other and pray for each other so that you may be healed. The prayer of a righteous man is powerful and effective. James 5:16*
109-144 **You Are Forgiven**	If we confess our sins, he is faithful and just and will forgive us our sins and purify us from all unrighteousness. 1 John 1:9
145-180 **Redeemed by God**	*I sought the Lord, and he answered me; he delivered me from all my fears (4). The angel of the Lord encamps around those who fear him, and he delivers them (7). The Lord redeems his servants; no one who takes refuge in him will be condemned (22).* Psalm 34: 4, 7, 22

181-216 **Repent and Seek God**	*Repent, then, and turn to God, so that your sins may be wiped out, that times of refreshing may come from the Lord, and that he may send the Christ, who has been appointed for you—even Jesus.* Acts 3:19
217-252 **Jesus Intercedes for You Daily**	*Whom will bring any charge against those whom God has chosen? It is God who justifies. Who is he that condemns? Christ Jesus, who died—more than that, who was raised to life—is at the right hand of God and is also interceding for us. Romans 8:33-35*
253-288 **Christ's Love is Endless**	*For I am convinced that neither death nor life, neither angels nor demons, neither the present nor the future nor any powers, neither height nor depth, nor anything else in all creation, will be able to separate us from the love of God that is in Christ Jesus our Lord.* Roman 8:38-39
Recovery Truth:	You can trust God to heal you, especially when you don't deserve it, if you confess and repent. With his death Jesus has already paid your sins.

Romans 5:8
But God demonstrated his own love for us in this; while we were still sinners, Christ died for us.

Lesson 3 – What is Recovery?

The Light of Scripture: Psalm 34: 17-18; 22

The righteous cry out, and the Lord hears them; he delivers them from all their troubles. The Lord is close to the brokenhearted and saves those who are crushed in spirit.

The Lord redeems his servants; no one who takes refuge in him will be condemned.

The Problem: **Reconciling with God, yourself and others is hard work that takes time**

The Solution: **Start today, take the first step and keep moving forward.**

The Procedure: **No matter what you think or how you feel, keep reading this book**

My Prayer

Father in Heaven I thank you for your almighty love for me. That you would redeem me while I was still a sinner is a true sign of your love. I am overwhelmed that you would recover me from my many bad decisions and actions. I praise your name for healing my broken heart, for healing my pain and shame. Lord Jesus may I be more like you and less like me every day. Help me to be a worthy servant in your service. Today I seek refuge in you. Thank you for helping everyone who calls upon your name.

As I stared at the phone, I suddenly lost the courage I had felt so strongly only moments before; back when I decided it was the right time to make the call. As a recovering addict, who had taken 12-steps I learned 'Making Amends" (Steps 8-9) was an important part of the healing process. I understood that by contacting individuals I had hurt and wronged with past behavior I would have an opportunity to express my sincere sorrow for the damage I had done to them. While I had sought forgiveness from others previously, it was never easy for me to do.

Looking down on the kitchen counter I reread a list of things that I had learned that made an apology more likely to be accepted. The list started with, "Always pray for both your victim and yourself". I had been doing that for days and felt led by God to call at this moment.

Next on the list was, "write out a statement God has given you to say" in case the person actually answers the phone. Sometimes hearing their voice freezes all of the words you intend to say and having it written out in front of you makes it easier to focus. My statement was printed out in very large letters in front of me.

Thirdly, I read "Be short and specific in the amend but not detailed about what you had done,". Restating the actual "offense" can re-victimize the person. I knew that she would know what I was expressing regret about.

Fourth, "Do not expect the person to be happy, grateful, understanding or forgiving about what you are sharing with them." The call was to state my responsibility and to let her know that I was accountable for wronging her. To tell her I was still remorseful for what I had done and to ask for forgiveness; not to please her or receive a favorable response.

Fifth, "Keep the call short, under 10 minutes, as it is a request for forgiveness not a conversation to explain anything." Reopening past relationships is not the purpose of the call and is almost always counterproductive to the healing process. I had my watch off and on the counter so I could see it clearly.

And lastly, "Thank them for their kindness in Jesus name and say good-by." Having done this process several times previously didn't make it any easier this time. I was feeling the weight, guilt and sorrow of my harm to this woman and I deeply regretted my actions with her. At my lowest, saddest point of shame I picked up the phone and began dialing. I felt like I was in a trance…hearing the phone ring on the other end, I wanted to quickly hang up…but God gave me the strength not to. I suddenly panicked, "What if someone else answers?"

The voice on the other end immediately brought me back into reality and the reason I was making the call. Her hello was no different than the many other hellos I had heard her say before. Reading my opening line, which told her who I was and asked for a minute of her time so I could apologize to her, went very quickly. I almost didn't hear myself speak.

She responded, "I don't understand, why you are calling me after all these years?" Suddenly

I felt God's presence and his peace as I told her, "It is very important that I ask for your forgiveness for the wrongs I have done to you. I am truly sorry for taking advantage of you when I should have been treating you with kindness and respect. I pray every day for your wounds and ask that God will give you forgiveness for my actions."

A long silence occurred on the phone; I knew she was still there from her breathing but I was not sure what she would say. I suddenly realized she was crying and I felt even more of a heel. I was wondering if I should just hang up when she said, "You know Everett, you were not the only man to hurt me in my life, there have been many...even one in my own family...but you are the only one who has ever asked me for forgiveness and admitted you were wrong." My heart was pounding very quickly; my head was absolutely empty as to what to say in response to her statement. Thank God I said nothing and just listened.

She went on, "I don't ever think of you when I think of those who have harmed me...until now I had forgotten what you...what we had done together...but I have been asking God lately to help me find my way back. I feel so lost and empty."

God spoke clearly through me when I said to her, "God has more healing than you have hurt. He has more love than you have hate. And he is begging you to trust Jesus who died for you. I have done so and God has restored my marriage and given me hope for becoming a decent man." She started crying harder and said she wanted to get right with God.

Realizing my time limit was almost up and that a strong urge to "rescue" her from her sadness (my co-dependency) was kicking in, I simply said, "Pray and ask God to take you to a church near you to get help. And you might want to read the gospel of John in the Bible; plus I gave her a title of a book (Love is a Choice) to help her with her recovery. Then I closed with, "Thank you for forgiving me. I will not be calling you again but God is more than able to provide healing to your heart if you seek him every day. He has healed me and I know he wants to do the same for you." Then I hung up and I have never talked with her since. I was one minute over my limit but somehow it didn't seem very important.

Recovery Truth # 11   I Agree _____ I Disagree _____
Reconciliation is recovery; healing occurs as you reconcile with God, Yourself and Others.

> **2 Kings 20:5b**
> *"...This is what the Lord, the God of your father David, says: I have heard your prayer and seen your tears; I will heal you."*

The order of reconciliation is very important

As my personal story indicates, making amends to others you have wronged is an important part of your recovery, but it is not the most important part. It is not where you start your recovery process. A secret to success in making amends to those you have offended lies in following the right order. First you must reconcile with God; then you must forgive you and learn to have mercy on yourself; and lastly you must ask others for forgiveness as God leads you.

Getting "right" with God is always the first "step" because he provides you with the Grace to heal so you can complete the other two amend processes. God's Grace provides you with <u>power</u> to do things you currently cannot do. Grace also provides you with the <u>love</u> you did not get when you were growing up and now need to give to others. Grace also helps us to <u>forgive</u> others who have wronged us even though they may not deserve forgiveness. Getting victimized never justifies you victimizing others. And lastly, God's Grace provides you with <u>wisdom</u> to understand what is acceptable to God and what is not. How to receive God's grace will be explained in Lesson 5.

After receiving God's power, love, forgiveness and wisdom you are ready to make amends with yourself and with others. You can receive God's Grace only through receiving God's Holy Spirit; it comes into you from God as you surrender your will daily and accept His will. You cannot will it to happen, buy it or get it from reading any book (even this one).

Recovery Truth # 12   **I Agree _____ I Disagree _____**
Your relationship with God is more important than any other relationship you have; it provides the power you need to forgive and love yourself.

> **Luke 10:27**
> *Jesus said, "Love the Lord your God with all your heart and with all your soul and with all your strength and with all your mind; and, Love your neighbor as yourself."*

The second step is learning how to forgive yourself for the harm you have done others and yourself. When you have "blown up" your relationships, health, credibility, finances and careers it is normal for you to be a tad critical of the person you have become. And that is good…you need to accept that you are dangerous to others and especially to yourself. But healing cannot occur when you refuse to forgive yourself for the damage you have done. Does anyone deserve forgiveness…no way! We never deserve forgiveness from God but he forgives us in Jesus name anyway, because he wants to heal our inner hurts. In the same way, while we never deserve forgiveness from others for wronging them, God's mercy mends both their hearts and ours.

Understanding and accepting "self-hatred" is a major stumbling block to you finding freedom from addiction, is a significant milestone in your recovery journey. Many seeking mental and emotional health have never found serenity because they could not get past this milestone. As you will learn in Lesson Four, self-condemnation is a main tap root in all addictions. It must be removed if you are to be restored to the person God created you to be. Many people going through recovery programs are bound by a lie that determines their success or failure; and that lie is, "You cannot be forgiven for your offenses, ever! " I am living proof that this is simply not true and millions of others have also found freedom in Jesus.

In summary, these three recovery steps taken in the right order are required in the reconciliation process. Receiving forgiveness and acceptance from God gives us the power to remove this crippling lie and to replace it with God's truth. Once you have learned to have "Mercy" on yourself then you can seek others and ask for their forgiveness. All of this is possible; not in your power but in God's mercy if you accept his gift of salvation in Jesus and receive his Grace through Faith.

Recovery Truth # 13   **I Agree _____ I Disagree _____**
Your relationship with others is your service for God, how you treat people reflects your level of recovery.

Galatians 5:13-14
You, my brothers, were called to be free. But do not use your freedom to indulge the sinful nature; rather, serve one another in love. The entire law is summed up in a single command: "Love your neighbor as yourself.

So what must you do to be reconciled with God?
Reconciliation with God consists of several factors, they are:

1. Seeking God and asking him for forgiveness in Jesus name.
2. Accepting Jesus as Lord because he "paid off" your debt, obligation to God
3. Understanding and agreeing with God on his truths (accepting his Word).
4. Changing from God's enemy to God's child, servant and friend.
5. Receiving God's forgiveness, favor and blessings upon you
6. Praising God for his mercy and grace
7. Serving God by telling others who Jesus is and how to be one with God

Listen to how God describes reconciliation, as you read underline the word every time he uses it in these verses.

2 Corinthians 5:17-21
Therefore, if anyone is in Christ, he is a new creation; the old has gone, the new has come! All this is from God, who reconciled us to himself through Christ and gave us the ministry of reconciliation; that God was reconciling the world to himself in Christ, not counting men's sins against them. And he has committed to us the message of reconciliation. We are therefore Christ's ambassadors, as though God were making his appeal through us. We implore you on Christ's behalf: Be reconciled to God. God made him who had no sin to be sin for us, so that in him we might become the righteousness of God.

So what does God tell us about Recovery/Reconciliation in these verses?

1. Spiritual Rebirth is required for Reconciliation

Therefore, if anyone is in Christ, he is a new creation; the old has gone, the new has come!

2. If you accept Jesus as your Christ, you must also accept Reconciliation as your Ministry (Christian Duty).

All this is from God, who reconciled us to himself through Christ and gave us the ministry of reconciliation; that God was reconciling the world to himself in Christ, not counting men's sins against them.

3. You need to commit to the Message of Reconciliation, becoming God's ambassador

God has committed to us the message of reconciliation. We are therefore Christ's ambassadors, as though God were making his appeal through us.

4. Your Reconciliation with God demands purity in your daily living.

We implore you on Christ's behalf: Be reconciled to God. God made him who had no sin to be sin for us, so that in him we might become the righteousness of God.

Recovery Truth # 14   I Agree _____ I Disagree _____
God isn't healing you to live your life separate from him or others. He is healing you to be a stronger, more obedient, loving servant of His.

Looking for a Few Good Men

I love this part of the recovery class I teach. I say to the men, "Imagine wanting to wear a United States Marine uniform really, really badly. You are so motivated to tell everyone you meet that you are a U.S. Marine that you go down and enlist. In doing so you surrender all your rights as a citizen, you literally give up your free will." Some of the men in class are already starting to smile, knowing I'm heading somewhere with this illustration …. They're just not sure where.

I continue, "You get sent to boot camp and on the very first morning the loudspeaker goes crazy with a very loud voice screaming in your ear telling you to get your sad behind out of bed and get ready for a 10 mile run. You look at your watch and it is only 4 am and then you look at the closest window and it is pitch black outside. Then you realize that the loud speaker screaming in your ear is actually a real live human who is very large and in charge, a guy who is affectionately called, "Yes Sir, Drill Sargent Sir!"

Bravely you raise your little hand and when he looks at it with great shock you reply, "Excuse me Sir but I don't run well this early in the morning, could you drop by after you get back, when I am ready?" Of course the Master Sargent is completely impressed with your courage and lets you sleep in for the rest of the morning while he takes the rest of the men out to be trained."

By this time most of the men are laughing and shaking their heads knowing that this kind of behavior would be totally unacceptable and severely punished. Yet we take a similar approach with God. We sign up to be Christians because we want to be forgiven and go to Heaven, but when Jesus asks us to obey God's commands we tell him to "call back later". Sadly we miss out on God's training which is where our healing and freedom actually come from.

When we surrender our lives to God we are signing up to be in his army. As in any army, we must obey our commander. The blessing we receive when we obey our Lord is that we get stronger, wiser, more loving and, for the first time for many of us, truly useful to others. God trains us up to be the person he intended us to be in the first place. We truly become "one of a few good men."

Recovery Truth # 15   **I Agree _____ I Disagree _____**
You can't keep it unless you give it away. What you receive from God He expects you to use to help others. The more you help others, the more He gives you.

2 Corinthians 1:3-5
Praise be to the God and Father of our Lord Jesus Christ, the Father of compassion and the God of all comfort, who comforts us in all our troubles, so that we can comfort those in any trouble with the comfort we ourselves have received from God. For just as the sufferings of Christ flow over into our lives, so also through Christ our comfort overflows.

Nothing motivates me more than realizing that what God has given me was intended to be given away. As I give what I have received, others are blessed and touched by God. And the really good news is that as I give what He has given me God gives me more to give the next time. God gives so we can give, God loves so we can love, God teaches us truth so we can teach truth, and God is faithful so we can learn how to be faithful.

WINNING THE WAR WITH YOUR FLESH!

A Testimony from a Brother in Recovery

Everett, my vocabulary does not have the words to express the level of gratitude I feel in regards to your faithfulness to the Lord in teaching Stand Firm. All I can say is, "Thank you for your obedience."

As a result of your faith and obedience there are three little children that get to experience life with a dad & mom who are healthy enough to let them be kids. As a result of your faith and obedience I am able to truly be a husband to my wife. God has used you to touch so many through your teaching.

Thank you for allowing him to use you.

God Bless, Lenny S.

So What Can You Do to Get Healed?

1. Read with an open mind.
2. Complete your inventory honestly
3. Trust in the Lord and keep turning the pages.

Please complete the Workbook activities for Lesson 3 before reading Lesson 4.

52 | Copyright: Everett T. Robinson

Lesson Three Inventory

What were you Thinking when you read Lesson 3?

How are you Feeling after reading Lesson 3?

How is what you are Thinking and Feeling now going to help you with your recovery?

What are you going to change in your behavior after reading Lesson 3?

What Bible verse in Lesson 3 will you commit to memorize?

Lesson 3: Activity 1 - 20 Choices for Recovery

Listed below are 20 choices for recovery. For each set of choices below circle the choice that your current behavior supports at this time in your life...only circle one of the two choices provided.

Do You _____ ?

1.	Obey/Work for God	or	Work for Self/World?
2.	Believe Jesus will forgive you	or	Think/feel condemned?
3.	Exhibit Joy	or	Live in Pain and spread it to others?
4.	Put others first	or	Put self-first above others?
5.	Have Intimacy with God & others	or	Live in Loneliness with self?
6.	Show Forgiveness for others	or	Show Bitterness, hate for others?
7.	Live in Honesty, Speak the truth	or	Live in Dishonesty, lie to others?
8.	Have Serenity under Stress	or	Have Stress without Serenity?
9.	Live by Healthy Boundaries	or	Habitually act out in sinful ways?
10.	Show Development in Christ	or	Show Immaturity, no improvement?
11.	Praise God daily	or	Complain about people daily?
12.	Act Interdependent	or	Act Co-dependent, dependent?
13.	Have Freedom in Christ	or	Live In Slavery to your flesh, World?
14.	Have Financially Security	or	Let Debt Control you?
15.	Demonstrate Generosity	or	Let love of money and possessions control you?
16.	Read the Bible Daily	or	Read TV Guide/Playboy/Sports Illustrated?
17.	Love others non-sexually	or	Seek/practice Sexual Immorality?
18.	Practice Humility	or	Stride in Pride, act arrogantly?
19.	Have Hope for your Future	or	Live in Regret about your Past?
20.	Live by A Recovery Plan	or	Live by a plan of self-destruction?

Areas circled on the right are areas where you still need recovery; please give them to God in prayer on next page:

Plug-in with Prayer - How would you like God to help you right now?

(in the space below please talk through writing directly with God...He is listening, ready, willing and able to help you.)

Lesson 4 – Power to Change Your Tree

The Light of Scripture: Ephesians 3:14-19

For this reason I kneel before the Father, from whom his whole family in heaven and on earth derives its name. I pray that out of his glorious riches he may strengthen you with power through his Spirit in your inner being, so that Christ may dwell in your hearts through faith. And I pray that you, being rooted and established in love, may have power, together with all the saints, to grasp how wide and long and high and deep is the love of Christ, and to know this love that surpasses knowledge—that you may be filled to the measure of all the fullness of God.

The Problem: **Either you control your flesh (self) or it will control you**

The Solution: **Accept God's forgiveness and Grace**

The Procedure: **Talk directly to God (prayer) and seek help from those who are experienced in recovery**

My Prayer

Good morning Father…I come to you in Jesus name…for there are no other names under heaven by which I can enter into your presence. Thank you for helping me today. I am not sure when or where I will need help but I am sure it will be often and without your power I just spin my wheels and go nowhere. Jesus, please be Lord of my life today and strengthen me so I can win my daily battle with my flesh. Thank you for your help and protection. Amen

In the Shadow of his Cross

It was the week before Easter and I was attending "Shadow of the Cross", a structured activity that Christ the King Community Church (in Bellingham WA.) provides during the week leading up to Good Friday. The main sanctuary is closed so only a few people may pass through at one time, creating a very personal, private and safe environment for each person. The inside of the sanctuary is very different than normal, lights are kept low and the music is very peaceful and inviting allowing for deeper personal reflection.

The theme for this year was emptiness…each one of the 7 activities at each station asked me to empty myself of things that God wanted to remove from my life. Things that I had held onto for years thinking they were of value but in reality they had been harming me. Each station reminded me of the fact that Jesus emptied himself for me during his life on Earth.

As I passed through the stations I chose to do the activities asked of me. While doing so I had a very personal encounter with the Holy Spirit. I was touched by God, washed clean by the Holy Spirit of wrong attitudes, feelings, intentions and memories. God was healing hurts that were still inside of me.

For instance, as I began to partake at Station One I could feel my emotions and troubles' raising to the surface…this was my second year going through. I was so blessed the year before that I had very high expectations of what God was going to do in me this time…I was not disappointed. I would like to share something that happened at Station Two that speaks directly to this Lesson.

During this activity there was a very large canvas board and I was asked to write my struggles and sins down on that board with a felt tipped pen. As I did so I also read the many other sins that had been left by others before me. The list was endless: adultery, lying, gossiping, witchcraft, selfishness, anger, rage, doubt, unforgiveness, regret, shame, stealing…so many things that I could relate to, so many things that I saw in me. As I read the big canvas board I realized how true it is that Christians will never be perfect, we still struggle with pain from wounds deep inside of us.

Recovery Truth # 16   **I Agree _____ I Disagree _____**
God never takes something unhealthy out of your personality that he doesn't put something healthy back in its place.

At this time during my self-examination God reminded me that he had created the Stand Firm class to help men empty themselves of these same poisonous things. Growing up we all had become polluted with toxic thoughts and feelings. And worst of all we believed the inner lie that it was OK to stay that way because we were "normal", like everyone else. The reality is God does not want you to be like everyone else, he wants you to be like Jesus.

You have become a slave to addiction patterns that are driven by the toxic things living inside

WINNING THE WAR WITH YOUR FLESH!

your mind and heart. If you are still under their control you are their captive, enslaved to repeat the same self-destructive patterns. Even though Jesus died that you might be free, often you choose to return to your "pain" instead of allowing God to take the toxins out of your personality, your relationships and your life. God wants to heal you, for that to happen you must let him heal your deepest pains. And that only happens when you are in the shadow of his Cross.

Colossians 3:4-11
When Christ, who is your life, appears, then you also will appear with him in glory. Put to death, therefore, whatever belongs to your earthly nature; sexual immorality, impurity, lust, evil desires and greed, which is idolatry. Because of these, the wrath of God is coming.

You used to walk in these ways, in the life you once lived, but you must rid yourselves of all such things as these: anger, rage, malice, slander, and filthy language from your lips. Do not lie to each other, since you have taken off your old self with its practices and have put on the new self, which is being renewed in knowledge in the image of its Creator. Here there is no Greek or Jew, circumcised or uncircumcised, barbarian, Scythian, slave or free, but Christ is all, and is in all.

So What Tree Are You Eating From?

Recovery Truth # 17   I Agree _____ I Disagree _____
The fruit of the Tree you eat from will either heal ya or kill ya.

Genesis 2:9
And the Lord God made all kinds of trees grow out of the ground—trees that were pleasing to the eye and good for food. In the middle of the garden were the tree of life and the tree of the knowledge of good and evil.

To keep the tree illustration of recovery simple I have put drawings of both the "Tree of Death" and of the "Tree of Life" in this Lesson for you to consider. Each one has branches and a root system clearly identified. The first drawing will be the Tree of Death and then we will review the Tree of Life.

The Tree of Death: Genesis 3:2-3
The woman said to the serpent, "We may eat fruit from the trees in the garden, but God did say, 'You must not eat fruit from the tree that is in the middle of the garden, and you must not touch it, or you will die.

We all know how all our troubles started; way back when Adam and Eve did the very thing God told them not to do. Just like them, we are still doing the very things God tells us not to do.

We often think God is being "Holy" and "Parental" and that he just wants to rain on our parade to ruin our fun. If you think this, you would be partly accurate. He does have a long history with rain storms ending parties.

The first time God sent rain to the earth was in the story of Noah when he flooded the whole earth. People back then were very evil and they did pretty much whatever they felt like doing… kind of like today. But God was so angry at their sin that, "he had all the great springs of the great deep burst forth and he opened the floodgates of the heavens and it rained on the earth for forty days and forty nights." (Genesis 7:11-12)

As we know from the rest of Noah's story, God destroyed all those who lived on the Earth at that time except for a very few. He actually restarted mankind hoping that people would learn to obey and stay away from the tree of death. Unfortunately, the human race has gone right back to eating from it. Let's consider the "Tree of Death" and see where you might have been grafted into it.

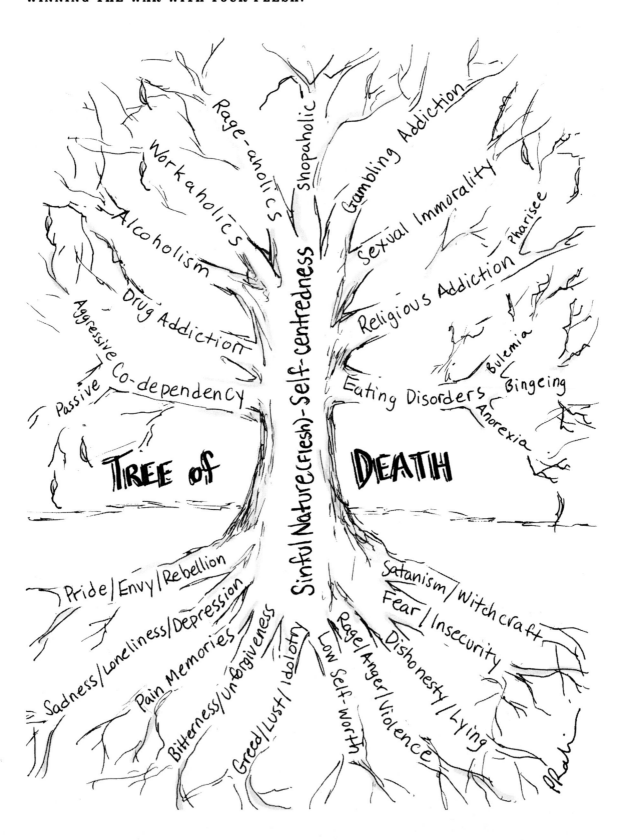

The Tree of Life

The really good news is that there is also a Tree of Life. When we trust God he does the miracle of changing the Tree of Death into the Tree of Life. It is important to realize that God cannot (will not) do this until you have accepted Jesus as your Savior and Lord. This is for our protection.

This can be very confusing but God does not want us to eat from the Tree of Life until we have been washed clean of all our sin which only occurs when we surrender our lives to Jesus. It is by his sacrifice that we are cleaned. He does not want us to live for eternity with sin in us or we would never be able to enter Heaven.

Genesis 3:21-24
The Lord God made garments of skin for Adam and his wife and clothed them. And the Lord God said, "The man has now become like one of us, knowing good and evil. He must not be allowed to reach out his hand and take also from the tree of life and eat, and live forever.

So the Lord God banished him from the Garden of Eden to work the ground from which he had been taken. After he drove the man out, he placed on the east side of the Garden of Eden cherubim and a flaming sword flashing back and forth to guard the way to the tree of life.

Many addicts want healing (Eternal life) but they do not want to submit to Jesus as their Lord. Praise God that He does not give us what we always ask for, as only He can see the Spiritual Consequences of our requests. Those that are good for our souls he grants and those that are bad for our spiritual development he doesn't. We need to help others in the same way He helps us so lost souls are won for God.

Proverbs 11:30
The fruit of the righteous is a tree of life, and he who wins souls is wise.

Just like any tree, the Tree of Life has roots, a trunk and branches. As you look at the Tree of Life picture please circle anything that you are having trouble demonstrating on a consistent basis. Also, circle the "roots" that you have difficulty with at the bottom of the tree.

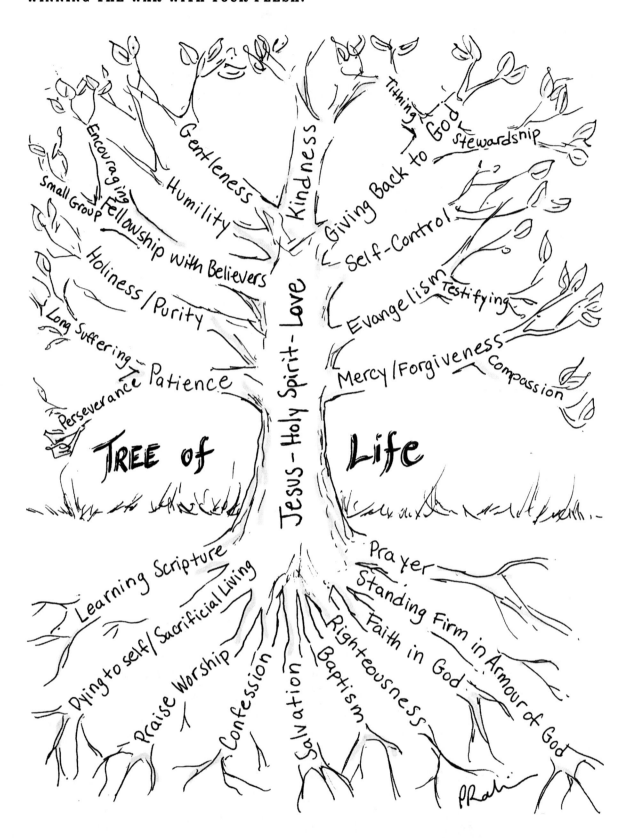

The Fruit of the Spirit (Tree of Life Branches) Includes Self-control

Galatians 5:22-24
"But the fruit of the Spirit is love, joy, peace, patience, kindness, goodness, faithfulness, gentleness and self-control. Against such things there is no law. Those who belong to Jesus have crucified the sinful nature with its passions and desires."

When I was first saved and read through the "fruit list" I didn't score very high on any of them. God understands this and exhibits all of these fruits with us so we know what they are. Over time, through prayer and submission, others begin to notice more spiritual fruit in our attitudes and behavior because of his mercy on us. Glory to God!

Recovery Truth # 18   Agree _____ I Disagree _____
Either you control yourself or your self will control you; it is a daily battle.

I grew up in the Sierra Nevada's in Northern California. I loved living there because there were lots of rivers, mountains and lakes. The smell of the big pine trees standing tall above us was overwhelming and our four definite seasons (Sun, Wind, Snow, & Rain) were awesome. Still growing up in "paradise" wasn't perfect; as a good friend used to say, "Some days you got the bear, other days the bear got you." Simply meaning that sometimes in life we win and sometimes we lose regardless of where we live.

So it is with our constant war with self; do we obey our inner desires to do what we feel like doing, or do what God would have us do? When we disobey God we "sin" before him and things tend to go downhill pretty fast. But when we admit (confess) we are wrong and seek his forgiveness God freely gives us his Mercy and Grace.

Remember: "If you're lying, you're dying".

1 John 1:8-10
If we claim to be without sin, we deceive ourselves and the truth is not in us. If we confess our sins, he is faithful and just and will forgive us our sins and purify us from all unrighteousness. If we claim we have not sinned, we make him out to be a liar and his word has no place in our lives.

Recovery Truth # 19   I Agree _____ I Disagree _____
If you repent God has more forgiveness and healing than you have sin and pain; ask and believe and you will receive.

Luke 17:3-4
If your brother sins, rebuke him, and if he repents, forgive him. If he sins against you seven times in a day, and seven times comes back to you and says, 'I repent', forgiven him.

I have always found safety and acceptance in this verse. Having sinned seriously and often I found peace knowing that I could always come to God through Jesus and find forgiveness and mercy. Just as we forgive others when they repent, so God forgives me when I repent. No one is perfect and we need help getting back on the right track. When I repent it is God who helps me get "healthy". Yet after he has forgiven me I must also forgive myself.

Recovery Truth # 20   **I Agree _____ I Disagree _____**
After God forgives your sins, you have no right to bring accusation and judgment against yourself. All self-condemnation statements need to be confessed.

> **1 Corinthians 6:19b-20**
> *....You are not your own; you were bought at a price. Therefore, honor God with your body.*

I often find that men's self-hatred (unforgiveness) towards themselves is a major block to them getting the blessings and healing God has for them. God says they are forgiven but they just keep on telling themselves how worthless and awful they are. This self-rejection and refusal to have mercy on yourself will keep you from being healed. It will keep you from experiencing God's power in your life. Section Two of this book will reveal why this is occurring in your head and in your heart. It will help you understand what is causing you to hate yourself.

A Testimony from a Brother in Recovery

I first learned the concepts in the book in a class with Everett called Stand Firm. The big eye opener was looking at the tree of death and the tree of life. As I understood the difference between fruit and roots things started to unfold. I soon realized I was lying to myself and others about addictions I had. As we started to talk about how we cope with pain I realized I had real problems. I started to pray to the Lord to reveal to me patterns that caused me to cycle. This class was good at helping me see that the Lord was holding my hand and that I was not going alone, Jesus was with me. It is so freeing to let the Lord remove the pig poop and start seeing the diamond.

The other big ah ha was the left brain and the right brain and how they operate in our daily lives. I was able to identify who was on my committee in the left side of my brain and I allowed Jesus to remove the ones with critical voices. I also faced the lies that I believed that have controlled me for so many years. I realized that as I forgave the people that have hurt me the Lord was silencing the voices on the committee. I learned that all of my videos that have been recorded from past damaging experiences were still playing in the right side theater of my mind. As I plugin daily I'm able to take every thought captive and make it obedient to the Lord; amazingly Jesus is taking away the bad memories. It is incredible to me how the Lord has all the love I needed and never got. It is more than I can hold; I guess that is why now I have so much to give away to my wife and kids.

As painful as it might be, please finish reading this book. Staying where you are at will not make your recovery easier, it will only get worse and hurt more people around you. God bless you. Joshua S.

So What Can You Do to Get Healed?

1. Read with an open mind
2. Complete your inventory honestly
3. Keep turning the pages-keep learning about what is destroying you
4. Exchange your will for God's Will; eternal life for eternal death

Please complete the Inventory activities for Lesson 4 before reading Lesson 5.

Lesson Four Inventory

What were you Thinking when you read Lesson 4?

How are you Feeling after reading this Lesson 4?

How is what you are Thinking and Feeling now going to help you with your recovery?

What are you going to change in your behavior after reading Lesson 4?

What Bible verse in Lesson 4 will you commit to memorize?

Lesson 4: Activity 1 - Which Tree do you currently live in?

The following information is can be used for group sharing in class.

What are five areas you circled on the Tree of Death sheet?

1.

2.

3.

4.

5.

What are five areas you need to improve on the Tree of Life sheet?

1.

2.

3.

4.

5.

Lesson 4: Activity 2-
How much time do you invest in your spiritual development?

1. How often during the week do you Pray (talk to God)?

1	2	3	4	5	6	7	8	9	10
Never		Once per week		Once per day		Daily for 30 minutes		Daily for more than 30 minutes	

What can you do this week to improve your Prayer time?

2. How often do you read God's Word (the Bible)?

1	2	3	4	5	6	7	8	9	10
Never		Once per week		Once per day		Daily for 30 minutes		Daily for more than 30 minutes	

What can you do this week to improve your bible reading time?

3. What 3 sections (books) of the bible are your favorite to read?

1.

2.

3

4. What are 3 things keeping you from sharing God's Word with others?

    1.

    2.

    3.

Lesson 4: Activity 3 - In the Beginning was the Word...

Recovery requires you learning and using God's Word...it is the POWER you need to heal what is sick, mend what is broken, and cast away what is evil inside of you. Review each verse provided and list down what you think the main learning points in that verse are.

Scripture Verses   **Learning Points**

1. John 1:1-3, 14:6; 17: 5

2. Genesis 1:1-3

3. Isaiah 55: 11

4. Matt. 4:4-11

5. Matt.24:35

6. Luke 8:11-12

7. Luke 24:25-27, 32

8. Luke 24:44-46

9. Romans 10:17

10. Romans 10:8-10

Scripture Verses   **Learning Points**

11. 1 Corinthians 2:12-13

12. Ephesians 6:17

13. Philippians 4:7

14. Hebrews 4:12-13

15. 2 Peter 1:20-21

Lesson 5 – Are You Plugged In?

The Light of Scripture – Romans 10:8-11

"The word is near you; it is in your mouth and in your heart," that is, the word of faith we are proclaiming: That if you confess with your mouth, "Jesus is Lord," and believe in your heart that God raised him from the dead, you will be saved.

For it is with your heart that you believe and are justified, and it is with your mouth that you confess and are saved.

As the Scripture says, "Everyone who trusts in him will never be put to shame."

The Problem: You are not connected to your Creator

The Solution: Plug-in to God's love, power and wisdom

The Procedure: Praise, Pray, Read and Sing

My Prayer

Dear Lord Jesus, please forgive me for being so clumsy with words. I have tried to tell the readers as clearly as I could how they can come find you and be healed by your Spirit. We both know that human words will not be enough, so I thank you for touching them as they read this book. I thank you for dying that they might live. And I thank you Lord for teaching them how to worship your Father in Heaven. Please touch them and inspire them to keep on reading. Amen

WINNING THE WAR WITH YOUR FLESH!

Way back in 1980 I was driving with my friend Terry down the freeway in Canada. He was ripping along at a very fast pace while trying to explain to me why I should become "Born Again". I had known Terry for about 3 years and every time we got together he would talk to me about Jesus. At first I found it amusing that someone would be so "into God". I thought, "Cool man…whatever turns you on!" Not to mention Terry and me both grew up in California, "The Land of Fruit and Nuts", where anything goes.

I soon realized he was telling me that I needed to be like him, that I needed to get "saved" and that really ticked me off. I got upset with him. I thought he should mind his own business, focus on his own sins rather than pointing out mine. But the madder I got with him the more he smiled. He was always HAPPY… disgustingly happy! You know the kind!

When Terry wasn't around, God was talking to me, by that I mean things that were happening around me seemed to have new meanings to them. At this time I didn't understand any of God's communication with me but I was feeling guilty of the lifestyle I was living. I remember distinctly thinking to myself, "Where did I go wrong? Somehow I must have taken a bad turn and am now someplace I never thought I would end up." I was emotionally exhausted, "burned-out" as we use to say…and nothing was getting me high anymore.

"Don't you understand that Jesus died so you can be saved?" said Terry loudly. Looking over at him in the driver's seat I snapped back angrily, "I am sick and tired of you talking about Jesus. The dude died 2,000 years ago, let it go…I know he died for everyone's sins up to the cross… but it's a little late for me!"

Terry crossed over the slow lane and onto the shoulder of the road so fast that my heart jumped up into my mouth. He stopped very suddenly and turned the car off; laughing out loud he just looked at me with a smile and said, "You think Jesus is dead! Nothing could be further from the truth."

Trying to breathe after the sudden shock of getting beached so fast on the side of the road, I tried to look somewhat intelligent and replied, "Well, of course he is alive in heaven somewhere but that isn't going to help me much now. I have done too much to be forgiven that easily!" Still laughing uncontrollably he said, "He is sitting in heaven next to God the Father and by dying on the cross he's already paid the price for all of your sin…all you have to do is accept him as Lord and you are forgiven."

At that moment God's spirit rushed through me confirming what Terry was saying…I suddenly felt hope…I suddenly saw a way out of the life I was living. As suddenly as Terry had stopped the car I spiritually turned a corner; for the first time in my life I understood just how important Jesus's dying on the cross was. For the first time in my life I knew I had a way home.

Did I pray and accept Jesus at that very moment? Nope…I wasn't about to give Terry that satisfaction, but it wasn't long after that when I was alone that I did ask God to put Jesus in my heart. My inaccurate concept of who Jesus was had been crushed and for the first time my view of Jesus became clear.

Who is Jesus?

Jesus is God's son whom he sent to Earth specifically to die in your (my) place. By dying for you on the cross he purified you of all your wrongful behavior (sins). You deserve to be tried and sentenced to death for your transgressions (sins, bad thoughts and behavior) but when Jesus died and rose again he paid your "sin bill".

God shows his Mercy and Love for all of us by sacrificing his only Son so we will not have to receive the punishment for our behavior that we deserve. We are purified by Jesus who obeyed God's will and went to the cross in our place. Then God raised Jesus from the dead and Jesus returned to Heaven as Lord over all of creation which includes you.

Hebrew 1:3
"The Son is the radiance of God's glory and the exact representation of his being, sustaining all things by his powerful word. After he had provided purification for sins, he sat down at the right hand of the Majesty in heaven."

Recovery Truth # 21   I Agree _____ I Disagree _____
Jesus paid the full price for your freedom; by his wounds you can be healed from the inner pain that drives you into self-destruction.

Isaiah 53:4-6
Surely he took up our infirmities and carried our sorrows, yet we considered him stricken by God, smitten by him, and afflicted. But he was pierced for our transgressions, he was crushed for our iniquities; the punishment that brought us peace was upon him, and by his wounds we are healed. We all, like sheep, have gone astray, each of us has turned to his own way; and the Lord has laid on him the iniquity of us all.

I Praise God every day that by his son's wounds I have been healed. He was pierced for my stupid choices and self-centered actions. He was crushed for my immorality and punished so I might have inner peace; which is often referred to as Serenity in 12-steps. Jesus carried my sorrows even after I had gone astray, not once but over and over again…he died that I might have eternal life.

Why Would Anyone Reject God's offer?

In short, if you reject Jesus sacrifice and God's free gift of forgiveness then you are saying you would rather pay the full penalty for your sins yourself. This is not a wise choice but one many people make, and suffer every day for making it.

I rejected God's greatest gift to us for many years. I did not accept Jesus as my Lord until I was 28. I resisted God's help because of many of the same reasons you and many others struggle with. Let's consider some of the main ones:

1. You do not understand the facts of who Jesus is or what his dying really means to your life.
2. You do not believe God wants you…just other people.
3. You don't believe God is real, just a concept made up to control people.
4. You do not want to accept something that most of your family and friends are rejecting because it will create stress in your relationships with them.
5. You do not want to stop living the sinful life you are living.
6. You are afraid God will do "bad things" to you once you are fully under his control.
7. You are too ashamed to allow Jesus to help you; you are such a bad person there is no hope for you.

You May Even Think there are "Other Ways" to God

You may be one of the many people in recovery who reject Christ. You want healing but you do not want Jesus. It is true that many people have obtained sobriety from the substances they were abusing but, sadly, they still haven't found the joy and inner peace that comes from being one with God. And while they are now not acting out; the deeper pain within them still blooms in other ways: such as bitterness, resentment, rage, fear, broken relationships and isolation. The very things Jesus came to set us free from still haunt them because they have been fooled into thinking there are others way to God rather than going through Jesus. God's word says otherwise because only Jesus died so you might live.

1 John 2:23
No one who denies the Son has the Father; whoever acknowledges the Son has the Father also.

Recovery Truth # 22   I Agree _____ I Disagree _____
God has a plan for your life and self-destruction and addiction isn't it.

Jeremiah 29:11, 13-14
I know the plans I have for you," declares the Lord, "plans to prosper you and not to harm you, plans to give you hope and a future.

I can state without a doubt in my mind that addiction is a one-way road to misery and death. It slowly kills your mind, your body, your relationships, your sense of hope and then it takes your life. When any man who has impulsive behavior patterns argues with me about their chosen "lifestyle" I simply ask them, "Would you want your children to become like you, to live like you, to do what you are doing, to suffer what you are suffering?" They all say the same thing, "No!" "So why then," I ask, "is it OK for you to destroy yourself?"

Their "thinking" tells them their children have a purpose in life, they are still young and will grow up to accomplish something, but their own opportunity to be somebody in life has passed them by. This mental lie keeps them in bondage. Lies like this one and many others will be discussed in the rest of the Lessons of this book. This will help answer the question, "Why do addicts slowly commit suicide, don't they want to live?"

The main point here is that God wants to heal you so He can use you. The really good news is God has already created a purpose and good works for you to do, and will give you the self-discipline you need to succeed. All you have to do is be reconciled with God to receive forgiveness, healing, wisdom, self-control, love and your purpose in life which is the reason God created you.

Recovery Truth # 23   **I Agree _____ I Disagree _____**
God created you for a purpose and you need God's power to complete it.

> **2 Timothy 1:7**
> *For God did not give us a spirit of timidity, but a spirit of power, of love and of self-discipline.*

Do You Plug-in Daily?

Looking at the many faces of the men sitting in the Stand Firm class that God allows me to teach twice a week, I suddenly realize that some of them just don't get it. They understand that God exists; they even have accepted that they have made bad choices and take responsibility for the suffering they have caused. And they know they must change if they want to be healed; but they are still confused and wonder, "How does God's power get into me so I can change?"

Reaching into my pocket I take out my cell phone. Holding it up I ask the group, "When I go home tonight what must I do to make sure my phone works tomorrow as well as it worked today?"

"Pay your bill," answers back Bill, one of the smiling faces I have come to love sitting in the back of the class each week. He's a Brother I pray extra hard for every day (grin).

"Ok, Ok," I laughing respond back, "you got me there. But what else must I do every night when I get home if I want my phone to work the next day?"

"Plug it into the charger," several other men answer in harmony.

"Exactly!" I reply. "It takes power every day for this phone to work as it was designed to do, and so it is for you and me. God has designed us, created us to function in a certain way. For instance, God has created me to teach and has given me the spiritual gift of teaching but for it to be effective I must be "plugged in" to His Spirit, His power."

I then move over to the wall and stand next to an outlet. I point down to it and tell them, "What if I had a power drill here right now and I wanted to drive a screw into a board using that power drill; would I not have to first plug it into the outlet first?"

Bill again responds with his usual wit and says, "Not if it is battery operated!" So to please Bill and some of the other comedians I ask, "So what happens when the battery runs out, how do you charge up the battery?" The answer comes back from Dave, one of several carpenters in the class, who yells, "Plug it into any power source."

I then say, "Each one of us has a human battery that needs to be charged everyday if we are to make it through the next day. We do so by sleeping, eating, protecting our bodies from physical harm, and so forth. But we also have a spiritual battery that cannot be charged back up with anything that is on earth. We can only do so by allowing God's power, his love, mercy and wisdom to come into us.

I then move over to the Cross that is in the classroom. It is large structure, towering above me and made of very rough wood…wrapping my arm around it I tell them, "This is God's outlet. It is here that you "plug in" to God's power so you can do what you need to do to stay sober.

"The cool thing about God's outlet," I continued, "is it has three holes in it. As you already know a three-pronged plug has a built-in ground wire so you don't get the shock of your life when you plug it in. We are made by God to plug into the Cross because it is a three-pronged outlet: Father, Son and Holy Spirit."

God's power is called Grace in the bible. Once we have plugged in, God downloads his Holy Spirit into us daily so we have the power to do all those things God tells us we must do; but cannot do while we are unplugged from him. We need power to obey and as we are plugged into God's power, his Holy Spirit passes through us healing us of all the pollution that is in us. Healing comes as the world's pollution (lies, pain, anger, greed, lust, etc.) is removed and replaced with love, light and power in the Holy Spirit."

1 Corinthians 1:18; 21-25
For the message of the cross is foolishness to those who are perishing, but to us who are being saved it is the power of God.

Jews demand miraculous signs and Greeks look for wisdom, but we preach Christ crucified; a stumbling block to Jews and foolishness to Gentiles, but to those whom God has called, both Jews and Greeks, Christ the power of God and the wisdom of God.

Recovery Truth # 24   **I Agree _____ I Disagree _____**
The Power to change the tree of death to the tree of life only comes when you "plug into" Jesus Christ daily. Recovery (your spiritual transformation), obeying God, and serving others all are a part of the Cross you must carry.

Luke 9:23
Then he (Jesus) said to them all: "If anyone would come after me, he must deny himself and take up his cross daily and follow me.

So How Do You Plug In?

1. Praise God all day long

Praising God simply means thanking God for everything and agreeing with him about who he says He is. When I get depressed, fearful, angry, critical of others (and I do) I start Praising God. Instead of asking for anything I thank him for all He has already given me, it can be anything that comes to mind whatever comes to mind. Here are some examples:

"Thank you Father in Heaven for being the Alfa and Omega, the First and the Last, the Beginning and the End."

"Thank you Lord Jesus for my shoes, my socks, my pants, my shirt, my comb, my razor, and thank you for everything you gave me today."

"Thank you Holy Spirit for protecting me, for teaching me, for leading me into your Holy Word."

When I tell God how much I appreciate him for who He is, and for what He does for me, I am plugging into His Holy Spirit. Soon after I am feeling much better and laughing out loud, even though nothing physical changed in my situation. I am now plugged into the Power of all creation so I realize how small my problems are compared to his POWER.

2. Pray for Others

I find that when I work with men who are struggling with compulsive behavior that they don't pray for themselves very effectively, because they don't like whom they are. But if I ask them to pray for another brother who is hurting or for someone in their family who is suffering they jump right to it and demonstrate the faith it takes to reach God through prayer.

When praying for others we demonstrate more faith that God can and will help…in short, we allow God's power to touch us. The more we let the Holy Spirit touch us the more our faith and human spirit increases in power.

3. Learn (read, memorize, and apply) God's Word

Jesus is the Word of God. Every time you learn one verse out of the bible you are putting Jesus into your mind.

John 1:1-5

In the beginning was the Word, and the Word was with God, and the Word was God. He was with God in the beginning. Through him all things were made; without him nothing was made that has been made. In him was life, and that life was the light of men. The light shines in the darkness, but the darkness has not understood it.

The word of God is Power. Repeating that verse over and over again brings God's protection and blessings on you. The more Scripture you learn the more access to God's Grace you have. Jesus gives us this teaching in Matthew 6:9-15 when he teaches us how to pray with the Lord's Prayer. Praying this prayer from your heart will plug you in if you also are willing to forgive those whom have hurt you.

In addition, God's Word (Jesus) scrubs out the pollution that lives within our minds so we can think clearly. This is important because our minds are where we make decisions. Bad decisions always indicate bad thinking, pollution in the mind. Learning scripture will clean up the "dirty workshop" in your head.

4. Singing and Listening to Praise Songs

When music enters our minds it goes into the right side of our brain (Google split brain), the part where our feelings, impulses, musical and artistic thinking comes from. Singing and Listening to music that praises God fills this side of our brain with God's light. It lifts us up in ways that reading and talking with others about God often can't. I love to sing the children's song, "Jesus Loves Me" because it immediately plugs me into his Holy Spirit as I am singing this song of praise.

5. Ask for Grace

We often pray as if God is an ATM machine or Santa Claus. We are so busy asking him for money, presents and other things that we miss out on the greatest gift which is access to his GRACE. God's grace brings love, power, wisdom, faith, patience and all the other internal "things" we need to succeed in life. These are more valuable than money or external objects; when asking God He touches us, proving he is real.

6. Ask God for a daily appointment time to talk with him

When I was having trouble praying on a consistent basis I asked God what I was to do. He took me to the following verse:

Mark 1:35

Very early in the morning, while it was still dark, Jesus got up, left the house and went off to a solitary place, where he prayed.

I was stunned by this verse. It was obvious to me that Jesus had the Holy Spirit as he was healing people and casting out demons. He was busy from sunrise to sunset with either teaching his disciples or speaking to the crowds. Everyone was after him for something. He must have been exhausted at the end of each day. He would have needed his sleep, knowing that the next day would be even more demanding than the previous one had been. Yet, while it was still dark he got up and prayed.

Even though I read the verse I wasn't about to get up while it was still dark. I loved sleeping in if you get my drift and believed praying at one time was just as good as praying at another time. The very next morning I woke up exactly at 5:55 am, no alarm clock was set and I had been in a very deep sleep. I got up and went into another room and knelt down and prayed. It was totally black outside. I had a great day.

That evening I told my wife and said I would set my clock for the same time to see if God would be there again. My clock never went off but exactly at 5:55 am I woke up with the verse in my mind. I again got up and prayed, this time I was more asleep than awake and mumbled more than prayed. Again my day was awesome; God was with me all day long.

About a week or so later I actually did not get up; I woke up right on time but decided I would sleep another hour as I was not feeling very good. I did pray an hour later but I felt alone and could not concentrate while praying. It just seemed dry. My day went badly. So the next day I awoke again at 5:55 am and prayed; the house was very cold and it was very dark outside and I fell asleep on my knees leading against the bed in our spare bedroom. When I awoke I was ashamed I had fallen asleep but I had a wonderful day with Jesus. God honors obedience and loves sacrifice.

Ask God for your appointment time so you can meet with him every day. Many men I have worked with who had great difficulty praying have done this and now have powerful prayer times. Not all of them were given morning times…God will tell you when and where he wants to meet with you. A key to meeting God at this time is to acknowledge that He is exactly who He says he is; and that we are exactly who He says we are.

I always surrender my will at this appointment, actually I beg God to take it from me for the day so I will not get in the way of his Spirit moving through me. It is God who plugs us in, it is not by our effort or intentions but by his Spirit. By keeping your appointment time you are more able to pray at other times during the day.

Recovery Truth # 25   **I Agree _____ I Disagree _____**
God is more than able to prove his existence to you when you are completely willing to surrender your will to him.

Do You Have the Courage to complete "The Big Experiment?"

All of the reasons to not go to God cannot be removed through "logic". You need personal proof that God is real and that his offer of salvation through his Son Jesus is real. You must know beyond a "Shadow of the Cross" that this is not some "trick" I am using to get control over you. The only way you know for sure God loves you is by completing what I call, "The Big Experiment".

The Big Experiment starts when you find a place where you can be alone with God. You tell God that you will surrender everything in your life to him if he touches your life in such a way that you know for sure he wants you. When you pray this you must be sincerely willing to completely surrender your will to him if he becomes real to you. God knows your heart better than you do and he will not engage with you if you really don't intend to surrender to him.

When I took the big experiment I was in my bedroom; my wife and kids were gone for the afternoon. I knelt down and said (more like told) God that if he could show me one sign within the next 30 days that he loved me I would be his forever. I then proceeded to also tell him that I would not go to Church or read the Bible but would do most everything else he wanted me to do if I saw the sign and knew it was from him. I was totally willing in my heart to "put all of my cards" on the table to see if he would pick them up.

Once I had finished praying I felt very strange, like I was not alone. I got up off my knees and sat on the edge of my bed. As I was sitting there my mind kept saying to me, "lighten up Everett…there is nobody here but you. God is not coming." At the same time I was habitually pulling my Marlboro box out of my shirt and taking out a cigarette. I smoked two packs a day so it was not unusual for me to light one up. As I put it in my mouth I took out my lighter and my mind said to me, "Let's get high, this is way too heavy to be thinking about…let's smoke a doobie and put on Zeppelin!"

Just then I lit the lighter and put it to the end of the cigarette but just before it touched the tip the flame flared up very brightly like a small torch. My lighter had never done this before so it scared me. I immediately felt God's presence in the room and dropping the smoke and lighter, I knelt down on my knees and prayed again. This time I was way more serious and respectful than I was the first time.

I begged God to take away my desire to smoke. I had tried so many times to quit but because I was stressed out so much I just kept on smoking. This time I felt an inner peace come over me. With God's loving touch I got up and went into the bathroom and flushed all the cigarettes I had left. I had never destroyed a "perfectly good" cigarette before but this time I did not hesitate. I have never had another cigarette since. And seeing others smoke always makes me want to pray for them.

But that was just the start of what God would do for me. In the next two weeks he touched me so many times I was begging him to stop…it was blowing my mind, freaking me out! How he touched me would not mean much to you but it spoke directly to me. I no longer doubted in any way that He was real and that He loved me.

Are you willing to "put all of your cards on the table" and find out if God is real? To be touched by God so that you know he loves and wants you? The best part of this experiment is that you are the only person there, so no one else will know you have done it…unless, of course, God shows up and touches you. God is more than able to prove to you that he exists. Here is how it might sound if you did pray to him.

"Dear Father in Heaven, I come to you in Jesus name and ask that you forgive me for harming others and myself. I surrender my will to you and ask that your Holy Spirit will come into me and take control over my life. Thank you, Lord Jesus, for dying in my place. Please come into my heart and help me to be the person you created me to be."

A Testimony from a Brother in Recovery several months after taking "the Big Experiment" while in class:

1. *I am a recovering sex addict.*
2. *I'm an imperfect human being.*
3. *Being in recovery in the "Stand Firm" class & being plugged-in daily with my Savior Jesus Christ; PRICELESS!*

Robert S.

So What Can You Do to Get Healed?
1. Read with an open mind
2. Complete your inventory honestly
3. Keep turning the pages-keep learning about what is destroying you
4. Exchange your will for God's Will; eternal life for eternal death
5. Plug into God's Holy Spirit and receive forgiveness and power to change.

Please complete the Inventory activities for Lesson 5 before reading Lesson 6.

Lesson Five Inventory

What were you Thinking when you read Lesson 5?

How are you Feeling after reading this Lesson 5?

How is what you are Thinking and Feeling now going to help you with your recovery?

What are you going to change in your behavior after reading Lesson 5?

What Bible verse in Lesson 5 will you commit to memorize?

Lesson 5: Activity 1 Creating a Daily Accountability Chart

Walking with Jesus daily is one of the hardest things to do because we do not prioritize our recovery above other daily tasks such as bathing, eating and working. By using the chart below you can create and stay focused on your "recovery ritual", the spiritual routine you need to do every day to stay sober and healthy. Check mark each one of the sobriety steps listed below every time you complete it, challenge yourself to fill out every box each week. Photocopy this page and start a yearly notebook for charting your recovery progress.

Date:	M.	T.	W.	Th.	Fri.	Sat.	Sun.
Today I did the following:							
Plugged-In Morning - PG10X							
Read Bible – 1 Chapter							
Called 1 Brother before falling							
Called 1 Brother to encourage/ pray with them							
Called a brother after falling							
Forgave myself after confessing							
Plugged-In at Noon- PG10X							
Memorized 1 Bible Verse							
Prayed for 10 other people							
Plugged-In Evening - PG10X							
Prayed for Saints in 1 other country in the world							
Thanked God for my life before going to sleep							
Praised God during the night when I woke up							

Who will you choose to be Today?

Christian	A man who is Plugged into God daily
Self-Centered	A man who is Plugged into his flesh (self) daily
Co-dependent	A man who is Plugged into controlling (or being controlled by) others
Addict	A man who is Plugged into something self-destructive daily

Lesson 5: Activity 2 –
God's Power removes Your Problems

List down 8 reasons you need God's power in your life. These will be the 8 areas you are feeling the most stuck and defeated in.

1.

2.

3.

4.

5.

6.

7.

8.

Section Two:
Your Flesh is Not Your Friend!

Lesson 6 – Who Really Controls Your Life?

The Light of Scripture: John 15:1-2; 5-6

Jesus said, "I am the true vine and my Father is the gardener. He cuts off every branch in me that bears no fruit, while every branch that does bear fruit he trims clean so that it will be even more fruitful.

"I am the vine; you are the branches. If a man remains in me and I in him, he will bear much fruit; apart from me you can do nothing. If anyone does not remain in me, he is like a branch that is thrown away and withers; such branches are picked up, thrown into the fire and burned."

⌐

The Problem: The "fruit" (your actions) you are growing is contaminated

The Solution: Trust God to "prune your character defects" from your personality so you can produce good fruit

The Procedure: Participate fully in recovery trusting God as you do

My Prayer

Thank you Father for your wonderful vine of life; my Lord and Savior Jesus, who died that I might live. And thank you for not cutting me off when I deserved to be cut off. Thank you Lord God for trimming me clean that I might bear fruit that is of value to others. Keep me in your vine Lord Jesus that I might be a part of your tree of life. Help me clearly write what you want me to say in this Lesson.

WINNING THE WAR WITH YOUR FLESH!

I can remember the first time I ever watched my wife Denise working with roses. We had several very tall rose bushes that had lots of flowers on them ...big, beautiful roses that were very fragrant. As I was standing there admiring the roses she took out her cutters and started hacking the branches off. One after another they dropped to the ground as I stared in horror.

"What are you doing," I yelled! "Those are my favorite flowers in the garden." You are killing them!"

"Calm down and stop yelling," she replied. "I am pruning them, cutting them back so that they will grow stronger and bigger. It is healthy for the bush if I cut away the disease that is in it."

As I stood there staring with my mouth hanging open she called me closer. "Come here and look at this leaf...see all the little black spots on this leaf?" she asked.

"Well...kind of...," I replied knowing that I was being taken to "school" on something I probably should have already known. Dreading the upcoming lecture I finished with, "but do we have to do that right this minute?"

Ignoring my weak attempt to escape she continued on, "It's a systemic disease in the plant, if I leave these little black spots on this leaf, and all the rest of them," she said pointing to the many other leaves that had the same blotches on them, "the poison will ruin the rose bush. Even the leaves lying on the ground will poison the bush, you don't want that now do you?" she asked with that cute little smile she always uses when she is right about something.

"No...of course not," I stammer, "But...why not just take all the leaves off? Why do you have to cut off all the branches as well?" I shot back thinking I had her where I wanted her.

"Quite simple actually," she began. "The poison travels up and down the rose bush through the branches, if the leaves are infected so are the branches. Look at this branch for instance; it has deterioration already in its joints. And this one and this one…" she continued as she snipped one branch after another.

Stunned by her deep understanding of horticulture I retreated to my inner mind for my next brilliant move knowing full well she had checkmated me even before the conversation had started. And just to drive the stake into my ego a little deeper she added, "And rose bushes love being pruned. It stimulates their growth and they produce more branches and roses after we show them some "tough love". Sure enough, about a month later those rose bushes came back with a vengeance and were loaded with new buds, a week after that we had more flowers than ever before. And of course, the leaves were very shinny and without spots.

I was not only humbled by my wife (AGAIN!) but also was impressed and touched by how such a simple illustration in nature could be applied to recovery.

Recovery Truth # 26   I Agree _____ I Disagree _____
God always heals (purifies) people from the inside out; removing the root system of sin first so our behavior patterns of self-destruction die from starvation.

Blackberries Make the Point Even Better than Roses Do

In the opening verses (John 15:1-2, 15) Jesus refers to himself as a Vine. Vines love to take over whatever is near them. They not only send up new branches at a fantastic rate but also go underground to reach other areas of your garden or yard. They are extremely prolific even if the ground lacks nutrients for the plant. Vines are very tough and hard to remove.

Take blackberry bushes for example, if you cut 8-foot high bushes (ours get at least that big out here in the Pacific Northwest) down to the ground without taking out their roots, they will grow back with a vengeance to be an even bigger bush within a year. You also must destroy the heart of its root system, the "root ball", if you are to keep them from coming back. This stops the underground migration throughout the yard.

True recovery programs identify and remove the "root balls" in your personality. Your root balls feed the compulsive, self-destructive behavior patterns which are currently destroying your life. These root balls are the real problems that need to be addressed in recovery but often are ignored because digging them up takes too much time. When it comes to inner healing, taking the time saves time (and lives).

Praise God that he is patient with us and takes his time when he is pruning us; this makes us "grow more productive". God's main method for pruning is called discipline.

Recovery Truth # 27   I Agree _____ I Disagree _____
God's discipline teaches you self-discipline because self-control is required to gain freedom from your flesh.

> **Hebrews 12:5-6**
> *And you have forgotten that word of encouragement that addresses you as sons:*
> *"My son, do not make light of the Lord's discipline, and do not lose heart when he rebukes you, because the Lord disciplines those he loves, and he punishes everyone he accepts as a son."*

WINNING THE WAR WITH YOUR FLESH!

My family lived in Southern California when I was very little. We moved a lot and the last town I lived in before moving to a little town in the Sierras was North Hollywood. Since we lived in the city and there were lots of cars my Mother would not buy bikes for my older brother and me. Every time we thought we had her talked into it some kid in the neighborhood would get dusted by a car and that was that.

I was in grade 5 right before we moved to Northern California. I was nine and thought I was pretty capable of riding a bike even though I had been on very few. I saw guys flying by all the time and it looked pretty easy to me. My friend Gary use to tease me about it about as he would have to ride very slowly for me to keep up with him when we were going someplace.

One day we were at his house and I was helping him by folding his papers and putting rubber bands on them so he could deliver them. On this particular day Gary brought out his older brother's bike. It was much better than Gary's bike, very shinny and had handle bars that were up high making me think it would be easy to ride.

Gary said, "Why don't you jump on TJ's bike and come with me. He won't be home for hours."

Stunned and feeling pressured I replied, "Get out of here...TJ would pound me in the ground if he knew I had been on his bike."

"I knew it, I knew it," Gary said laughing at me, "all this stuff about your Mother not letting you ride a bike is a bunch of junk...you're too scared to ride one."

Now I was getting mad. My mind kept telling me, "go ahead, who's going to know?" And the smirk on Gary's face was really "frying my bacon".

"O.K., I'll tag along but I ain't carrying any of your papers. I'm just going along for the ride. And you can't tell anyone I did it, especially TJ...agreed," I said sticking out my hand.

Laughing out loud Gary shook my hand saying, "This I gotta see!"

We took off down the street and the first block was not too bad. I was going slow enough to keep my balance and I loved the feel of the "wind in my hair". Ok, Ok so I had a crew cut, the wind still felt good in my face. But then Gary hit another gear and was gone, flying up and down the blocks with me far behind him. I almost ran into a couple of parked cars as moving cars were passing me on the street. I was glad Gary had not seen me. I started to think this was not a good idea and that I should take the bike back when we hit the boulevard.

Gary had already gone around the corner and was a block down a very busy boulevard when I stopped. He yelled at me to hurry as no cars were coming at that moment. So I took off and was pedaling down the street weaving back and forth in and out of parked cars. Cars were ripping past me going very fast (cut me a break, 30 mph is fast when you are 9). When I made it to the end of the block and turned the corner I saw Gary sitting on someone's front lawn laughing his head off.

Soon it was all over and we were back at his house (Thank God) and I told him I had to go home to eat dinner. I was later getting home than I had said I would be so I ran home as fast as I could. When I got there my Dad was sitting in the living room with my Mom. He never got home this early so I was surprised to see him. He stood right up and came at me. As he walked up to me he asked me "the question."

"Were you riding a bike on the boulevard in heavy traffic about 30 minutes ago?"

Like any red blooded American boy who had just done something wrong I lied straight to his face.

"Not me Dad, you know I can't ride a bike. I don't even own a bike."

Grabbing me by the arm he yelled, "I just drove by you and saw you. Now tell me the truth or I will beat you within an inch of your life!"

So I told him it was me (thinking I wouldn't get it if I admitted what he already knew) and he really let me have it. Moral of the story: "if you're lying, you're dying."

Recovery Truth # 28　　　　　　　　　　　　　　　**I Agree _____ I Disagree _____**
While discipline sometimes hurts like sin, it won't kill you like sin.

> **Hebrews 12:10-12**
> *Our fathers disciplined us for a little while as they thought best; but God disciplines us for our good, that we may share in his holiness. No discipline seems pleasant at the time, but painful. Later on, however, it produces a harvest of righteousness and peace for those who have been trained by it.*

God prunes us with Discipline to produce the fruit of righteousness

Discipline when delivered from a spirit of love is LOVE. Without discipline from God and loving parents when we are "growing up", how can any of us expect to have self-discipline, another name for self-control?

Whether we are Christians or not God expects us to have self-control. This simply means God expects us to control our self which is: our flesh, minds, emotions, words, bodies, and behavior. God tells us that this is not humanly possible without his Holy Spirit in us.

For instance, we are to love our enemies. A pretty tall order especially if they have hurt you and your family. God has stacked the deck so to speak so that we have to come to him to receive the power we need to do what he commands us to do. The awesome thing is God is real and so is his Spirit which puts the power in us, if we submit to God in Jesus name.

Our behavior during life is measured by God according to his "rules" or "laws" not by our intentions, opinions, best wishes, or civil laws. This really upsets our three adversaries: Satan, the World, and our Flesh. All three do not want us listening to or obeying God. They tell us that self-control brings internal happiness and external success, when we let our Self be in control. Many different religions actually teach that there is an inner god within us that we need to trust if we are to find true peace in life.

Nothing could be a bigger lie. Our flesh is not our friend for many good reasons. To help you better understand how dangerous it is to surrender your life to your Self - let's take the Flesh apart piece by piece to see how it sabotages your health, relationships and recovery.

What exactly is the Flesh?

As we learned in Lesson 2, the Flesh is one of three enemies that would destroy us. It is one of three obstacles keeping us from plugging into God and being spiritually transformed for our trip to be with Jesus in Heaven. Our flesh is also referred to in the bible as: **flesh**, **body**, **sinful nature**, **old nature**, and **self**. For the purposes of this book these terms are equal in meaning and will be used as such.

> **Matthew 26:41**
> *"Watch and pray so that you will not fall into temptation. The spirit is willing but the body is weak".*

Even though this is a short verse it contains a ton of wisdom for those who wish to recover. Let me quickly highlight the key words:

Watch	Keep looking for, be ready, be prepared, and be on the alert
Pray	Talk to God, be connected to God, Submit to God
Temptation	Threats to you and your family's well being
Spirit	Your spiritual self, protection for your soul
Body	Your mental, emotional and physical being

Recovery Truth # 29   I Agree _____ I Disagree _____
Temptation is the back door that Satan uses to enter your flesh so he can lure you into doing things you will regret later.

> **2 Corinthians 2:11**
> *"...in order that Satan might not outwit us. For we are not unaware of his schemes."*

Temptation is Satan targeting the weaknesses of our flesh, to trick us into thinking, talking and doing sinful things. Since Satan cannot make us do anything against our will he must use tricks or what the Bible calls "schemes" to make us think sinning is a good thing for us. He uses our own flesh to lead us away from God's Light and into his darkness where we (and others) suffer the consequences of our choices. From God's perspective temptation is simply an invitation from Satan for us to sin; an invitation we do not have to accept and can overcome if we have self-control.

1 Corinthians 7:5

"Do not deprive each other except by mutual consent and for a time, so that you may devote yourselves to prayer. Then come together again so that Satan will not tempt you because of your lack of self-control."

Make no mistake about it; your flesh is not your friend. Your flesh is not only weak but it is hungry and wants what Satan promises it. Our bodies like pleasure and most sin is very pleasurable at first, then it turns on us and causes great pain. The key is to have self-control over our flesh so it cannot connect with those people and things outside of us that will take us down into darkness. Let's use the everyday sin of adultery as one example of how a man lacking self-control and discipline can go down into destruction.

Proverbs 5:20-23

"Why be captivated, my son, by an adulteress?
Why embrace the bosom of another man's wife?
For a man's ways are in full view of the Lord, and he examines all his paths.
The evil deeds of a wicked man ensnare him; the cords of his sin hold him fast.
He will die for lack of discipline, led astray by his own great folly."

So How Does Your Flesh Ensnare You?

I have identified many factors so far in the book that you will need to win the on-going battle with your flesh. You must have a power greater than you to win this battle so plugging into God through Jesus and the Cross brings the Holy Spirit (God) into you. The longer you are plugged in the more power (Grace, Love, Forgiveness, Self-control, Wisdom, etc.) you will have in your daily fight.

You also need to surrender your life to God so he can "clean it up" and "straighten it out". To do this you will need to take your flesh apart piece by piece so the Holy Spirit can "overhaul it"; just like taking your car in to have the engine rebuilt. For it to work properly the parts that aren't working must be replaced with parts that are. And God is the only personality mechanic I know who never gets the job wrong.

Here is a list of parts that make up your flesh (personality included) that God has to heal for you to have full recovery. After some of them I have put a number that indicates the Lesson coming up that will give you more specifics about how God will heal you. Let's briefly review them:

1. **Your Free Will**

   This includes your pride, spirit of rebellion, spiritual stubbornness and need to be in control of your life so only you make the choices you think are best.

2. **Your Self-Worth (C.12)**

   Self-Worth is the level of value you place on yourself. It is also a measure of the level of respect and friendship you have with yourself.

3. **Your Brain (mind: C. 7, 8, 9)**

   We never behave without thoughts and decisions occurring first. If we are to win the battle of "acting out" we must first win the battle of "acting in" which occurs in our thinking processes.

4. **Your Heart (C. 10)**

   The center of your personality, your soul, your character.

5. **Your Emotions (C. 11)**

   Feelings we experience every day that strongly influence our decision making and choice of behavior.

6. **Your Desires (C. 11)**

   Your "I wants", "Gotta Haves", and "Gimme, Gimme, Gimmes".

7. **Your Eyes (C. 11)**

   Everything you see using your vision is recorded in your mind.

8. **Your Tongue (C. 11)**

   Every word that comes out of your mouth.

9. **Your Body Parts (C. 11)**

   What you do with your hands, where you go with your feet, and I can't mention the other parts in public.

In the Lessons coming up you will understand how the flesh takes control over you and makes you do things you know are wrong. Not just once or twice but over and over and over again you make the wrong choices because you trust your flesh. Your flesh is your #1 enemy and must be controlled by you…this is what self-disciplined means.

When we were children and we came back in from "Trick or Treat" on Halloween night we would always dump all our "goodies" on the floor and start eating. Along comes Mom or Dad and tells us to slow down. They explain that if we eat it all at once we will be very, very sick. They usually take it away and let you have some every day while they watch our "haul". Now our flesh says they are lying and just want to get some of it for themselves but over time we come to realize that too much of a "good thing" can be very bad.

Like the two pieces of pie I had last night, the first one was more than enough and was so good my flesh said one more must be better. But the second one put me down like a mad dog and I had a stomach ache all night. At three in the morning my flesh was not anxious to go back for thirds.

Recovery Truth # 30   I Agree _____ I Disagree _____
The Dog You Feed the Most Wins the Fight Every Time so Feed your Spirit and starve your flesh.

Steve, a pastor in my past and brother in the Lord today, use to tell a story of a man who had two dogs in Alaska. He would fight them against each other and always won his bet. But he never bet on the same dog, each time he would change which dog he would bet on and that dog would win. A man asked him one time how he knew which dog was going to win. "Simple", he answered, "I only bet on the dog that I fed that week".

So it is with our battle with our flesh. You can't feed your flesh and your spirit at the same time; whichever one gets fed the most during the week grows the strongest and wins the battle. You need self-control (self-discipline) to feed your Spirit and starve your flesh. Only when you are plugged-in will you have power to overcome your flesh.

I had a long period of recovery because I did not understand this principle. I kept feeding my flesh with spiritual pollution (worldly pleasures) but spent little time feeding my spirit with God's Grace. Every time I was tempted I swore to God I would not do the same sin over and over again, and every time I went right ahead and did it again. I was depressed and felt hopeless, like I would never find the healing I needed.

On the outside it appeared that I was doing all the right things: going to Church, tithing, in prayer groups, reading the Bible when I had time, but nothing seemed to work. Then I started "plugging in to God", seeking him and submitting my weaknesses to him. I stopped begging him to help me and started thanking him for what he had already done for me. I learned how to Praise his name and stopped focusing on me and my mistakes. I learned how to accept his forgiveness and stopped hating myself each time I failed. I stopped feeding my sinful nature (flesh) and started feeding my spirit. Now that my spirit is one with the Holy Spirit I have control over self. Wouldn't you like to have that too?

A Testimony from a Brother in Recovery

Living so many years of my life just for me and doing things my way was not working for me. My life was destructive and hurtful for myself and others. These destructive patterns eventually led me to years in an 8 x 10 cell. For a long time I thought I could fix myself but I could not do any of this on my own. It was during this time when I met God face to face that my healing began. With this healing I found that life was worth living. I still am learning how to truly love and to live the life God created for me to live.

Having been released from a physical prison of bars and razor wire I came to realize that one does not have to be "locked up" to be in prison. I needed to be "Plugged in", connected to God's power, outside of those bars as much as I did inside. I also needed others and the tools available to help me become a man of God. Taking the Stand Firm class Everett teaches helped me more than I can say.

In this class I learned many things that keep me sober and moving straight towards God. One was how plugging in to God every morning is vital to my daily walk. I also learned that my negative inner voice was setting me up to fail and how I could change my negative thoughts and feelings into loving statements towards me.

Another valuable lesson was how my past "Trails of Shame" were still pulling me down spiritually. In class I found very useful information and solutions for leaving these trails behind. And being challenged in class to be honest and "transparent" about my struggles and weaknesses with other men who have similar issues has really helped me to trust again. Trust God, trust others but more importantly, to trust me.

I am really looking forward to using the many things God has taught me through this class to help other men who are on the same journey of recovery that I am on. It is now my purpose for living. I can't wait to get copies of this book as I know so many men who need direction and support.

Bill B.

So What Can You Do to Get Healed?

1. Read with an open mind
2. Complete your inventory honestly
3. Keep turning the pages-keep learning about what is destroying you
4. Exchange your will for God's Will; eternal life for eternal death
5. Plug into God's Holy Spirit and receive forgiveness and power to change
6. Trust in the Lord more than you trust your flesh which is not your friend

Please complete the Inventory activities for Lesson 6 before reading Lesson 7.

Lesson Six Inventory

What were you Thinking when you read Lesson 6?

How are you Feeling after reading Lesson 6?

How is what you are Thinking and Feeling now going to help you with your recovery?

What are you going to change in your behavior after reading Lesson 6?

What Bible verse in Lesson 6 will you commit to memorizing?

Lesson 6: Activity 1: How much Control do you have?

Circle your level of control for each part of your flesh listed below.

A. Your Free Will

This includes your pride, spirit of rebellion, spiritual stubbornness and need to be in control of your life so only you make the choices you think are best.

No Control   50%   80% Control

B. Your Self-Worth

Self-Worth is the level of value you place on yourself. It is also a measure of the level of respect and friendship you have with yourself.

No Control   50%   80% Control

C. Your Brain

We never behave without thoughts, decisions occurring first. If we are to win the battle of "acting out" we must first win the battle of "acting in" which occurs in our thinking processes.

No Control   50%   80% Control

D. Your Heart

The center of your personality; your soul, your "true" character, your passion.

No Control   50%   80% Control

E. Your Emotions

Feelings we experience every day that strongly influence our decision making and choice of behavior; such as fear, anger, confusion, loneliness, frustration, etc.

No Control   50%   80% Control

_____

F. Your Eyes

Everything you see using your vision is recorded in your mind.

No Control   50%   80% Control

_____

G. Your Tongue

Every word that comes out of your mouth.

No Control   50%   80% Control

_____

H. Your other Body Parts

What you do with your hands, where you go with your feet, and I can't mention the other parts in print.

No Control   50%   80% Control

_____

I. Your Needs

What you need to feel satisfied in life; safety, security, love, acceptance, etc.

No Control   50%   80% Control

_____

J. Your Wants

What you "think" you must have to be successful, happy; usually things such as fame; cars; houses; money; trips; eating out; new electronic "stuff".

No Control   50%   80% Control

_____

Lesson 6, Activity 2: Which Dog do you feed the most?

Under each category below list down what you are currently doing that "feeds" (makes bigger, stronger) that part of your personality.

A. To make my Flesh bigger and stronger (Spirit weaker) I currently am:

    1.

    2.

    3.

    4.

    5.

B. To make my Spirit bigger and stronger (flesh weaker) I currently am:

    1.

    2.

    3.

    4.

    5.

Lesson 7 – Something to Be Mindful Of

The Light of Scripture: Romans 1:21

For although they knew God, they neither glorified him as God nor gave thanks to him, but their thinking became futile and their foolish hearts were darkened.

~

The Problem: **Your brain causes you to be a "double-minded" man**

The Solution: **Let God give you a "Brain Bath"**

The Procedure: **Surrendering both sides of your brain to God**

My Prayer

I praise you today Father for opening my mind to your truth. Thank you for healing what little brain I have from all the pain and pollution that was in it. You are a great and loving God who helps me every day, often when I don't even know you are doing so because I am so near-sighted with my own problems. Help me think clearly in writing this Lesson, I need to be clear and write useful things for the many readers who are insane like me. LOL

One of the biggest discoveries in my recovery was realizing that I actually was not in control of my mind but that my mind was in control of me. I had always prided myself on being quick witted, able to think fast and "figure out" any problems I was having. Unfortunately, this self-perception really was the foundation for my spiritual fall time after time.

The first time I really understood that my mind was my enemy I was sitting in a 12-step class at my church. I was overwhelmed by the number of men and women who had showed up for the first class. There were around 160 people. After we had received our books and the opening lecture was finished we were assigned to small groups of no more than 12 per group.

In my small group I looked around and saw eleven men who were total strangers. I didn't even know the group leader which made me feel totally out of control. We were facing each other as we sat in a tight (way too tight) circle. I remember thinking to myself, "This is stupid, I'm not sharing my problems with a bunch of guys…where are all the women?" Fortunately, the women had been removed to another area where they were meeting in groups without men.

Going home that night I told my wife Denise I was not going back because there were only men in my group and that all we would do is talk about sports. I told her real loudly that I was "serious" about getting better. She quickly replied, "Praise God there are no women in your group and you are going back…do I make myself perfectly clear?"

Next week in group we were reading the 12-steps aloud and I had Step 2. As I read it one word exploded in my head. It said, "Came to believe that a power greater than ourselves could restore us to sanity." The word that hit me like a ton of bricks was SANITY! I had never thought of myself, in all my acting out and blowing up my life, as being insane.

Hearing the word coming out of my mouth was emotionally overwhelming for me. I wanted to laugh out loud as it was a simple answer to why I was messed up…I was crazy, but of course …why hadn't I thought of it before? Then I got angry and wanted to throw the book across the room as I felt insulted…these people think I'm nuts! I'll show them they're wrong. And lastly, I wanted to cry because I believed I had to be insane to have done all the damage I had done to those I loved so much. Case closed, I was guilty and now sentencing would take place.

Praise God I stayed in the group and worked the program as those strangers became my brothers. We all shared our tears and fears as we learned how to become "transparent" with our inner pain. We came to understand that there was a power greater than our "thinking", a power who was loving and full of mercy. I also soon realized that there was much more work to be done if I was to be restored to sanity. I needed to learn how to control my thinking.

What Makes Us Go Insane?

When it comes to answering the question, "How do people become addicted?" there are three main reasons: Biological Influences, Psychological Damage and Spiritual Pollution. In this book I will discuss all three, but I will only talk about Biological influences for the rest of this lesson. Let's start with this quote on sexual addiction.

"A sex addict is a man or a woman whose sexual behavior (view pornography, masturbation, fantasy, sexual and/or emotional affairs, humiliating and demanding sexual behavior) is harmful to their finances, intimate relationships, careers, self-esteem and probably to their families as well.

Some people use sex as a coping mechanism for their personal problems. There are three reasons why people become sexually addicted; they are biological, psychological, and spiritual. The three building blocks of sex addiction are 1) sexual fantasy, 2) pornography, and 3) masturbation.

Studies have linked a deficit in the neurochemistry of the limbic system in those patients that have been diagnosed as sexually addicted. Apparently these patients have sex to restore the dopamine levels in their bodies. People can recover from sexual addiction learning about the roots to their addiction and by attending the 12 step recovery program." (From internet: "Can sex be an addiction?" http://www.csun.edu/~psy453/addict_y.htm)

Biological Factors Impact Decision Making

The first source is what is commonly called **Nature** or how we are "hardwired" from birth. This response focuses totally on all of the "biological" reasons we become addicted. They would include: DNA, health of the body at any given age, gender differences, hormonal influences, diet, exercise, etc. There are many research studies examining how the brain actually works. The mind is a new frontier for investigation; many of these studies have to do with the biochemistry of the brain.

Recovery Truth # 31   **I Agree _____ I Disagree _____**
One reason you act insane is because your brain is always on chemicals.

Our brains have all kinds of biochemical "stuff" going on in them. We simply call it thinking but it really is more complicated than that. Thinking is just the outcome of all of the biological processes which are in operation within our heads. More importantly is the fact that this "stuff" is working inside us without us even knowing what it is.

When it comes to sexual behavior cycles, the following neurochemical factors play a key part in how we get sexually aroused and then cool back down.

Biological Factors: Five "Neurochemicals" to be considered

Serotonin   A neurotransmitter that influences most of the 40 million brain cells to relay brain messages within your brain including levels of sexual desire/arousal.

Testosterone   Sexual hormone in men, determines the strength of sex-seeking behaviors.

Oxytocin   A pituitary hormone that leads to attraction, affection, attachment, and pair bonding

Dopamine   A neurotransmitter that stimulates sexual arousal, provides the biochemical reward for sexual contact, the main source of the sexual "rush" or orgasms

Prolactin   A pituitary hormone that counteracts the "dopamine high", it brings the person back down to their "pre-rush" level, often to the point of relaxation or wanting to sleep

Our body's function using a complicated system of bones, joints, muscles, tendons, ligaments, nerves, veins, blood, and biochemical substances called hormones, neurotransmitters and whatever else they are called. A main player in our sinning and in our recovery is Dopamine. This little beauty gives us the super feelings we have when we do certain things: drinking caffeine, eating chocolates, taking dangerous risks and surviving, shopping when depressed, and of course, sexual contact of any or all kinds. For example, kissing alone can really start the dopamine ball rolling within your head leading you to wanting more. Even flirting releases dopamine making you want to "take the next step".

Dopamine is very powerful and creates in us the super urge to repeat whatever sets the dopamine off in our heads even if it is destroying our minds, bodies, relationships and futures. Dopamine is the "payoff" for acting out and is one of the most powerful acting-in problems addicts have because it causes your own mind to betray your better judgment.

Dopamine creates habits (addictions) in you so that you keep feeding the brain dopamine. Smoking, for example, illustrates just how simple this chemical sabotage works. Most smokers I have met (and I smoked from 18-28) say they wish they could quit. They know it is really destructive to their lungs which pump oxygen into their blood so it goes into their brain so the mind can function. Nurses, of all professions, understand this but many of them smoke like chimneys setting a terrible example of health to their patients. They can't stop because they work in a high stress occupation; to relieve the stress they need something that will calm them down and make them feel good even if it only lasts for a few minutes. That something is Dopamine which is triggered by nicotine.

Coffee is no different; people drink gallons of coffee every week just to let the caffeine trigger Dopamine in their minds so they can feel good. The problem with all of these substances is when the Dopamine wears off you have to come back down and then you want to do it again to get back up. This repeated pattern of behavior is called the addiction cycle. As we know: acting-in leads to acting-out.

One last example, I think the alcohol and drug patterns are clear to understand but what about shopaholics (spending money to feel good)? They get depressed because they are in debt, things at work or home are not working out the way they want them to, or they feel hopeless because they are unplugged from God. And to deal with depression they must find a "high" so they go spend money they do not have on going to movies, clothes, cars, eating out, electronics, internet specials …you know the drill. When they spend they feel a sense of power which is really the dopamine rushing through their minds. Of course, by the time the first payment comes around they are more depressed than they were to begin with so the cycle starts over. They have to go buy something else to get their next dopamine fix.

So how do you break this cycle? And more importantly, how do you find "inner peace" without addictive substances? The answers to these questions lies in plugging into God so that He can give you the power to overcome your body's demands to get high. I never thought this would be possible but it is. God's Spirit touches our human spirit and we have a spiritual high that is beyond understanding. This happens when we let God teach us how to win the battle for the mind.

Recovery Truth # 32   I Agree _____ I Disagree _____
To win the battle for your thinking you must control "both" of the super computers in your brain.

Right Brain and Left Brain Characteristics

It is simply amazing how God created the human mind. All human beings have two sides (called hemispheres) to their brains, the left and the right. Each side functions like a "Super computer". You can access some very clear and easy to understand articles on thinking on the internet, just Google the term Left-Right brain (also called Split-Brain). You cannot control something if you do not understand what it is; so for our purposes I am going to give a quick overview of the main differences between the Left-side brain (LB) and Right-side brain (RB).

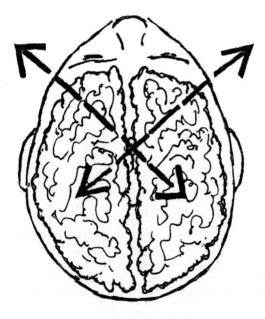

1. The LB and RB control different sides of your body

It is hard to fathom but God has created the two sides of your brain each to operate the opposite side of your body. So your LB controls the right side of your body and the RB controls the left-side of the body. This is very evident when someone has a stroke (which is like a heart attack in the brain). If the stroke does not kill them, they are often crippled on one side of the body. If the left side of the body is handicapped we know the stroke occurred in the RB; and if the right side is damaged then it reveals the stroke occurred in the LB

2. The LB and RB process information totally differently

All day long you are taking in new information from your environment. This happens through your five senses: smell, taste, sight, hearing and touch. But as the information comes into your brain both sides do different things with that information. The LB breaks it down into categories, identifies it and labels it and places meaning or value on it; basically it analyses the data strategically to see how useful it is for future goals. For example, you enter a room full of people at a meeting. Your LB immediately breaks down the incoming data as to how many people are there, what time is it, how long has the meeting been going on, what the purpose of the meeting is, and, who you need to connect with to get what you want. In short, the LB takes the whole and breaks it down into many categories and parts.

The RB gets the same information, but instead of breaking it down, it lumps it all together and evaluates it emotionally, how it relates to helping people and relationships, and how it can be used for creative action. So at this same meeting your RB gets excited because there is a buzz going on in the room, people seem very upbeat and are talking a lot, there are lots of possibilities to connect with everyone in the room, and, there are some creative approaches to the agenda. In short, the RB takes all the parts and creates a whole.

3. The LB is Goal and Time Driven while the RB is Relationship-Oriented

Your LB demands that you use all information to reach goals by certain timelines, regardless of how it impacts people's feelings or needs. It is very competitive and wants to "win" in whatever it is doing. The RB demands that you be sensitive to others feelings and ideas, that you be respectful and kind, that you take time out to be playful and to enjoy the experience whatever it happens to be.

4. The LB is purpose driven while the RB is driven by people & pleasure

The LB inspires you to be task-oriented and value production; what needs to be done now and how much will it cost. The RB is into living life, experiencing it to the fullest which means having fun with others. The LB seeks high quality results and is critical of people and situations, less trusting and therefore more controlling. The RB leads you to be overly trusting, to think the best of everyone, and to give in on quality and achievement standards if it brings more people together and they are happy.

5. Everyone uses both the LB and RB but not in the same way

God created our minds to be divided into two "super computers" that are operating at lightning fast speeds processing incoming data with staggering complexity. We call this thinking. Each individual uses both sides of their brains but certain people naturally operate out of their LB

80% of the time while others operate out of their RB 80% of the time. Men, as a large group, tend to be more LB while women, as a large group, tend to be more RB. Now having said that, I have met many men who were totally RB thinkers and many women who were LB thinkers so it is not determined by gender.

You will know for sure which side you prefer to use before you are done reading this book so relax and stay in a learning mode for right now. To help you keep this "split-brain" information straight here is a chart summarizing some of the major differences between the LB and the RB.

Left Brain/Hemisphere	Right Brain/Hemisphere
Controls right side of the body	Controls left side of the body
Center for Language/vocabulary	Center for Emotions/ feelings
Rational, systematic, logical	Impulsive, creative, experiential
Task/time focused, driven	People focused, relationship driven
Looks at differences, advantages	Looks at similarities, common ground
Analytical, sequential, problem solvers	Musical, Artistic, Athletic
Competitive, challenge driven	Non-competitive, team driven
Very organizational, hierarchical	Very spontaneous, friendly, playful
Prefers Predictability & Production	Prefers Variety and Innovation
Focus is mostly on past and/or future	Focus is mostly on the "now"
Identity – Who you Think you are and should be	Actor – Who you want to be, dream of becoming
Self-Concept –everything you think about self	Self-Esteem – everything you feel about self
Routine allows for better quality control	People, variety, invention are the spices of life
Planned, structured developers	Open minded, cross-cultural travelers
Draws on previously accumulated, organized information that often is factual, proven, tested, documented, etc.	Draws on unbounded qualitative patterns that are not organized into sequences, but cluster around images, looks for new solutions to old problems
Logical decision makers: Splits info into categories: distinctions are important, thinks logically, sequentially, sees cause and effect, problem solving is key focus and drive is towards task completion	Emotional decision makers: Lumps info together: Is a holistic, global thinker Sees associations, resemblances, connectedness to people is highly important, relationships are main focus

So Left is Right and Right is Left...Color me confused!

As more than one brother has said to me when going over the left and right brain information, "Who cares, what does it have to do with recovery!" And I always answer the same,

"Everything…even right now your LB and RB are tricking you into thinking none of this information can help you when it is exactly what you need to get right with God so you can get the healing you need." So readers, be patient, I will explain in great detail how both sides of your brain can sabotage your recovery in Lessons 8 (LB) and Lesson 9 (RB).

Recovery Truth # 33   **I Agree _____ I Disagree _____**
The garbage you let in your brain will be the garbage that makes all your decisions in life.

Even before you were born your mind was recording information from the outside world. Like a computer it stockpiles data into files that you access for daily decision making. It also creates extensive picture albums of everything you see as you are growing up. Both of these systems of retaining information we call "memories".

The left side brain accesses information through words and vocabulary. The location of our language development and storage center is on the left side of our brain. The more we learn to speak, read and write using words the more this center in our brain grows. Much of the information comes in through our eyes or visual learning.

The memories stored in the right side of our brains consist of sounds, images, emotions, experiences and fears. These memories are directly related to touching, smelling, tasting, doing, hearing and feeling.

Regardless of which way the information comes into our minds it comes in from the world we live in. We do not live alone in a vacuum. Our world consists of other people, animals, things, relationships between us and others, plus between other people without us, situations and events, the weather, acts of nature, etc.

We want to think the "World" is a paradise that has no problems, when in fact it is a fallen world. Wars, disease, famine, corruption, rape, dishonesty, earthquakes, hurricanes, pornography, good friends and family members all infect us with fears, insecurities, anger, lust and what I call corruption or garbage. Most of this garbage comes in without us even knowing it has entered our minds.

It is this corruption that I call mind pollution; much like a "Trojan Worm" that has entered the operating system of your computer, it requires a power greater than you to "wipe your hard drive (brain) clean". The process of wiping your mind clean is a major part of recovery and cannot be "skipped" if you want to be healed.

Recovery Truth # 34   **I Agree _____ I Disagree _____**
To have your "super computers" refurbished you must give them back to your Creator.

About a year ago I opened up an email from someone I did not know, the message said urgent so I clicked on it without "thinking". As soon as I did it, my computer went nuts. My security program started sending me messages that a Trojan worm had invaded my computer and was taking over. I freaked out until I remembered what my good friend Ron told me, "Do not turn your computer off, if you think you have a virus call me first."

I called Ron immediately; he had me check my virus program to see if the invader had been quarantined, which it had been. He then told me it was OK to turn it off and bring it to him. When I brought it in, I figured it would only take a few minutes for him to kick the worm out and I would be on my way. After examining it he told me that he would need to keep it for a couple of days so he could wipe the hard drive clean. I was very upset at first. I thought that wiping my hard drive clean would destroy all my valuable files, documents and programs. Ron just laughed and told me to leave it to the "Master."

Now I wasn't sure if he meant God or himself but I was sure I had no ability or skills to deal with the problem. I had to trust him to do what he said he would do and Ron returned the computer back in its proper working order (without losing my files). Ron always resolves computer problems: first, because he is a true Man of God, and second, because he knows what he is doing. Unfortunately he is also a raving Arizona Cardinal football addict and desperately needs help but that is a story for another recovery book, I just don't have the time or space to address that one here (LOL).

When you have viruses in both of the computers in your brain you need to go to the "Master" for help. Removing these "Trojan Worms" from your thinking requires expert skill as they are totally different viruses. Praise God that he is the Creator and knows exactly how to wipe your "hard drives" clean without losing any of your important memories. Praise God that he can and does "renew" our minds, removing the things that for years have kept us from praying to him; lies that keep us "unplugged".

> **1 Peter 4:7**
> *"The end of all things is near. Therefore be clear minded and self-controlled so that you can pray."*

As I have been telling you over and over again, it is your flesh that has sabotaged your dreams, your relationships, your health, your finances and your soul. To win this battle you must retake the "high" ground, you must win the battle for your mind. Your mind is the command post for your flesh. To retake this command post you need help from other "Brothers in the Lord".

Recovery Truth # 35   I Agree _____ I Disagree _____
"As Iron Sharpens Iron, so one Man Sharpens Another." Proverbs 27:17

A Testimony from a Brother in Recovery

My name is Dave and I am in my mid-fifties, married with grown children. All my life I have been listening to a voice in my head that has brought me nothing but fear and worry. I have been always questioning everything, such as: "Where is God?", "Is this as good as it gets?", "Why am I here?" I felt so alone that even though I knew 100's of people I always felt isolated, unable to connect to people and to God. I had major anger problems and had hurt many of my family members deeply.

Then I took the Stand Firm class and learned how to "plug-in" to God. Every day I surrender my life to Jesus and God pours his love into me. My negative inner voice is no longer controlling my life and now I can understand God's Word. I actually have gotten past the self-hatred and know that God has created me for a purpose. Through this amazing information I am now taking a journey that I only thought happened to others, never to me. God's plan is so much better than the one I have been listening to. I have learned to let God's Holy Spirit transform my mind and heart. I know you can find the same inner peace if you let God take control of your life.

Dave Z.

So What Can You Do to Get Healed?

1. Read with an open mind
2. Complete your inventory honestly
3. Keep turning the pages-keep learning about what is destroying you
4. Exchange your will for God's Will; eternal life for eternal death
5. Plug into God's Holy Spirit and receive forgiveness and power to change
6. Trust in the Lord more than you trust your flesh which is not your friend
7. Control your mind through God's power or it will control you with Satan's power

Please complete the Inventory activities for Lesson 7 before reading Lesson 8.

Lesson Seven Inventory

What were you Thinking when you read Lesson 7?

How are you Feeling after reading Lesson 7?

How is what you are Thinking and Feeling now going to help you with your recovery?

What are you going to change in your behavior after reading Lesson 7?

What Bible verse in Lesson 7 will you commit to memorizing?

Lesson 7 Activity 1: Which Brain Chemicals are Which?

Match the correct names for each neurochemical described below:

_____ A neurotransmitter that influences most of the 40 million brain cells to relay brain messages within your brain including your levels of sexual desire/arousal.

_____ Sexual hormone in men, determines strength of sex-seeking behaviors.

_____ A pituitary hormone that leads to attraction, affection, attachment, and pair bonding

_____ A neurotransmitter that stimulates sexual arousal, provides the biochemical reward for sexual contact, the main source of the sexual "rush" or organism

_____ A pituitary hormone that counteracts the "dopamine high", it brings the person back down to their "pre-rush" level, often to the point of relaxation or wanting to sleep

Dopamine   Oxytocin   Prolactin   Serotonin   Testosterone

Lesson 7 Activity 2: Separating Left from Right

Place a checkmark under the brain hemisphere (left or right) you think that personality characteristic comes from.

	Right Brain	**Left Brain**
Task/time focused, driven		
Controls right side of the body		
Actor – Who you want to be, dream of becoming		
Very spontaneous, friendly, playful		
Planned, structured developers		
Self-Concept –everything you think about self		
Musical, Artistic, Athletic		
Center for Emotions/ feelings		
Competitive, challenge driven		
Focus is mostly on past and/or future		
People, variety, invention are the spices of life		
Looks at similarities, common ground		
Very organizational, hierarchical		
Identity – Who you Think you are and should be		
Focus is mostly on the "now"		
Routine allows for better quality control		
Open minded, cross-cultural travelers		

	Right Brain	**Left Brain**

Logical decision makers

Looks at differences, advantages

Non-competitive, team driven

Self-Esteem – everything you feel about self

Prefers Predictability & Production

Analytical, sequential, problem solvers

Prefers Variety and Innovation

Emotional decision makers

Controls left side of the body

Center for Language/vocabulary

Impulsive, creative, experiential

People focused, relationship driven

Rational, systematic, logical

Now go back to Lesson 7 and see how many you marked correctly.

Lesson 8 – Just Because You Think It Doesn't Make It True

The Light of Scripture: Romans 7:21-25

So I find this law at work: When I want to do good, evil is right there with me. For in my inner being I delight in God's law; but I see another law at work in the members of my body, waging war against the law of my mind and make me a prisoner of the law of sin at work within my members. What a wretched man I am! Who will rescue me from this body of death? Thanks be to God-through Jesus Christ our Lord!

The Problem: **Your brain lies to you so it can control you**

The Solution: **Replacing the lies in your thinking with God's truth**

The Procedure: **Learn (memorize) God's word**

My Prayer

I praise you Father God for the insights you have given me about my flesh being my enemy. I ask that you will remove anything from my mind that does not honor you. I surrender my thinking to you and ask that you give me the "brain bath" my mind needs to clear it of all worldly pollution. And please protect me daily from the evil one's schemes as he tries to reenter my brain so he can control my emotions and actions.

Thank you Jesus for dying for my sins that I might live. You are my Lord and I seek your help as I write this book today…open my mind to your scriptures so I can provide answers to men's questions about how they got so screwed up living in this world. Help me to show them how they can find you and be cleaned of all the toxic waste that is in their minds.

Thank you Father.

I remember back when I was younger, and it seems like only yesterday, when I would get together with a bunch of guys to have a few beers. Personalities changed and guys would open up with things that they would never say when they were sober. Somehow we all of a sudden had the courage to speak our deepest thoughts and feelings. We use to call it "liquid courage" and we would get all the heavy things in our minds off our chests. We spilled our "guts" about women, politics and of course every sport that was ever invented. We were going to stop the war, shut down the government and win the heart of that special girl whatever her name was. We were going to "be somebody!"

The truth of the matter was the next day, suffering from hangovers and still broke; we woke up to the reality of our lives. The war raged on, the government was still there doing things we hated and not doing anything we wanted, and all of us were lousy athletes. To make it even more tragic, most of us couldn't even get a date for Friday night because we were so "stuck in our heads". Our solution back then was to drink more beer! Beer always washed away our fears and tears…at least to the next day when we woke up and were face to face with "reality" again.

Recovery Truth # 36   I Agree _____ I Disagree _____
Transparency requires having the Courage to Honestly Share Your Fears and Tears without the Beers

I found the same thing to be true when I started getting stoned. I was much more particular about whom I shared my thoughts with as not everyone was "cool" back then. Whether I was flying high with "Bombers" rolled with Acapulco Gold or choking down "Skinnies" filled with Bakersfield Brown I shared my opinions with everyone in the room who would listen. I even shared my opinions when no one was listening. While lost at the University of Addiction I thought I was in "real classrooms" for expanding my mind into greater consciousness. After all, we weren't called "heads" for nothing.

It is so tragic that men just seem to enjoy being open and honest with each other when they are high on something. The problem is nothing ever gets fixed, nothing ever gets better, and no one ever changes for the positive. The truth is most men are "Slip-sliding away" into darkness, laughing as they go, believing the many lies their minds tell them. One such lie is, "This is the best it will ever get, so enjoy it while you can." How sad it is to realize that our own minds deceive us into choosing self-destruction over life; that our own brains would lie to us!

Let me say here and now that if God can take a guy like me and clean him up and heal him of his inner fears and tears without using alcohol, drugs, women, cars, money, power, or violence to do it, he can definitely save your sorry behind. The starting place is the cross; once you are plugged into Jesus you will have the power of the Holy Spirit to help you regain control of your life from your flesh. To gain this power you need to learn how to be transparent (brutally honest) with God, yourself, and significant others.

Transparency: getting off the Zeppelin before it's too late

Major goals in recovery are: seeing the truth, accepting the truth, telling the truth and living the truth. This is because most people with compulsive behavior patterns are self-centered, self-destructive and dishonest. And what keeps them primarily this way is a huge river in Egypt called "Da Nile"...actually its denial and it's not only in Egypt.

Denial is simply your mind lying to you. It tells you "up is down and down is up"; and you believe it. It tells you things are "really not that bad" when they are and you believe it. It misleads you into thinking, "I got myself into the mess I'm in and I can get myself out." Now nobody who knows you and cares about you believes any of these lies. They try to get you to get help but your mind keeps telling you everything is really OK, when in fact you are going down like a "Zeppelin in flames". When the levee of lies breaks your whole life becomes flooded with pain.

The beginning of recovery starts when you stop lying to yourself and accept the facts and consequences of your behavior. It starts when you begin to be transparent with those who can help you (and not with those who can't help you).

The practice of "Transparency" refers to: not hiding anything, being open about your strengths and weaknesses, and appropriately sharing your "stuff" with people who need to know. Transparency is the life blood of recovery because it requires you to "look in the mirror" of your personality and behavior and accept everything that is reflected back at you, the good as well as the bad. To be transparent you must accept responsibility for your self-destructive actions and stop playing the "Blame Game".

Recovery Truth #37   **I Agree _____ I Disagree _____**
When you Blame you stay the Same.

Taking responsibility for who you have become is very difficult because your mind is working against you. It does this right in the middle of your thinking. While you are trying to figure out how to stop destroying your life your "inner voice" is talking to you about how much you deserve to keep doing the self-destructive things that you have been doing. Remember, acting-in (thinking) leads to acting-out (doing). Overcoming this kind of contradiction in your thought patterns is the main learning point in this Lesson.

Your Inner Voice is Crucial to regaining Sanity

Your "inner voice" (also called Self-talk) is that part of your thinking that speaks to you inside your head. It is located inside your left-side brain where your vocabulary center is found. Everyone has an inner voice; and it has nothing to do with mental illness where someone has multiple voices in their heads talking to them. The inner voice is simply your mind talking to you when you are alone or when you are speaking with others.

For example, I am driving down the highway and I am messing around with the FM presets trying to set a new station when all of a sudden my mind yells inside my head, "Watch out Everett, you're too close to that car! Slow down and pay attention!" In this case my mind is helping me be a safe driver which is a good thing. But it could be just the opposite…I might be driving down the road and my inner voice says, "Look at the new Lexus driving by," and I turn my head away from where I am heading and run into the back end of the car in front of me.

God gives your mind the ability to "talk directly and only to you (inside your head) without anyone else being able to hear". This is what I call your inner voice. Verbalizing using language is one of the major things that separate people from animals. What is even more interesting is that you can have a conversation going on in your head at the exact same time you are having one with someone else. This happens most of the time. For instance, when any two people are having a conversation there are actually three conversations going on at the same time. Each person has a conversation going in their head (that's 2) and then there is the conversation that is happening between the two individuals (that makes 3).

This makes listening, comprehension, and communication very difficult as inner conversations talk louder than outer conversations. So communication often becomes distorted since both people's inner voices are replacing the words being spoken with new words that are not being spoken by the speaker. For example, here is a short exchange between a husband and wife that might sound familiar to most of you:

Husband: "Wow…nice dress!" (his inner voice saying she looks good in that dress)

Wife: "Really…well forget it; I haven't got time to make love now." (Her inner voice saying he is only commenting on the dress to have sex and I am too busy now)

Husband: "Ok, Ok…calm down. I just said I like the dress." (His inner voice saying that is the last time I tell you I think you look good)

And of course this conversation keeps going sideways for the rest of the day as both their inner voices keep setting them up for more arguments and hurtful statements.

In and of itself your inner voice is neither good nor bad, it just tends to talk to you the way significant others around you spoke to you as you were growing up. So if you grew up with people who talked to you in very positive ways you will more likely talk to yourself in positive ways; and if not, you will talk to yourself in negative ways. When you were born your mind and inner voice were empty and both develop as you learn words, vocabulary and judgmental phrases.

As humans we tend to personalize people's statements even when they are not directly talking about us. For example, you are a child and your Dad and Mom have the following exchange:

119

Dad talking to Mom: "I hate kids, they are so stupid."

Your Inner Voice: "Dad hates kids, Dad must hate me. He thinks I am stupid." Or

Dad talking to Mom: "I love watching Kids; they are so smart in how they figure things out."

Your Inner Voice: "Dad is cool, he likes me. He thinks I am smart."

The negative inner voice begins at the same time we learn to talk and think; it happens from people talking to us, with us and at us. If that word exchange (conversation) was positive our thinking overall tends to be positive, if it is negative then we will think of ourselves more negatively. When we list our negative inner voice messages we can often identify where we first learned that "negative tone of voice" or "putdown" from. These significant "teachers" are still in our heads and are often called our "Committee Members".

Your committee consists of both positive and negative role models who left "taped messages" inside your head. Possible committee members would be: Mom, Dad, Older Siblings, Grandparents, past employers - especially some of your first bosses, teachers, coaches, military superiors, spouses, teenage friends, etc. You learn to perceive and talk to yourself the way these people teach you to. If that was positive then it is a good thing but if it was devaluative then it has disastrous impact.

Negative inner voice statements don't just happen; they come from somewhere and have purpose. And that purpose is to destroy everything you think about yourself and others. Removing your negative committee members and replacing them with positive ones is essential to recovery. The key to success is understanding this truth, "Just because you think it doesn't make it true."

Recovery Truth # 38   **I Agree _____ I Disagree _____**
Freedom from negativity begins when you trust what God says in the Bible more than you believe what your inner voice (mind) is telling you.

Like a computer program the Inner Voice will talk to you the way it was programmed to talk to you. Most of this programming occurs during the first ten to twenty years of your life. Your inner voice functions like an "operating system" (OS) for the two super computers inside your brain. For better or for worse, it dominates your thinking, decision making, behavior and relationships. Basically, what goes into your mind is what comes out in your behavior.

For instance, if your OS has lots of negativity programmed into it; viruses like hatred, prejudice, jealousy, and revenge will create self-destructive behavior patterns which will increase and dominate your life. In short, we end up doing what we swear we will never do. Your mind, and more specifically, your thinking deceives you into becoming someone you can't stand and someone God never meant for you to be.

How Your Left-Side Brain Works Against You

In the previous lesson, I identified the fact we all have two sides to our brains. The inner voice, positive or negative, is in your Left-Side Brain. This is where your vocabulary (word) center is.

The negative inner voice has many characteristics that identify it: lying to self and others, fearfulness, worrying, critical thoughts of self and others, jealous thoughts, severe judgmentalness, pride, selfishness, and all devaluations reveal its true purpose...to destroy your life and the lives of others. In recovery it is often referred to as "stinking thinking".

As your inner voice gets trained by others and the world to become negative it takes on very self-destructive techniques. In short, instead of being your best friend it becomes your worst enemy. Please consider the following characteristics of a negative inner voice.

Negative Inner Voice Characteristics

1. It is judgmental; highly critical of you and others
2. It is jealous, unforgiving and vengeful
3. It hurts others while telling you it's for their own good
4. It is manipulative and deceitful
5. It lies like a rug
6. It isolates you from positive people and from God so it can control you
7. It sets you up to fail repeatedly by choosing toxic relationships
8. It is fearful, worries excessively and tells you there is no hope for you
9. It is controlling of you and others
10. It is verbally abusive towards you

My negative inner voice did not want what was best for me, it wanted to destroy me. It wanted me to get high so it could make a fool out of me which it certainly did. And worse than that it used me like a pimp to hurt others I loved, telling me that I was in the right when I was really wrong. For instance, these lies told me my wife did not love me when she really did. The lies it put in my head bound me over to addiction. Those lies tormented me day and night. Those lies also kept me from coming to Jesus sooner than I did so that I could be healed.

Perfectionists are really Worry Worshippers

Many of you worry, worry, and worry about everything. Your negative inner voice keeps hounding you day and night telling you one lie after another and you believe every one of them. Some of its biggest lies are:

- you have to be more than you are
- you have to be better looking than you are
- you have to be smarter than you are
- you have to be holier than you are

- you have to be kinder than you are
- you have to be more fun than you are
- you have to be "Perfect" if you want to be successful

This type of thinking is highly stressful and leads to repeated failures in relationships and major health issues. It never ends in your mind; you can never be satisfied because you always fall short of being perfect. You will never be happy because you are so imperfect. And your mind keeps piling it on you no matter how good a job you do. In short, listening and agreeing with your negative inner voice will destroy everything you hope to have in life.

Your "negative inner voice" is nothing but a Big Bad Bully.

Once I started trusting Jesus I stopped putting garbage into my body. Then my mind started to work the way it was created to work. As I praised God more and read his word daily I suddenly realized just what my negative inner voice really was…a Bully! Bullies rule with fear and intimidation but by plugging-in to God's power you can receive the spiritual power to Stand Firm against all of your bully's threats.

Make no mistake about it, your flesh is no friend of yours…in fact, it is a persecutor of your soul. And within your mind (the main computer running your flesh) your left-brain and right-brain are full of viruses that need to be removed. The major virus in the left-side of your brain is your negative inner voice. Praise God, removing mental pollution is His specialty!

Take a Brain Bath; Let God wash away your negative inner voice every day!

Romans 12:2
"Do not conform any longer to the pattern of this world, but be transformed by the renewing of your mind. Then you will be able to test and approve what God's will is—his good, pleasing and perfect will."

In recovery we must examine how our minds keep leading us back into self-destructive behavior patterns over and over and over again. The main answer is, "Your negative inner voice." It has been programmed to destroy you from an early age and with God's power you can reprogram it before it is too late. Remember, you must win the battle for your mind if you are to stop your compulsive acting-out.

What goes on in your head strongly influences your decision making and that directs your behavioral choices which in turn decide your success in life. Let's take a closer look at how you can turn your negative thoughts into positive ones.

1. Read, memorize scripture daily. God's Word will wash your mind clean.

2. List down what your inner voice is telling you…seeing it on paper gives you an

opportunity to see how negative it is and to change it. We will be held accountable for what we think as well as for what we say and do.

3. Tape record yourself talking...the negative inner voice speaks through your mouth all the time...decide if what you hear coming out of your mouth honors God and those you love, if not then change it.

4. Identify Who is On Your Committee. These are the most significant people who first programmed your operating system (Inner Voice)...figure out where the negative thoughts first started...what person, what event led to you thinking each thought. Replace the negative thoughts with positive ones. Replacing negative devaluations with scripture verses helps restore your mind to God's will.

5. Learn to discriminate between God's voice and your committee member's voices...who is really talking to you and is the message helping or hurting you/others?

6. Your negative inner voice can also be controlled by Satan who enters through what others say and the media, such as: pictures, books, movies, TV shows, music, newspapers, lectures, etc.. Temptations are projected into our thoughts every day through these sources. Limit anything that is putting negativity into your mind faster than you are learning scripture. For example, when I stopped listening to rock and roll my acting out decreased noticeably.

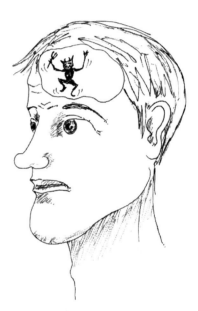

7. Stop hanging around people who tell you negative things about you and about others. Spend time with those who are positive in their outlook on life and who praise God rather than curse men.

8. Get help with your negative inner voice. It will always tell you that you can do it alone which is how it wins out against you. You must work with men who have more sobriety than you do, not less. They will help you with your "stinking thinking".

9. Read Christian articles and books that will help you control your thinking. You will find many of them under the title of "Self-talk".

Praise God by thanking him for everything you have, by doing this daily you will be plugging into the power you need to clean your hard drive. You also will be able to better identify the negative thoughts that have been hiding inside your thinking for years.

Recovery Truth # 39   I Agree _____ I Disagree _____
God does not negotiate with terrorists; and your negative inner voice terrorizes you every day. It is holding you for a ransom that will never be paid.

When you start to let God change your negative inner voice it will freak out, rebel, and fight back to keep control over you. Do not be worried, all worrying is just your negative inner voice trying to keep you locked into fear. It will kick, bite and rip you up for surrendering your will to God instead of trusting in it to guide your life back into self-destruction. Don't panic, just trust God more than you trust your own mind. One of my favorite quotes comes from St. Augustine, "Do not try to understand so that you may believe but Believe that you might understand."

God is very aware of how your mind is polluted by the world and how that pollution convinces your mind it is really powerful, when in fact, it is just a bully that is picking on a weakling (you). But besides being a bully it is also a terrorist. Terrorists are bullies that take captives and hold them for ransom by threatening to kill their captives if they do not get their demands met. Lucky for us, God does not negotiate with Terrorists. God destroys the destroyer.

So your inner voice is already saying, "Wait a minute…what if…? One of your negative inner voice's tactics is to always question God's abilities to help you. By undermining your thinking it continues to hold valuable territory within your mind, and therefore can still influence you to relapse back into your self-destructive patterns. It uses you to block God from giving you the help you need to take control over it and the other self-destructive parts of your mind.

Get mad, attack the negativity in your mind…it is not who you were created to be. Fight back by plugging in to God's Spirit to get spiritual power to override the lies in your head. Read God's Word and memorize scripture to replace the world's lies with God's Truth. And let God teach you to love yourself mentally; all self-hatred statements in your inner voice do not come from God. They are poisonous to you and to all of your relationships.

Recovery Truth # 40   I Agree _____ I Disagree _____
You become what your mind focuses on and thinks about the most.

"Watch your thoughts, they become words
Watch your words, they become actions
Watch your actions they become habits
Watch your habits they become character
Watch your character it will become your destiny."
Frank Outlaw (poster sold at www.jaguared.com)

A Testimony from a Brother in Recovery

Relief! I have finally found Relief! One evening I discovered just how trapped in my mind, in my "stinking thinking" I was. In a moment I realized just how poorly I had valued myself daily my whole life. I believed all the lies in my inner voice was telling me and finally understood how trapped I was inside my own thoughts.

When I was recording my self-worth inventory I could see just how negative all the lies in my inner voice really were. How those thoughts were destroying me and all that I loved. But I soon discovered empowerment as God handed me a roadmap for healing my mind. The joy I felt when I discovered that I wasn't a misfit, that God didn't want to destroy me...that he loved me. My stronghold of fear-my oldest and cleverest foe-was loosened. Somehow, the truth of God not sparing his Son Jesus for my sake rescued me from all the lies...from Satan's lies that repeatedly told me that God did not really want me. But God's perfect love drove out my fear and I now know that I can have success from addiction.

On that evening I also found out how to read the roadmap to healing through learning about specific and identifiable prayer. What drove me to control my external environment was fear. So now I pray, "Father in Heaven, please remove this fear from me." Sometimes I ask God to, "Hold my hand while we both walk down this road of fear together." I am so strengthened when God is holding my hand and encouraged when He carries me along the path I am now walking. God's love strikes at the core of my fear and renders it powerless in my life. The truth has set me free.

It is amazing how in one evening, while taking inventory of my self-worth, self-concept and negative inner voice, the Truth got ahold of my insides and I experienced freedom from addiction by surrendering my flesh to my Father in Heaven in Jesus name. I now have hope where I once had anxiety, love where I once had anger and faith where I once had fear. Praise Jesus!

David C.

So What Can You Do to Get Healed?

1. Read with an open mind
2. Complete your inventory honestly
3. Keep turning the pages-keep learning about what is destroying you
4. Exchange your will for God's Will; eternal life for eternal death
5. Plug into God's Holy Spirit and receive forgiveness and power to change
6. Trust in the Lord more than you trust your flesh which is not your friend
7. Control your mind through God's power or it will control you with Satan's power
8. Replace your negative inner voice (lie machine) with God's word

Before reading Lesson 9, please complete the Workbook activities for this Lesson.
Please complete the Inventory activities for Lesson 8 before reading Lesson 9.

Lesson Eight Inventory

What were you Thinking when you read Lesson 8?

How are you Feeling after reading Lesson 8?

How is what you are Thinking and Feeling now going to help you with your recovery?

What are you going to change in your behavior after reading Lesson 8?

Plug-in with Prayer - How would you like God to help you right now?
(in the space below please talk directly with God…He is listening.)

What Bible verse in Lesson 8 will you commit to memorizing?

Lesson 8: Activity 1 - Stopping the Negative Inner Voice

1. Rate the following **Negative Inner Voice Characteristics in your mind.**

   NT = Not there   ST = Sometimes There   AT =Always There

   ___ It is judgmental; highly critical of you and others
   ___ It is jealous, unforgiving and vengeful
   ___ It hurts others while telling you it's for their own good
   ___ It is manipulative and deceitful
   ___ It lies like a rug
   ___ It isolates you from positive people and from God so it can control you
   ___ It sets you up to fail repeatedly by choosing toxic relationships
   ___ It is fearful, worries excessively and tells you there is no hope for you
   ___ It is controlling of you and others
   ___ It is verbally abusive towards you

   Now take 5 minutes to quickly write answers to the following questions.

2. What are some of the most powerful negative things your mind tells you?

3. How do you "Stand Firm" when Satan attacks your inner voice with lies and other negative thoughts?

4. What can you do to take the offensive in the spiritual fight within your mind?

Lesson 8: Activity 2 - The Truth Will Set You Free

In the spaces numbered below write out five negative statements (lies) that your inner voice (self-talk) tells you about yourself in regards to your recovery. After you have done this, go back and write one of God's truths related to each lie. If you are not sure what God's truth is leave it blank for now.

Inner voice lies: example = I can never be forgiven for what I have done, it is too late.

God's truth: example = "Forgive, and you will be forgiven" (Luke 6:37)

1. Lie Number One =

    God's truth is =

2. Lie Number Two =

    God's truth is =

3. Lie Number Three =

    God's truth is =

4. Lie Number Four =

    God's truth is =

5. Lie Number Five =

    God's truth is =

Lesson 8: Activity 4 – Who's On Your Committee

Take 5 minutes to write down your 5 most significant committee members (mental programmers) and list down how they, through your negative inner voice, still influence your decision making and behavior today.

Identify one negative thought each committee member planted into your mind and discuss how it still affects you today.

Example:

Mother You are just like your father and always will be!
(Your Dad was an alcoholic)

Committee Members Negative Thoughts/Behaviors from them

1.

2.

3.

4.

5.

Lesson 8: Activity 5 -
Who did you learn that negativity from?

List below at least five ways your flesh is sabotaging your health, relationships, and recovery through your "negative inner voice". List what the negative message is and which committee member it originated with.

	Negative Statement	Committee Member
1.		
2.		
3.		
4.		
5.		

Lesson 9 – When Right is Wrong

The Light of Scripture: Proverbs 14: 12

"There is a way that seems right to a man, but in the end it leads to death."

The Problem: **The Right-side Brain seduces you with pictures wrapped in feelings that trigger bad decisions.**

The Solution: **You must surrender your feelings and "Video Vault" to God**

The Procedure: **God wipes off toxic feelings and pornographic images from your hard drive (brain) so you can't be seduced by them**

My Prayer

Dear Lord Jesus I praise you for your kindness and mercy. I am strengthened by how gracious you are to all of us who are struggling to serve you by helping others learn about your Father in Heaven. I am very grateful for you opening up my mind to just how it deceives me with pictures, feelings and past experiences.

I surrender all my thoughts to you. I thank you for taking away the many images in my mind that misled me into self-destructive behavior that hurt others as well as me. I am so pleased that your Holy Spirit brings me peace, your peace which transcends all understanding. Help me to accurately tell each reader how he can find your Holy Spirit and your peace even while they are still suffering. Help me Lord to bring them to you.

This is weird, but interesting!

fi yuo cna raed tihs, yuo hvae a sgtrane mnid too.

Cna yuo raed tihs? Olny 55 plepoe out of 100 can.

i cdnuolt blveiee taht I cluod aulaclty uesdnatnrd waht I was rdanieg.

The phaonmneal pweor of the hmuan mnid, aoccdrnig to a rscheearch at

Cmabrigde Uinervtisy, it dseno't mtaetr in waht oerdr the ltteres in a word

are, the olny iproamtnt tihng is taht the frsit and lsat ltteer be in the rghit

pclae. The rset can be a taotl mses and you can sitll raed it whotuit a pboerlm.

Tihs is bcuseae the huamn mnid deos not raed ervey lteter by istlef, but the wrod

as a wlohe. Azanmig huh? yaeh and I awlyas tghuhot slpeling was ipmorantt!

The words above seem scrambled and so mixed up that they make no sense but the message is actually quite easy to read if you do so with the right-side of your brain rather than your left-side. Remember that your vocabulary center is on the left side of your brain. The left side identifies every letter and assesses what order they are in to match it with a word in its memory banks that has that exact spelling. But the right side of your brain, once a word has been learned correctly by your left side, can recognize the scrambled word by its "picture". If you could not make out the message the left-side translation is provided below:

If you can read this, you have a strange mind too. Can you read this? Only 55 people out of 100 can. I could not believe that I could actually understand what I was reading. The Phenomenal power of the human mind, according to research at Cambridge University, it doesn't matter in what order the letters in a word are, the only important thing is that the first and last letter be in the right place. The rest can be a total mess and you can still read it without a problem. This is because the human mind does not read every letter by itself, but the word as a whole. Amazing huh? Yeah and I always thought spelling was important!

Quick Right-Side Brain (RB) Review

Along with your left-side brain, your right-side of your brain is another wonderful super-computer that has been programmed by God to do some amazing things. For example:

- Your emotions exist in the right side of your brain. All feelings originate from here.
- RB dominate people tend to be "experiential" (learn by doing) learners

- Your mental pictures, images& imagination come from this side
- RB dominant people tend to be more relationship oriented; caring and merciful; talkative; and like talking with their hands and actions.
- It is in the RB that you see animals as friends and family members rather than just pets
- It's on this side that you have all your "creativity".
- RB dominant people tend to be very artistic and love painting, sewing, etc.
- RB dominant people tend to be very athletic and love playing sports
- RB dominate people tend to be very musical and love playing instruments and singing
- RB dominant people tend to smile more, laugh louder, and touch more.
- RB dominant people also tend to love cooperation, teamwork, win-win thinking; they are more non-competitive.
- RB dominant people tend to prefer variety in most things; they prefer friends that are different from them.
- RB people also are more impulsive and have difficulties with self-discipline and critical comments about them.

Understanding how the right-side of your brain influences you for good and for bad is just as important as comprehending how the left-side of your brain impacts your decision making. On the right side there are some very powerful characteristics that are either working with you to find healing; or are working against you, taking you back down into slavery (addiction).

Let's consider one of the most powerful factors below (others will be examined in Ch. 10):

RB provides thinking with Pictures, Feelings, and Sounds & Actions

As I went up and down the rows and rows of videos every one of them held a strong attraction for me. Each one had very specific images in it that I wanted to see again. Even though I had seen every one of them many times I still revel in watching them again and again. They made me feel alive in a strange way.

One was of a young boy who went over to a friend's house and they watched a SCARY movie. It was a true Horror flick and the young boy almost wet himself as he sat there "wide eyed and terrified". He went home and had nightmares for weeks imagining he was one of the victims in the movie.

Another one was about the Alamo and the battle that took the lives of all the men who stood in the way of the Mexican army moving across Texas. In it a young man was fighting next to Davy Crocket and was shooting just as fast and straight as Old Davy was. In the end he gives his life to save Davy from a bayonet thrust.

And another film was a swashbuckler that had good pirates fighting off bad pirates in big sea battles. And of course, the hero saves the beautiful woman held captive by the bad guys and sails off into the sunset with her in his arms.

And who can forget all the Bond movies, where James defeats every villain and beds every woman in his path. The image of Ursula coming up out of the surf in a white two piece and walking up the beach always brings strong emotions every time I watch her.

One of my favorites is of the small high school football team being picked for last place in their league only to win the Championship. It wasn't easy as they had to work very hard just to win every game by one point. One player in particular stands out scoring most of the touchdowns and making many game saving tackles. The best part of his heroics is that he is the smallest player on the team.

The movies titles just keep flashing in front of me. Which one to choose is always the challenge but soon I get to the "special" flicks. These ones are what you might call "mature" or "adult" in their themes and pictures. These all contain nudity and sexual content. Suddenly I feel a stronger urge to pick one of these.

One is of teenage lovers who fight and break up yet are drawn back together by their passion for each other. It is often referred to as "Young Love". First time kissing and touching always creates a power within that can be extremely engaging. These moments seem cemented within the mind. Another one is of a first year college student who finds out that besides classes and studying, real education comes from young ladies who love to experiment with drugs and love. He soon drifts farther and farther into learning about what the "humanities" is really all about.

A film that always grabs my attention is the one about the university student who is very poor and meets an older woman who "befriends him". She is 35, divorced and lives in a very nice home while he slums it with three roommates who smoke, drink and sleep most of the day. He finds himself drawn into her world and experiences romance in very erotic ways.

The list of films goes on and on. There are so many and all of them seem to say the same thing over and over again each night, "Pick me, Pick me…you know you want to watch me!" And sure enough I chose one and again go into the "dark room of my mind" to replay that memory over and over again till it fulfills the need I have. For you see, I was the young boy, the teenager, the hero, the college student, the university student, and the "Hero" in every movie that ever played in my mind.

Recovery Truth # 41   I Agree _____ I Disagree _____
Most men are legends in their own minds but seldom in anyone else's.

Mental Masturbation
I have often heard that, "Most men are legends in their own minds." All of these types of movies are in the "Video Vault" of your mind for a reason, to keep your legend dream alive. All day long and every night you go through the playlist to select which memory you will mix with which fantasy for your cerebral "validation" fix. Men need to feel valued, important, powerful

and significant; when these feelings do not occur in reality we go to fantasy to get them. These trips to the "Theatre of the Mind" fuel most of our self-destructive habits.

Remember, acting-in (thinking) leads to acting-out (compulsive behavior patterns). Behavior doesn't just happen…it is a result of thinking that leads to decisions on how to act. So when you are sitting in your mind watching your "movies" you are "priming the pump" to take action out in reality. If the internal images are pornographic (yea, yea…I know you never have any of these) then they will feed your desires to go do whatever you are thinking about.

For example, before you masturbate (sure you don't and never have) you fantasize or "dream" of who you will be with and what you will be doing with them. All of this pornographic thinking is what I call mental masturbation and is based on what is already in your video vault. It only stands to reason that if you want to end the pornographic feelings and lustful images in your thinking you must first eliminate the stockpile of videos you have in your mental vault.

Stocking Your Mind with "New Movies"

You have a "Theatre of the Mind" in the right side of your brain. In it you are the director and producer of whatever images are "playing". You mix and match memories from your past with other images you have put in your "Video Vault". All your experiences provide your "Production Company" with new material. Watching TV shows, playing video games and looking at pornography can greatly increase the number of corrupt "movies" in your mind. And not all of these polluted images are sexual in content.

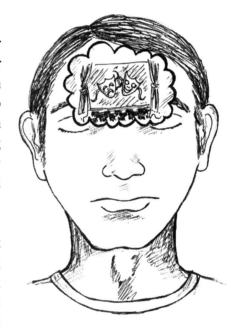

For instance, many dreams are of retaliation against someone who hurt you or wronged you in some way. In these fantasies you are telling them exactly what you think and how you feel. You are doing things to them that you would never do in reality but in fantasy it sure feels good to "get even" with them. Other fantasies may focus on making millions of dollars, paying off all your debts and still having lots of money left over for traveling, buying things and helping the poor.

And many times your Theatre plays horror movies. Images that scare you to death are presented and really evil things are happening to you. Sometimes these images come from real horror movies or events you have seen in reality and other times they are created by horrific things that happened to you as a child. Your mind uses these images to frighten you, threaten you and control you with fear. Like the negative inner voice you also have a negative movie director who uses mental images to punish you.

Daydreaming, Mind Tripping and "Astro Traveling"

"Daydreaming" is simply dreaming during the day. In the 60's it was often called "mind tripping" and "astro-traveling" (LOL...well it was). As we have learned, the right side of the brain operates with pictures and sounds, colors, dreams, images, and voids (blank spaces in your thinking) rather than with language/talking/planning (left-side brain). Daydreaming manipulates you with "movies" of what could have been and what should be. It is replaying past events with different outcomes, imagining fantasies to replace the many realities you hate facing every day.

For instance, when you find reality "boring" or unsatisfying you take a mental trip up into your Theatre to watch something more uplifting, more enlightening. In these mental vacations you always win, always get the girl, always get the promotion, and always get justice for past wrongs. Unfortunately, when you return to reality you realize that nothing has really changed... life is still "boring" and disappointing.

The most destructive part of these types of mental vacations is that they all require you to leave the "now". So even while your body is sitting in reality (school, work, home, church, etc.) your mind is a million miles away. This means you are not concentrating with what is happening around you in the present...you are lost up in your gray matter and that leaves you in a very vulnerable place.

I already used the example of how the negative inner voice can cause a traffic accident if you listen to it rather than pay attention to driving safely. Well the exact same thing happens driving with the right side of your brain only this time you don't hear anything, you just see pictures of you being somewhere other than in your car. When this happens your concentration is not on operating the vehicle as much as it is on what you are "imagining", leaving you and others at great risk.

One of things I stress in the Stand Firm class is being "grounded" which is the skill of "living in the now". I help the men learn how to stay focused on the now, whether it is good or bad, so they can stay in control of their minds. If you cannot control your mind you will never be able to control your behavior. If you cannot stay focused in the now you will be misled into making bad decisions.

Recovery Truth # 42   **I Agree _____ I Disagree _____**
Isolating from others by withdrawing into the fantasy keeps you mentally sick, emotionally crazy and ineffective in all relationships.

One of the most self-destructive parts of leaving reality is that you can't stay on your mental vacations for very long unless you use something else to prolong the "trip". All people, when they are unhappy, love to "medicate" which is a recovery term meaning you need to put something into your body that makes your mind go into dream mode and stay there longer.

Alcohol, drugs, sex, gambling, shopping, smoking, eating sweets and many more behavior patterns release Dopamine (explained in Lesson 7) which gives you the feeling of elation or a "high" offsetting the drudgery of living in reality. When you use these escape patterns repeatedly they stop being just self-reinforcing negative compulsions and become harmful habits called addictions. At this point your bad habits control you rather than you controlling them; which means you are out of control.

When your mind becomes controlled by negativity and other world pollution, your reality becomes a "living nightmare". Your health, wealth and stealth (a lie in your head that the real you cannot be seen by others) all come crashing down leaving you worse off than when you first started living in your "head", or should I say, in your "Man Cave".

So why does watching Mental Movies feel so right, so good?

Giving up these mental movies is never easy as men become very attached to their private collections. Over the years these "bad boys" have become your most prized procession. While others have let us down in real life, your fantasies remain loyal to you. They keep on giving you everything you want to see and hear. They make you feel "good" even when you are being bad. As we use to say in the 60"s, "If it feels good do it! This concept works right up until you hit the wall and crash; and all addicts hit the wall while accelerating into darkness.

Letting your feelings make your decisions is letting your feelings control your behavior. Sooner or later you will want to get your fantasy life to merge with your reality. For example, when men repeatedly look at sexual images they soon start thinking about hiring a professional to give them the sexual rush they think they need. Prostitutes make big money helping men (and women) fulfill their fantasies. They are trained to do things with them that they can't do in their real world, but think about every day.

Many men have secret lives where they spend some time every week going and doing something that they do not want others to know about. This secret life gives them a false sense of power and of freedom. This acting out often matches the mental fantasies they are having with their mental images and, in turn, add to their Video Vault collection. Secret lives are very addictive until the secret is uncovered. I have spent many an hour with men who were caught in their secret life and now must face the consequences (jail, divorce, STD's, loss of employment, etc.) that are guaranteed to follow.

Little Boys and Their Toys

Most of this acting out is justified in men's thinking by the feeling of entitlement. This feeling lives in the right-side of the brain and does not care about "facts" such as God's laws. Many men believe that since they work hard they have earned the right to do what they dream of. Often it is not even sexual pleasure they are seeking but objects and thrill-seeking experiences such as racing 4-wheel drive trucks up muddy hills. Cars, boats, electronic equipment, bigger TV's, shopping to get more clothes, eating in high end restaurants and trips to far away locations all are examples of this entitlement rationalization. While very costly, these things are all considered great "fun" that doesn't harm anybody. Believing this lie only fools us.

A familiar saying that women have for men acting badly is, "they are just little boys playing with their toys." Unfortunately, these toys often determine their destinies and eternal future. Knowing this, men still refuse to give up their toys because these toys are also their "best friends". These mental friends have been with them since childhood when they first suffered pain and loss in relationships. Withdrawing into their minds was the only place they had a sense of being in control. To give up such friends is the same as having to give up their right arm.

Most addicts have few, if any, friends so these mental images fill in for the loss of companionship. The Theater of the Mind is like a friend's house where you can always go for comfort. This is especially addictive after a hard day trying to make it in reality. But the more you go there the more you become a prisoner of fantasy and the less you are able to function successfully in reality. But to receive healing you must first be willing to leave these old friends who are now your worst enemies, and to give up your "mind toys".

Recovery Truth # 43   I Agree _____ I Disagree _____
Television, Motion Pictures, Video Games and Adult Internet sites feed your "Fantasy Factory" with pollution; creating a Virtual World in your mind that will destroy you.

By now you realize that you have a Theatre of the Mind in which you are the director of whatever images are "playing"; you create these images (fantasies) to satisfy the unmet needs (desires) in your life. All your experiences provide this Theatre with new material...watching TV and video games or looking at pornography can greatly increase sinful "movies" in your mind. These kinds of movies are really just a toxic dump which pollutes your thinking and actions. To escape reality you actually bring that same reality into your mind causing "twisted thinking".

Your success in life is directly related to how mentally focused you are on reality, not fantasy. The more time you spend in fantasy the fewer opportunities you will have to be successful in life. Computer/TV generated reality is no reality at all. It is all just "Smoke and Mirrors". Entertainment is full of slick tricks to get your money by selling you a "service" that ultimately destroys you and your family's lives.

Recovery Truth # 44   I Agree _____ I Disagree _____
When it gets too tough to stand before men kneel before God; you'll stumble and fall less when you are on your knees.

Whatever the images are, if they do not honor God you must allow him to "wash your mind clean" of them. Asking God to take them out of your brain and to replace them with thoughts that are affirming to Him and to you is a superb way of taking back your mind.

Freedom from this mental prison only comes when you ask God to wash your mind clean of memories, emotions and fantasies that dishonor him. God will lead you away from the unwholesome thinking which leads you into sinful actions when you surrender your will to him.

Recovery Truth #45   I Agree _____ I Disagree _____
Nothing changes until you ask God to change it.

Men, being prideful and stubborn almost always drag their feet in giving over to God the very things that are killing them. They still hang on to the lie that tells them they can do it themselves with a little help from God. Another year goes by and they find themselves right back where they were the last time I talked with them; Still going down in flames, hurting themselves and others as they go. And they often blame God for their choices and failures.

Sadly, when I work with men to help them clean out the pollution from their minds I often run into very strong resistance. I remember this resistance in myself all too well when I was trying to get straight. I soon encounter their flesh trying to "negotiate" the terms of their surrender with God while helping them eliminate the mental thoughts and images that are destroying their lives.

You cannot negotiate the terms of surrender; until you surrender your life to GOD you will suffer and unfortunately, so will everyone else who cares about you; watching you destroy yourself always takes a terrible toll on those who love you. The good news is once you have completely surrendered God is more than willing and able to put your personality and life back together the way it was supposed to be before you surrendered your mind and life to the world. Either God controls your life or the world will control you; thinking you can control either is "insanity".

A Testimony from a Brother in Recovery

Going into this program I was at a point in my life that I needed more than counseling, everything was broken, I was off my spiritual track and headed to isolation and living with fear. I wasn't sure what I'd get out of it - hoping for change and fellowship with others, what I came away with was a revelation, not only identifying the addictions but stripping layers of hurt, layers of embarrassment and layers of heartache, finding the road back to the real me.

What I got from this program was that God loves me and Jesus died for me and that I had to stay plugged in to his word to stay focus on HIM. Once I let God cleanse myself, my marriage, my job, my Christian walk, and this life everything got better.

M Walker

So What Can You Do to Get Healed?

1. Read with an open mind
2. Complete your inventory honestly
3. Keep turning the pages-keep learning about what is destroying you
4. Exchange your will for God's Will; eternal life for eternal death
5. Plug into God's Holy Spirit and receive forgiveness and power to change
6. Trust in the Lord more than you trust your flesh which is not your friend
7. Control your mind through God's power or it will control you with Satan's power
8. Replace your negative inner voice (lie machine) with God's word
9. Purify your Video Vault by letting God give you a brain bath

Please complete the Inventory activities for Lesson 9 before reading Lesson 10.

Lesson Nine Inventory

What were you Thinking when you read Lesson 9?

How are you Feeling after reading Lesson 9?

How is what you are Thinking and Feeling now going to help you with your recovery?

What are you going to change in your behavior after reading Lesson 9?

Plug-in with Prayer - How would you like God to help you right now?
(in the space below please talk directly with God…He is listening.)

What Bible verse in Lesson 9 will you commit to memorizing?

Lesson 9: Activity 1 –
Inventorying the Theater in Your Mind

Please answer the following questions:

List 3 non-sexual fantasies (mental movies) that you frequently replay in your mind?

1.

2.

3.

What "sexual" fantasies (mental movies) stimulate you to sinful actions?

1.

2.

3.

What emotional memories haunt you (replay in your mind)?

1.

2.

3.

What are 3 memories (Mental toys) you do not want to give up to God?

1.

2.

3.

Lesson 9: Activity 2 – Assessing Mental Pollution Sources

Rate your activity using each one of the sources for acquiring mental pollution listed below; according to how much time you spend using each one gaining impure thoughts, words and images for your "Theater".

Sources for mental pollution	No Problem - Use very little	A Struggle -Hard to put it down	It Owns Me – I am addicted to it
Magazines			
Books			
Television Shows			
VCR Movies			
Internet			
Video Games			
Laptop, Notebook, Tablet			
Cellphone			
Smartphone			
Car Radio			
Motion Pictures			

Lesson 10 – Welcome to Open Heart Surgery

The Light of Scripture: Romans 1:24-25

Therefore God gave them over in the sinful desires of their hearts to sexual impurity for the degrading of their bodies with one another. They exchanged the truth of God for a lie, and worshiped and served created things rather than the Creator—who is forever praised. Amen

---

The Problem: Our Hearts are full of Pride, Fleshly Wickedness and Worldly Pollution; all of which feed our compulsive acting in and acting out.

The Solution: All of these toxins in our flesh need to be spiritually scrubbed clean by God.

The Procedure: God gives us a new Heart by washing our spirits clean with His forgiveness through His Holy Spirit.

My Prayer

Dear Father God, only you can open a heart to your truth and your Spirit. I pray today that those who read this Lesson will be filled with your light in their hearts. And that your light will drive out the darkness that is controlling them. Please touch them with your truth and call to love just as you opened Lydia's heart in Acts 16:14 to receive your spirit.

I was driving to work on Highway 1 in Canada way back in 1988. It had two lanes going into Vancouver and two lanes coming back out. It was around 8 a.m. and I was in the middle of morning rush traffic which was moving along at a good clip. It was a gorgeous day; blue skies, warm and all the trees around the freeway were very green. I had wished I had another day of vacation off but I didn't. It was time for me to get back to work…or so I thought.

I was getting close to the Port Mann Bridge which crossed the Fraser River. I was in the fast lane listening to the radio and thinking of what I had to do when I got to work when I passed a big tanker truck on my right. Right before I got completely past him the driver suddenly switched lanes. As he did so, the front of his bumper slapped the back end of my Plymouth Reliant station wagon and suddenly my day took a turn for the worse.

The force of the blow spun my rear end around and the speed I was traveling moved me into the slow lane. I was now going backwards at 65 miles per hour looking directly into the eyes of the driver that had been directly behind the truck. I read profanity on his lips as I saw him pulling his wheel hard to get over behind the truck before he hit me head on. It was then that I noticed the back of the tanker was inches away from the side of my station wagon. I remember thinking to myself, "if I keep spinning my front end will catch his back end and I will be t-boned by the car coming at me".

At this same instant I was also aware that my car was still moving towards the side of the road. I knew that I was going to go off the road and hit something very soon…and that it was really going to hurt. I suddenly let go of the steering wheel and said, "Jesus Save Me!" very loudly. Then my car went off the pavement and flipped over. I was traveling through the air when I suddenly and violently came to an immediate impact. The force threw my head and left arm against the side window and glass was flying all over the inside of the car.

I soon realized I was stopped. I was choking on all the dust inside the car. I remember turning off the radio as it was blaring very loudly. I immediately felt my legs thinking maybe I had been cut or broke one of them but they were fine. I then turned off the ignition in case of fire. I could hear cars hitting their brakes and coming to a screeching halt outside my car. I panicked thinking to myself that one of them was going to pile on top of me and that I needed to get out of the car as soon as possible.

I reached over and undid my seat belt and landed with a big thud on my head, it really hurt both my neck and my shoulder. For a moment I was stunned and then I fully realized that the car was completely flipped over and I was upside down. I fought to get my feet out from under the dash and soon was on the inside of the roof flat on my belly, lying between the front bucket seats. Yes, hard to imagine, I had a station wagon with bucket seats and a stick shift. I use the word "had" because this was the last time I ever drove it.

As I looked around I could see nothing but dirt on both sides. The roof was crushed down almost to the tops of the seats. I heard many loud voices outside and a pair of very big black shoes was next to my rear left door window which had not broken. A hand was banging against the glass as the man told me to roll the window down. I actually had to roll the window up which I did with much pain from my neck. As I did so this wonderful breeze came in, fresh air and I lay my head down and wanted to go to sleep. I thought this is all a big dream and I was going to wake up and tell my wife Denise I just had a really scary dream. Only it wasn't a dream.

The voice was from a Mountie (US translation = State Trooper) and he told me to cover my eyes as they were going to use the Jaws of Life to cut me out. I freaked out hearing this and rose up quickly yelling, "NO!" I looked around quickly and saw the back door of the wagon was not broken so I passed the keys to him and told him to open the back up. As he did so I crawled to where the back door was and it opened down about half way before it hit the telephone pole I had just missed.

A firefighter on the scene ripped off his gear down to his t-shirt and started into the car which freaked me out completely and I immediately told him to stop. He had so many muscles that his muscles had muscles. You know the type…a Calendar boy. He was so big he couldn't get all the way in which was a blessing as I did not want anyone inside with me…claustrophobia had gripped me big time. He backed out of the opening and I crawled very slowly to it. When I reach it very strong hands reached in and jerked me out like I was a rag doll. I was strapped to a board, hauled up an eight-foot embankment and shoved into an ambulance which drove away with sirens blaring.

Now I told you all of that, to tell you all of this. When I got to the emergency room a nurse came in and looked at my left arm which was bleeding in many places. She immediately grabbed a bowl and a brush and started scrubbing all the cuts to remove the many small pieces of glass buried in my arm. As she did so I began screaming like a little kid and she actually told me to be quiet. She went on to explain that if she did not get all of the glass out my arm it would become infected and I could lose it. She also scolded me by saying, "the pain you are feeling now is far better than the pain you will feel later if I don't do it!" And to this day those words of wisdom have stuck with me.

Recovery Truth #46   I Agree _____ I Disagree _____
If you want to avoid the pain of self-destruction you have to suffer the pain of recovery; so get ready for it daily by plugging in to God.

Remember that recovery is a day by day journey towards God. Recovery is simply God removing from you all the negatives the world has placed in you and receiving all the spiritual positives He has created for you. On this road to recovery we all must stop in God's "emergency ward" for this "transplant".

Removing all the toxic poisons that have been planted in your personality, especially those that are embedded deep in your heart will be a painful, but very necessary, operation. For without this "open heart surgery" you will stay the same, suffering and causing agony for many others. Praise God, He is the heart surgeon and not you. This is not a do-it-yourself procedure. This Lesson explains how and why you need to let God create in you a "new heart".

The Day My Surgery Began

Over fifteen years ago I was face down on my living room floor crying and feeling like life was pretty much over. Denise had left me for the second time and this time we both agreed she should never come back. We both had given up on thinking that I was ever going to "get it right". God repeatedly gave me chances to repent and each time, after several months of not sinning, I would turn right around and do it again. Each time I relapsed I felt more defeated, more hopeless and more disgusted with myself. On this day I was at rock bottom and felt it was over when God did an amazing thing.

As I lay sobbing on the floor our two little dogs, Arlo and Sweetie came over to me. One on each side of my head and at the same time both started licking my face. At first I tried to push them away, pesky little critters who just wanted outside I thought to myself. But each time I pushed them away they came back and started licking my face again. As they did so, I felt like I was being "comforted" by God, I could feel his presence in the room.

After petting and hugging my two little friends I got on my knees and prayed. I told God I didn't know what to do and that only he could deliver me from my disastrous choices. God followed by saying in my mind… David. I immediately knew he meant King David who had committed adultery and murder. I didn't understand what I was to do but still crying I found my bible and when I opened it I was at Psalm 51.

I had read this Psalm before without much conviction but as I read it this time my mind completely exploded with hope. I prayed every line back to God and based my recovery on it. I did not read anything else for weeks, just Psalm 51. The following section, in particular, really gave me strength. God touched my spirit with His Spirit every time I read it.

> **Psalm 51:10-13**
> *Create in me a pure heart, O God, and renew a steadfast spirit within me. Do not cast me from your presence or take your Holy Spirit from me, Restore to me the joy of your salvation and grant me a willing spirit, to sustain, me. Then I will teach transgressors your ways, and sinners will turn back to you.*

I came to understand that for me to recover I had to receive a new heart. That mine was totally a wreck and it was actually polluting my life rather than making it healthier. But I felt new joy because I also realized that God could and would create a new heart in me. And that I also now had a purpose for living, once I went through recovery I would help other men who were "down and out" like I was. The funny thing about this was, I didn't really like men very much but at this point if God wanted me to help them then I was going to do it.

Recovery Truth #47   I Agree _____ I Disagree _____
Your heart is the driving force within your personality; it is either driving you towards God or away from him.

So why do you need a new heart?

1. **Your heart is prone to be full of evil from Childhood**

   Genesis 8:21
   Then Noah built an altar to the Lord and, taking some of all the clean animals and clean birds, he sacrificed burnt offerings on it. The Lord smelled the pleasing aroma and said in his heart: "Never again will I curse the ground because of man, even though every inclination of his heart is evil from childhood."

One thing that really got me upset before I gave my life to God was the concept of people having a "sinful nature" from birth. I would think what many people think and that is "how can a baby have sinned?" Adults I understand, even teenagers but babies and young children were beyond comprehension to me. That was taking "genetics" just too far. I had trouble grasping this reality because I was looking and evaluating people from a physical viewpoint rather than from a spiritual (God's) view point.

We cannot understand how holy and pure God is so it is difficult for us to comprehend just how unholy or evil we are. We are so locked into performance equaling goodness that we think only those who do really bad things will be punished. Well scripture tells us the opposite. We are all born with a sinful nature inside of us. Going back to the "fall", Adam and Eve (the greatest grandparents of them all) sinned before God, thus allowing "uncleanness" to enter into all mankind.

What we now call "Original Sin" is not a choice we make or a belief system we have developed over time, it exists because God told A&E to obey and they did not. They chose to listen to Satan and their hearts which got them booted out of paradise. Only Jesus' sacrifice on the cross removes this spiritual uncleanliness, nothing you achieve in life can remove it; it is a gift from God because of his love for you. Anyone who rejects this gift (Jesus) rejects God and will remain controlled by their sinful nature, which operates out of your heart, even if you are the nicest person on earth.

   Romans 3:22-24
   This righteousness from God comes through faith in Jesus Christ to all who believe. There is no difference, for all have sinned and fall short of the glory of God, and are justified freely by his grace through the redemption that came by Christ Jesus.

2. The heart you have now is not curable because it is so deceitful.

Jeremiah 17:9
The heart is deceitful above all things and beyond cure. Who can understand it?

What the bible calls your heart is not to be trusted. In fact, it says it is deceitful beyond all "things". This is a pretty strong statement considering how many things there are in this life. But when you think about it more closely, only people are deceitful. I don't believe animals and plants lie or are dishonest, just you and I and everyone else we meet. Deceitful means dishonest, untrustworthy, misleading, unfactual, cunning, devious, fraudulent, corrupt, greedy, insincere…shall I go on?

One of the main reasons the world is so messed up, and this has been true throughout history regardless of time or nation or location, is that people have a great capacity to be self-centered, which always leads to dishonesty and deceitfulness not to mention violence. Only when God enters our lives and creates in us a new heart do we begin to act like Jesus who had no deceit in him at all.

3. Your Heart is the Fountain for your Poisoned Personality

Proverbs 4:23
Above all else, guard your heart, for it is the wellspring of life.

Water is essential for all life and for growth. Most natural wells collect pure water in them because the water has been filtered by minerals in the ground. But if something toxic is put in the well the pure water goes bad and poisons all those who drink from it. Your personality is like a well and what goes into it will be what comes out of it. Worldly pollution in your heart cannot satisfy anyone (including you) who is thirsty for forgiveness, love and truth which are God's spiritual water. Only drinking from God's flowing river of mercy can do that.

Recovery Truth #48   **I Agree _____ I Disagree _____**
What comes out of your mouth reveals what is in your heart.

4. Your Mind, Mouth and Behavior are all directed by your Heart

Mathew 15:16-19
"Are you still so dull?" Jesus asked them. "Don't you see that whatever enters the mouth goes into the stomach and then out of the body? But the things that come out of the mouth come from the heart, and these make a man 'unclean'. For out of the heart come evil thoughts, murder, adultery, sexual immorality, theft, false testimony, slander.

Trying to stop the flow of self-destructive behavior coming out of you without getting a new heart in Christ is never going to happen because the source of that flow (your heart) is still pumping from a toxic well (your sinful nature). Just like people's hearts keep circulating blood regardless if they are doing good or evil, asleep or awake, are tall or short, young or old; so does your "heart" keep circulating compulsive thoughts, feelings and desires that lead to acting out. To stop this circulation of selfishness requires a "new heart implant".

5. If God does not replace your heart Satan will continue filling it with evil.

Acts 5:3
Then Peter said, "Ananias, how is it that Satan has so filled your heart that you have lied to the Holy Spirit and have kept for yourself some of the money you received for the land?

Many people, like Ananias and his wife, want to please God but only after they please themselves first. Again, the sinful nature dominates our commitment to God opening up God's discipline upon us. We say Jesus is Lord but only mean it when we are trying to impress others. When "push comes to shove" we resist God by disobeying his commandments and teachings. Jesus says directly to us, "If you love me you will obey what I command." When our "sinful nature" (our flesh) hears this it laughs and tell us we don't have to obey and so we don't. When this happens not only do we suffer but so do many others.

6. You need a new heart from God to fulfill His two greatest commands

Mark 12:28-31
"One of the teachers of the law came and heard them debating. Noticing that Jesus had given them a good answer, he asked him, "Of all the commandments, which is the most important?'

"The most important one," answered Jesus, "is this. Hear, O Israel, the Lord our God, the Lord is one. Love the Lord your God with all your heart and with all your soul and with all your mind and with all your strength. The second is this: 'Love your neighbor as yourself.' There is no commandment greater than these."

No human ever born can keep these two commandments without God first "creating in him a new heart", one that is controlled by his Holy Spirit and not by the flesh. You cannot keep the Ten Commandments without God empowering you with his grace. And you will never be able to "love your enemies" while your flesh rules your mind and your heart. Only with God's Grace can we do this.

Recovery Truth #49   I Agree _____ I Disagree _____
You will receive inner peace, joy and compassion for others when God purifies your heart.

7. **You need a new heart so you can be filled with God's Love, Power and Joy!**

John 16:21-22
A woman giving birth to a child has pain because her time has come; but when her baby is born she forgets the anguish because of her joy that a child is born into the world. So with you: Now is your time of grief, but I will see you again and you will rejoice, and no one will take away your joy.

Recovery is similar to a woman having a child (I understand you are a man but hang with me on this one) in that there is great pain and suffering during the process but afterward there is great joy. And when great joy floods your being, the hard work of the process is soon forgotten. When we are "born again" into God's Spirit we also receive freedom from past pain and deep grief, two of the main roots for compulsive behavior. By plugging into God's Spirit every day we continue to be renewed by the Spirit as He cleans out the worthless things in our hearts and replaces them with Joy, Love and Power. Jesus promises it and I testify its true.

Just One little problem: Your Human Heart is not the Heart mentioned in the Bible
The bible has hundreds of scriptures that mention the word "heart" but none of them are talking about the human organ that we call the heart. Our hearts are powerful pumps that force blood throughout our bodies 24-7 regardless of how we are living. Our human "pumps" cannot make decisions because they have no intelligence. For example, many humans who are classified as "brain dead" can still have fully functioning hearts with the help of life support. And the opposite is also true, many people who have very high levels of intelligence die of heart attacks at early ages regardless of how mentally clever they are. So what's up with that? It is obvious that the "physical" heart has nothing to do with your "spiritual" heart.

Recovery Truth #50   **I Agree _____ I Disagree _____**
All that emotional pain you feel really comes from the right side of your brain, not your physical heart.

Hebrews 4:12
For the word of God is living and active. Sharper than any double-edged sword, it penetrates even to dividing soul and spirit, joints and marrow; it judges the thoughts and attitudes of the heart.

So if your heart is not in your Heart, where is it? It's in your Mind!

For the heart to have "thoughts and attitudes" as is described in Hebrews4 it must be in your thinking which is in your mind. So I believe that the "Spiritual" Heart mentioned in the bible is all of the following:

1. The "center core" of your personality or your soul

2. The main essence of who you are; your human spirit
3. The total sum of all your character
4. Your capacity to love the Lord, others and yourself
5. Your willingness to serve God and others as much as God helps you

6. And it is the "human house" in which your sinful nature now lives. When God's Holy Spirit moves in the sinful nature must move out.

The really good news is that even when you do not fully understand where your heart is, God does. By giving him permission to "operate" he scrubs your "heart" clean of all the poisons that have been put into the well of your personality since you were born. In doing so he really changes your personality so you can become the person you are meant to be. In our culture romance sells big time; so we are told our hearts are supposed to be the center for our feelings and emotions…but as you will read in Lesson 11, it just isn't so!

A Testimony from a Brother in Recovery

Dear Everett (sent as an email)

Did you notice I was early for the class...life is so much better when you walk in his light...thank you again for a wonderful lesson and presentation...please, please get your lessons to as many people as I can...it is needed...I was amazed at how everything discussed in group were issues that I face every week, every day and every hour...I refuse to allow fear to control my life any longer...or shame or a false belief that I am not worthy of God's love or forgiveness and I must forgive myself and MOVE on...

Please continue to give me "tough" love whenever I need it, deserve it and am a distraction in class...thank you for helping me focus and grow...I will bear fruit someday but I am not doing everything I need to do yet to produce the best fruit for the Lord... Lord please continue to "prune" me...God's class through you is great...And brings me great energy, joy and happiness (no fear)

Thank you brother Everett

Rich B.

So What Can You Do to Get Healed?

1. Read with an open mind
2. Complete your inventory honestly
3. Keep turning the pages-keep learning about what is destroying you
4. Exchange your will for God's Will; eternal life for eternal death
5. Plug into God's Holy Spirit and receive forgiveness and power to change
6. Trust in the Lord more than you trust your flesh which is not your friend
7. Control your mind through God's power or it will control you with Satan's power
8. Replace your negative inner voice (lie machine) with God's word
9. Purify your Video Vault by letting God give you a brain bath
10. When you need open heart surgery race to the hospital, don't stroll

Please complete the Inventory activities for Lesson 10 before reading Lesson 11.

Lesson Ten Inventory

What were you Thinking when you read Lesson 10?

How are you Feeling after reading Lesson 10?

How is what you are Thinking and Feeling now going to help you with your recovery?

What are you going to change in your behavior after reading Lesson 10?

Plug-in with Prayer - How would you like God to help you right now?
(In the space below please talk directly with God...He is listening.)

What Bible verse in Lesson 10 will you commit to memorizing?

Lesson 10: Activity 1 –
Rating The Greatest Commandment

Mark 12:28-31

"One of the teachers of the law came and heard them debating. Noticing that Jesus had given them a good answer, he asked him, "Of all the commandments, which is the most important?'

"The most important one," answered Jesus, "is this. Hear, O Israel, the Lord our God, the Lord is one. Love the Lord your God with all your heart and with all your soul and with all your mind and with all your strength. The second is this: 'Love your neighbor as yourself.' There is no commandment greater than these."

Using this verse rate how well you are Loving God:

	Not at All	10%	25%	50%	100%
Loving God with Your Heart					
Loving God with Your Soul					
Loving God with Your Mind					
Loving God with Your Strength					
Loving your Neighbors as yourself					

Lesson 10 Activity 2: Taking Your Pain/Wound Inventory

Identify up to three examples for each of the following pain (wound) categories. Be brief; if you have nothing to write down for a category leave it blank. These categories are in no particular order. Use relationship names only (not personal names) to ID people such as Mom, Dad, first wife, old employer, etc.

A. Neglect by another person (being ignored, unattended to, not provided for, etc.)

1.

2.

3.

B. Verbal Abuse by another person (lying, gossiping, criticalness, slander, etc.)

1.

2.

3.

C. Physical Victimization (physical abuse, rape, beatings, theft, threats with weapons) by others

1.

2.

3.

D. Self-Inflicted Abuse or Victimization (acts of self-sabotage, suicide attempts, cutting, over-indulging, destroying relationships, debt, etc.

1.

2.

3.

E. Grief due to loss (of relationships, jobs, pets, opportunities, health, respect)

1.

2.

3.

F. Physical pain (due to illness, injury, accidents or anything else)

1.

2.

3.

G. Regret due to a missed or lost opportunity in life

1.

2.

3.

Lesson 11 – God is Real No Matter How You Feel

The Light of Scripture: Titus 3:3-7

At one time we too were foolish, disobedient, deceived and enslaved by all kinds of passions and pleasures. We lived in malice and envy, being hated and hating one another. But when the kindness and love of God our Savior appeared, he saved us, not because of righteous things we had done, but because of his mercy. He saved us through the washing of rebirth, and renewal by the Holy Spirit, whom he poured out on us generously thorough Jesus Christ our Savior, so that, having been justified by his grace, we might become heirs having the hope of eternal life.

The Problem: Our feelings, moods and passions are all controlled by our flesh that uses them to deceive us into thinking we are sailing towards safety when we are really heading into dangerously deep water.

The Solution: Stop living in an emotional "FOG"

The Procedure: Rely on "GPS" to navigate you out of the "FOG".

My Prayer

Father God you are so awesome. You are so perfect in your kindness. I love it when you touch my life and lift me up. I am so grateful that I am not afraid of you anymore like I once was. Thank you for taking my fears away and helping me to receive the gift of life, love, light and liberty that is in your Holy Spirit. Please help my brothers who are lost at "sea" to find safe harbor within your loving arms. Amen

For years I was a business consultant. Many moons ago (late eighties) I provided services and programs for companies that were interested in improving Leadership, Team Building and Customer Service within their organizations. One such company invited me to meet with them to discuss possible programs for their employees. All my inquiries regarding what they did for business went unanswered, all they would tell me was "When you get here you will understand."

When I arrived at their building I could not tell from the name of the company what services they provided. They were fairly new, had a very low profile and there was no literature in their waiting room explaining who they were or what they did. Once I got past the "meet and greet" I told them I needed to know something about what they did if I was to shape the program to fit their staff.

At first they didn't want to tell me specifically what their business goals were. They explained they were working on "cutting edge" technology and asked me to sign a non-disclosure form before we could continue our conversations. After doing so they took me to the heart of their operations…inside their main work area were many employees who were busy examining maps and photos and putting information into computers. Today we might call them a "Geek Squad".

They showed me their new invention which was a "black box" about the size of three size-14 shoe boxes. They told me their product would be installed in large ships giving them valuable navigation information. They explained that their system used a Global Positioning System (GPS) navigation process to take information from satellites circling the earth to tell the ship's crew exactly where they were and what was around them at all times. This would be invaluable as they would be able to "see" in the blackest darkness, most violent storms and thickest fog.

I was amazed at the system and its applications. I was even more amazed that they said that if it worked successfully in ships they would make it smaller and put them into cars. I remember thinking to myself…cars, why would we need them when we have maps, roads and traffic signs…little did I know.

The illustration here is that, like ships in a heavy fog, we often get lost, hurt and misled because we cannot see into the unknown (future). We do not know what our decisions and actions will bring. We also are at high risk because we cannot foresee the dangers that lie in our path. We make decisions based on current feelings, needs and desires only to find out later that the consequences of those choices are too high a price to pay for the immediate gain.

What if we could have a GPS system installed in our brains, hearts and relationships? We would be able to see ahead into the future so we could navigate around dangerous people, events and situations. We would have valuable information to make better decisions. We would make fewer mistakes; hurt fewer people and waste less time. Well, we do have such a system if we allow God to install it in us.

Romans 8:12-14

Therefore, brothers, we have an obligation—but it is not to the sinful nature, to live according to it. For if you live according to the sinful nature, you will die; but if by the Spirit you put to death the misdeeds of the body, you will live, because those who are led by the Spirit of God are sons of God.

Recovery Truth #51   **I Agree _____ I Disagree _____**
The only thing keeping you from receiving your GPS system from God is the F.O.G. that you are living in.

When we surrender our wills and lives to Jesus we receive God's Perfect Spirit (GPS). As it states in the verse from Romans you just read, GPS can put to death the misdeeds of your body; but only if you stay "plugged in" to God. Every time we put something in the world between us and God we unplug ourselves from his perfect Spirit leaving us back in the dark. For example, if my job is more important than my relationship with God I will become unplugged leaving me to work in my flesh rather than in His Spirit.

You need something internal that is very powerful to overcome external invitations to self-destruction which is what addictions are. You not only need power but also vision to succeed in such a treacherous world. The world constantly baits you with temptations to do wrong; these temptations always feel good at first and meet the deep desires of your flesh.

In such a world we all have many fears. We are afraid of failing, of being rejected, of being poor, of being sick, of being hurt, of being sued, dying; you name something in life and there is probably a fear for it. Personally, I am afraid of snakes!

But there is a fear that is even bigger than all those fears, and that is the FOG you live in…the FOG I am talking about stands for "Fear of God". While some people see God as something good and holy most people have a deep, deep fear of him. And that fear keeps us from coming to him, from surrendering our lives to him and from letting Him put his Perfect Holy Spirit (GPS) into us. This fear comes in the form of many lies that your negative inner voice (Satan) tells you; lies such as:

- If I let God into my life he will punish me for all the wrongs I have done
- If I let God control my life it will be boring, unexciting
- If I let God control my life I will lose all my friends
- If I let God put his Spirit into me I will become a "Jesus Freak"
- If I surrender my life to God he will send me to a very poor country to die
- If I let God control my life he will make me stop drinking and drugging
- If I let God control my life he will make me stop having sex outside of marriage
- If I let God control my life he will make me confess and I will suffer for what I have done wrong, maybe even go to prison.
- If I let God control my life I will have to sing in Church

- If I let God Control me he will make me vote Republican (grin; actually not...God doesn't support any political party, just people who serve him and others through his Spirit...which leave's 90% of both parties out)

All of these lies I hear every day from men I am trying to help find freedom in Christ so they will have the power and wisdom to stop destroying themselves and others. But these lies also keep men "sailing in the FOG" where they will be shipwrecked upon the rocks of life.

Personally, I was one of these men. I believed many of these lies. I put off surrendering my life to Jesus for three years when I knew in my Spirit it was the right thing to do, the only thing I could do to get out of the mess I had made of my life. Still I resisted out of Fear. I was very afraid of an unloving God.

In my mind (my flesh, not my Spirit) I saw God as a vindictive, unforgiving, punishing God who was going to take me out behind the "wood shed" for all the bad things I had done. Instead, when I did surrender my life to him, I was filled with overwhelming love and security...like I had never experienced before. It was the biggest rush I had ever had up to that point in my life. God actually was just the opposite of who Satan had told me he was. And I wasted so much of my life being controlled by my negative inner voice instead of trusting Jesus who, after telling me how much his Father loved me, died to pay the penalty for my sin.

God hears your prayers through his Holy Spirit

Psalm 55:16-17
But I call to God, and the Lord saves me. Evening, morning and noon I cry out in distress, and he hears my voice.

When you pray to God it is just like you calling someone on your cell phone, which you do all day long. God answers if you really surrender your will to him. God doesn't take calls that are insincere and deceitful; calling to get something just for your personal pleasure, for instance, doesn't make it through. Knowing your heart and mind he assesses you to see if you really want to talk to him because you care about him. When we do the Holy Spirit actually translates everything we say, no matter how badly we are saying it, into beautiful prayers that reflect God's will for our lives.

Romans 8:26-27
In the same way, the Spirit helps us in our weakness. We do not know what we ought to pray, but the Spirit himself intercedes for us with groans that words cannot express. And he who searches our hearts knows the mind of the Spirit, because the Spirit intercedes for the saints in accordance with God's will.

This kind of praying, by Faith and Love for God, brings us peace and a knowledge of his wanting us in his family no matter what we have done or not done. It is never too late to call upon the name of the Lord. He is always listening, always watching, and always loving us in spite of our choices in life. He is ready to pull us out of the "emotional quicksand" we find ourselves in, if only we call in the name of Jesus.

When I use my cell phone I have to go through T-Mobile because that is the service I chose. When I call God (prayer), the only phone service that reaches into Heaven is the name of Jesus. There is no other name you can connect with God through…Praise God because I have so many needs no other service could handle it. It is like calling 911 for immediate help.

Recovery Truth # 52   **I Agree _____ I Disagree _____**
Those addicted to sexually acting out are emotional cripples imprisoned by the shame within their brain (RB).

As I stated in the last Lesson, you do not experience emotions in your human heart. The control center for your emotions, feelings, and experiential memories (movies with people, sounds, smells and actions) are all in the right side of your Brain (RB). Many of your memories are recorded under emotions (anger, fear, happiness, etc.) and have very powerful influences on your desires, impulses and decision making. The old expression, "if it feels good do it" is an example of how feelings play a big part in our acting out. God wants you to obey his commands rather than the demands of internal forces inside of your flesh which will lead you into trouble and shameful behavior.

Your center for emotional pain is also in the right side of your brain. Each memory is filed under an emotion filing system. So if I ask you to tell me about the five scariest moments in your life, you would go to the file drawer labeled FEAR located in the RB. If I wanted to know what things really, really make you mad then you would look in the file drawer labeled ANGER. In those drawers would be all of your fear and anger moments from your life, many lumped together. Every one of your negative emotions is directly connected to a negative experience in your past; the more powerful the negative feeling in you, the more traumatic the experience was in your past.

Temper, Temper, Temper

I have a big yard and the only working outside faucet is on the back of my house. To reach the front yard I have to connect two 100 ft. hoses together so I can water the plants up by the road. One day, I drug the hoses up to the area I was going to water and squeezed the trigger on the water nozzle and nothing but a small drip came out. Getting mad I threw my hose down and marched down the length of the hose to find where it was kinked. Of course, the hose was fine until I got all the way back to about three feet from the hookup on the back of the house where, sure enough, the hose had a kink in it stopping the flow of water.

Still angry, I grabbed the hose and started twisting it to get the kink out and it soon reappeared farther up the hose about five feet. So then I had to unkink that one which created another one just up the hose, and my temper kept on increasing to the point where I had to stop and "give myself a timeout".

I learned a long time ago that the best way to deal with my Irish "temper-ment" was by giving thanks to God. So I stopped, took off my baseball cap, and thanked God for the hose, water, plants and for the patience I would need to fix the problem. Once I had "calmed down" all the kinks were removed and the plants got watered.

So it is with our personalities, we have many "kinks" in them that need removing but doing so requires prayer, patience and practice. It took a long time for those character flaws and habitual ways of behaving to be cemented into your character and there are no quick fixes but there is hope and an answer.

So How Do You Overcome Your Negative Emotions?

Our flesh attacks us during life mostly with emotions like anger, fear, depression, discouragement, sadness, and many other feelings we experience when upset. These negative "feelings" occur mostly because we did not get something we needed (not wanted) when we were growing up. These are some of the "roots" to your acting out and must be replaced if you want to be healed. Each one listed needs to be surrendered to God so he can heal the wounds you have related to emotion.

I will go into this more in Lesson 12 as we examine more deeply the, "Fruit of the Root." But first let's consider some of the most powerful negative feelings that keep you trapped in slavery and what God's Holy Word tells you about each one. I am going to move over each one very briefly and primarily use God's word to illustrate the impact they have upon our heads, hearts and habits.

A. Stand Firm against Anger, Bitterness, Unforgiveness

A1. Confess and Surrender Your Anger/Rage to God daily

> **Proverbs 19:3**
> *"A man's own folly ruins his life, yet his heart rages against the Lord."*

> **Ephesians 4:26; 29-31**
> *Do not let the sun go down while you are still angry,...*
> *Do not let any unwholesome talk come out of your mouths, but only what is helpful for building others up according to their needs, that it may benefit those who listen. And do not grieve the Holy Spirit of God, with whom you were sealed for the day of redemption. Get rid of all bitterness, rage and anger, brawling and slander, along with every form of malice.*

A2. Trust God and give Him your Bitterness/Unforgiveness/Vengeance

Romans 12:17-21
Do not repay anyone evil for evil. Be careful to do what is right in the eyes of everybody. If it is possible, as far as it depends on you, live at peace with everyone. Do not take revenge, my friends, but leave room for God's wrath, for it is written:

"It is mine to avenge; I will repay," says the Lord. On the contrary:

"If your enemy is hungry, feed him;
If he is thirsty, give him something to drink.
In doing this, you will heap burning coals on his head."
Do not be overcome by evil, but overcome evil with good.

A3. Use God's Forgiveness for you to forgive others

Ephesians 4:32
Be kind and compassionate to one another, forgiving each other, just as in Christ God forgave you.

Recovery Truth #53   I Agree _____ I Disagree _____
If you are truly sorry for hurting people, then unload your gun (stop your anger, unforgiveness, foul language, criticalness) <u>before</u> you attempt to make amends with them.

B. Stand Firm against Fear, Worry and Anxiety

B1. Eliminate Fear by Living in Love

1 John 4:16-18
And so we know and rely on the love God has for us. God is love. Whoever lives in love lives in God, and God in him. Love is made complete among us so that we will have confidence on the Day of Judgment, because in this world we are like him. There is no fear in love. But perfect love drives out fear, because fear has to do with punishment.

2 Timothy 1:7
For God did not give us a spirit of fear, but a spirit of power, of love and of self-discipline.

B2. Worrying is a Waste of Your Time and Energy

Matthew 6:31-34 (Jesus speaking)
So do not worry, saying, "What shall we eat?" or "What shall we drink?" or "What shall we wear?' For the pagans run after all these things, and your heavenly Father knows that you need them. But seek first his kingdom and his righteousness, and all

these things will be given to you as well. Therefore do not worry about tomorrow, for tomorrow will worry about itself. Each day has enough trouble of its own.

B3. Cast Your Anxiety on the Lord and find Peace

1 Peter 5:6-7
Humble yourselves, therefore, under God's mighty hand, that he may lift you up in due time. Cast all your anxiety on him because he cares for you.

C. Stand Firm against Sorrow, Guilt and Shame

C1. Repent and leave Sorrow (sadness, loneliness, grief) in God's Hands

2 Corinthians 8:10
Godly sorrow brings repentance that leads to salvation and leaves no regret, but worldly sorrow brings death.

Psalm 34:18
The Lord is close to the brokenhearted and saves those who are crushed in spirit.

C2. Repent when you feel Guilt

Guilt is extreme thoughts of regret, remorse, conviction, responsibility. It is your positive inner voice telling you a negative judgment about yourself based on something bad you have done, or something good you should have done but did not do, giving you a chance to make amends. It is God calling you to repentance.

Psalm 38:4
My guilt has overwhelmed me like a burden too heavy to bear.

C3. Shed the Shame (extreme feelings of disgrace, humiliation, uncleanness)

Shame is emotional rejection (damnation) of self because of strong feelings of unworthiness and self-hatred related to bad things done to you by others (abuse) and by yourself (self-abuse). Shame is located on the right side of the brain. It is removed through inner healing by accepting and living by God's word.

2 Corinthians 4:2
Rather, we have renounced secret and shameful ways; we do not use deception, nor do we distort the word of God.

Solution: Take a Spiritual Shower!
God's Love washes away inner pain; it's one of His specialties!

Psalm 51:1-3
Have mercy on me, O God, according to your unfailing love; according to your great compassion blot out my transgressions. Wash away all my iniquity and cleanse me from my sin. For I know my transgressions, and my sin is always before me.

Learning to Love and Forgive Yourself

A major "kink" in your personality hose is not forgiving yourself and others as Jesus has forgiven you...without his forgiveness you cannot enter his rest so you can heal, get your minds right and receive the Grace (power) to do God's will in your life. Forgiveness from God removes this snarl from your "spiritual hose".

We treat ourselves quite poorly when we aren't as good at doing something as we think we should be. When we don't accept ourselves for who we are, we often develop a sense of self-rejection. We don't like what we look like, or how we talk, or how we walk. We even get down on ourselves for getting down on ourselves, which is the ultimate self-defeating trap.

And just as important, you must learn how to have mercy on yourself when you have not lived up to your own expectations. Your self-esteem is also often down because you won't forgive yourself when you make a mistake. At such times you don't show kindness and understanding to yourself, when those are the very qualities you need the most to improve and not make the mistake again. By not caring for yourself you have to turn to others and hope that they will give you that kind of nurturing. This often leads to dependency and more hurt if they can't or won't help you.

Seek God's Love and Comfort

2 Corinthians 1:3-4
Praise be to the God and Father of our Lord Jesus Christ, the Father of compassion and the God of all comfort, who comforts us in all our troubles, so that we can comfort those in any trouble with the comfort we ourselves have received from God.

Are You Spiritually Stubborn?

Recovery Truth #54   I Agree _____ I Disagree _____
Spiritual Stubbornness is you wanting God's love, forgiveness, and healing while still refusing to bend your knee to His authority so you can become his servant.

Romans 2:5-6
But because of your stubbornness and your unrepentant heart, you are storing up wrath against yourself for the day of God's wrath, when his righteous judgment will be revealed. God "will give to each person according to what he has done."

There are several key reasons why men won't bow to God and receive his help.

1. They are afraid of God due to the lies that were identified earlier in this Lesson.
2. They are still "hooked" by the sins they are committing and won't quit doing what is destroying them
3. They think they have lots of time to "think about it"
4. They don't believe their flesh is really their enemy
5. They believe they are "in control" and can stop when they chose to
6. They don't believe God is actually there, he doesn't really exist.
7. They don't believe God will forgive them, others yes, but not them
8. They don't want to forgive those who have hurt them
9. They are still too prideful and self-centered to worry about God
10. They don't "feel" anything; they have become "hard-hearted" due to "frozen feelings"

Recovery Truth # 55   **I Agree _____ I Disagree _____**
You can't heal what you don't feel because you can't leave what you don't grieve.

Most all of your problems in life come out of your negative feelings, evil passions and emotional memories of traumatic experiences from your past. Again, these are all stored in the right side of your brain. They are in emotional filing drawers and logic (left brain thinking) cannot find them or make them go away. They are "accessed" (brought out of memory and into reality) by the following:

1. **Emotional Triggers**
   Anything that brings an excessively strong negative emotional reaction from you. A trigger is always outside of you, such as: someone else's behavior or words; any sounds, smells, or tastes; or something you are watching.

2. **Emotional Grenades**
   Any action you take towards others to keep them away from you especially if they are trying to help you or care about you.

3. **Emotional Nightmares**
   Often called nightmares, these mental videos of past traumatic experiences in your life can occur at any time of the day. These memories are events and experiences you were scared by earlier in your life and they now suddenly appear in the Theatre of your mind and start playing all too vivid images of what occurred to you. You become victimized all over again each time you watch the movie.

Being abused repeatedly, especially as a child, can leave you living as an "emotional cripple". This means that you cannot connect with other people in positive relationships, prefer to isolate, tend to live in your head, and have extremely low self-worth having little or no hope you can ever be healed. In short, you are controlled by emotional triggers, grenades and nightmares.

It also means you have become so "self-centered" that you have trouble understanding and respecting other's ideas, feelings and boundaries because you are totally stuck in your own emotional quicksand. You "use and abuse" people and things (alcohol, drugs, food, sex, shopping, work, etc.) to find release but nothing ever relieves the agony in your heart.

In recovery inappropriate acting out is called "medicating" which addicts do in an attempt to make their shame and pain go away, even if only for a few minutes. The negative inner voice tells you abusing yourself and/or others will erase the abuse you suffered by others…of course, this is a lie that always leads you into destruction not health.

Frozen Feelings indicate a Heart of Stone

Frozen feelings indicate repressed memories of traumatic experiences. This is a natural way humans deal with trauma. For instance, many men (and women) who have been in combat come home and are unable to connect with their loved ones the way they did before they left to fight. They often seem distant, emotionally unavailable, often are restless with fits of anger coming out of nowhere; they are in need of "something" to end their inner pain but nothing in reality seems to work. Other examples would be anyone who suffered child abuse, sexual abuse, abandonment by loved ones, and extreme pain due to loss that was uncontrollable.

While men (or women) with frozen feelings can function physically they cannot give or receive love. They also have great difficulty "playing" and having fun. This problem indicates what we might call a "Heart of Stone" or "Hard Heartedness". This term traditionally means a person who "lacks compassion for others" or who is "unable to demonstrate mercy". I think the root to this would be a person who is "unwilling to access any emotion that would trigger pain from past traumatic experiences". In short, by avoiding emotions people avoid replaying the painful videos from their past.

Remember, your heart is in the right side of your brain and all your emotions, visual memories, and ability to have fun originate from there. Trauma represents an event overwhelming our five senses (hearing, seeing, touching, smelling and tasting) in such a negative way that the event bombarded our sanity, threatening to destroy it. So when your personality comes under this kind of "attack" you "shut down emotionally" which is called repression.

This decision to repress emotions is actually a survival process that kicks in so you can survive the traumatic experience while it is actually happening. And if the abuse happened over a long period of time then it only strengthens your "insensitivity" after the event has ceased. Your mind, to defend its survival, shuts down your ability to feel…unfortunately, it is far easier to shut it down than it is to turn it back on again. Inner healing is letting God restore your mind and heart to you without the trauma which is crippling you and poisoning your relationships.

Mark 2:3-12

Some men came, bringing to him a paralytic, carried by four of them. Since they could not get him to Jesus because of the crowd, they made an opening in the roof above Jesus and, after digging through it, lowered the mat the paralyzed man was lying on. When Jesus saw their faith, he said to the paralytic, "Son, your sins are forgiven." Now some of the teachers of the law were sitting there, thinking to themselves, "Why does this fellow talk like that? He's blaspheming! Who can forgive sins but God alone?"

Immediately Jesus knew in his spirit that this was what they were thinking in their hearts, and he said to them, "Why are you thinking these things? Which is easier: to say to the paralytic, 'Your sins are forgiven,' or to say, 'Get up, take your mat and walk'? But that you may know that the Son of Man has authority on earth to forgive sins..." He said to the paralytic, "I tell you, get up, take your mat and go home." He got up. Took his mat and walked out in full view of them all. This amazed everyone and they praised God, saying, "We have never seen anything like this!"

Key Lessons learned from this scripture verse

1. Jesus is moved by Faith to heal you, not by pity
2. Jesus can and will forgive you sins
3. Jesus knows what you are "thinking" in your heart (RB)
4. Jesus heals people who have been crippled for a long time so he can help you when you surrender...stop being spiritually stubborn

A Testimony from a Brother in Recovery

Everett,

I wanted to let you know how much the Standing Firm class has helped me. I have struggled for years with an addiction to internet pornography. Going to church, praying and talking to other men has never brought me any victory. But when we discussed the negative inner voice something clicked. I was able to identify where the messages were coming from and how to reprogram my thinking using God's word.

Then last week we talked about all the images and videos we have stored in the right side of our brains. I asked God to do a "brain wash" of those memories after that class and for the first time I found some relief. Thank you for sharing the lessons God taught you through your recovery.

By more prayer and God's grace I know I am becoming a new creation in Christ Jesus.

God Bless you,

Joel B.

So What Can You Do to Get Healed?

1. Read with an open mind
2. Complete your inventory honestly
3. Keep turning the pages-keep learning about what is destroying you
4. Exchange your will for God's Will; eternal life for eternal death
5. Plug into God's Holy Spirit and receive forgiveness and power to change
6. Trust in the Lord more than you trust your flesh which is not your friend
7. Control your mind through God's power or it will control you with Satan's power
8. Replace your negative inner voice (lie machine) with God's word
9. Purify your Video Vault by letting God give you a brain bath
10. When you need open heart surgery race to the hospital, don't stroll
11. Don't ever make decisions based on how you feel; pray and ask God first

Please complete the Inventory activities for Lesson 11 before reading Lesson 12.

Lesson Eleven Inventory

What were you Thinking when you read Lesson 11?

How are you Feeling after reading Lesson 11?

How is what you are Thinking and Feeling now going to help you with your recovery?

What are you going to change in your behavior after reading Lesson 11?

Plug-in with Prayer - How would you like God to help you right now?
(in the space below please talk directly with God…He is listening.)

What Bible verse in Lesson 11 will you commit to memorizing?

Lesson11: Activity 1 - The Emotional Checklist

Please rate how well you manage (control) each negative emotion (feeling) listed below using the categories provided (check only one):

Emotion/Feeling	I manage it	It controls me	It Dominates me
Anger			
Apathy			
Bitterness			
Boredom			
Confusion			
Depression			
Envious			
Fearful			
Frozen Feelings			
Grief			
Guilty			
Indecisive			
Loneliness			
Lost			
Lustful			
Prideful			
Rejected			
Sadness			
Trapped			
Unappreciated			
Unforgiven			
Ungrateful			
Unhappy			
Unlovable			
Unworthy			
Uselessness			

Lesson 11: Activity 2 – Which Fears Block Your Recovery?

If I let God into my life he will:	I believe this	I don't believe this
Punish me for all the wrongs I have done		
Take away all my non-Christian friends		
Make me a "Jesus Freak" like Everett		
Send me to a very poor country to die		
Make me stop drinking and drugging		
Make my life boring, unexciting		
Make me stop looking at porn		
Make me stop having sex outside of marriage		
Make me confess to my wife, be divorced		
Make me suffer for what I have done wrong, maybe even go to prison		
Make me read the Bible		
Make me go to Church		
Make me sing in Church		

Lesson 11: Activity 3 – How Resistant to God Are You?

Key Reasons for Resisting God's help	This statement is true about me	This statement is not true about me
I am afraid of God due to the lies identified in Activity 2		
I am still "hooked" by the sins I am committing and don't want to stop		
I have time to "think about it" before making a commitment		
My flesh is not my enemy		
I am "in control" and can stop anytime I choose to		
God is not actually there, he doesn't really exist		
God will not forgive me, others yes, but not me		
I don't want to forgive those who have hurt me		
I don't worry about God		
I am too "hard-hearted" to care what happens to me		

Lesson 11: Activity 4 – What Emotionally Controls You?

A. Emotional Triggers (list 3 examples)

Anything that brings an excessively strong negative emotional reaction from you. A trigger is always outside of you, such as: someone else's behavior or words; any sounds, smells, or tastes; or something you are watching.

1.

2.

3.

B. Emotional Grenades (list three examples)

Any action <u>you</u> take towards others to keep them away from you especially if they are trying to help you or care about you.

1.

2.

3.

C. Emotional Nightmares (list 3 examples)

Often called nightmares, these mental videos of past traumatic experiences in your life can occur at any time of the day. These memories are events and experiences you were scared by earlier in your life and they now suddenly appear in the Theatre of your mind and start playing all too vivid images of what occurred to you. You become victimized all over again each time you watch the movie.

1.

2.

3.

D. Frozen Feelings (list 3 situations where your lack of emotion has dominated you)

Inability to show emotions in your present and/or remember emotions from your past.

    1.

    2.

    3.

Lesson 12 – I Kid You Not, They Will Kill You!

The Light of Scripture: Romans 6:11-14

In the same way, count yourselves dead to sin but alive to God in Christ Jesus. Therefore do not let sin reign in your mortal body so that you obey its evil desires. Do not offer the parts of your body to sin, as instruments of wickedness, but rather offer yourselves to God, as those who have been brought from death to life; and offer the parts of your body to him as instruments of righteousness. For sin shall not be your master, because you are not under law, but under grace.

$\backsim$

The Problem: **Your desires influence your body parts into doing self-destructive behaviors that hurt you and others.**

The Solution: **Surrender your desires to Jesus so he is in control of them.**

The Procedure: **Accept God's Grace, it is His power to do what you cannot do without His Holy Spirit living in you.**

My Prayer

Thank you Lord for saving me. Thank you Lord for healing me. Thank you Lord for freeing me from the power of my flesh. Thank you Lord for giving me power through your Holy Spirit to overcome my evil desires. Thank you for teaching me how to control my body so it does not sin and hurt others. And thank you for the person who is reading this book right now, may you bless them as you have blessed me. Amen

WINNING THE WAR WITH YOUR FLESH!

Summer brings out the little beggars every year; black ants, running around our kitchen like they pay the mortgage every month. Tiny scouts show up first. They are the ones who are out in front leading the charge; loners running ahead of the troops to seek out the best goodies to be had. They are equipped to send out wireless signals to the colony that food is available. The tasters come next, the ones who don't just take a lick or two but actually dive in for the full sample. They are there to make sure the grub is worth calling out the army. And then the real troops arrive, hundreds of them scrambling all over the counter answering the "bell" for the next round. Soon all of the hordes are "bellying up to the bar" for their fair share of the loot.

Ants are a fascinating species of insect to watch. They are highly organized into large groups of workers, each group having its own assignment for which they are programmed. They travel over many difficult terrains and obstacles to get to their next meal. They are persistent workers who find the food source and after much effort break it down into pieces so they can carry it all back to their family, the colony.

To keep the colony, and more importantly the Queen, alive they must transport large amounts of food to the many hungry mouths waiting for it. Their self-sacrificing endeavors keep the colony growing. There is much to admire about the ants drive and commitment to family. But it is this drive that leads to its destruction. Ants drive is driven by their inborn desires. They are programmed by nature to stay alive and multiply but that same programming also leads to their destruction.

Much like pigs hitting the trough they just can't slow down long enough to know that today's chow is Terro, an ant poison that doesn't kill them until they get back to their colony. Then it kills all who are there. Ants are committed to working hard together to accomplish what is best for their community…dedicated, persistent and loyal. Great team workers, yet they just can't leave that sweet "poison" alone. If it tastes good they just have to ring the alarm for others to "come and get it" so it can be taken back home with them.

Humans are very similar to ants in that we are motivated and driven by desires; a major part of our inner nature to survive. Most of the time we just can't help it; we must obey our inner demands called "desires, needs and fears". It is these inner impulses that often get us killed because we just can't say no to that "sweet poison" put out just for us. It all seems so innocent at first: excessive nicotine, alcohol, and drugs; sexual contact with multiple partners; eating as much food as you want whenever you want; spending money you don't have; risking your health and your body for thrills…what could possibly be wrong with all of that?

The answer is simple: alcoholism, drug addiction, and sexually transmitted diseases; diabetes; divorce, lost relationships, and family rejection; the death of jobs, careers and homes; not to mention court time, jail and prison. Millions of hours of your life down the drain with nothing good to show for letting your flesh control you.

Recovery Truth #56   I Agree _____ I Disagree _____
You fall into destruction when your evil desires unite with worldly temptations that God has specifically warned you to stay away from.

When I am working with men I always get "push back" on this kind of teaching. As one brother told me, "I work hard every week and my wife just can't meet all my desires. What she doesn't know won't hurt her." So I ask guys like this how they are acting out. They tell me specifics, and regardless of what it is, I ask them the following question, "If your 15-year old son or daughter was doing the same thing you are doing, but not telling you about it, would that be OK with you?"

Immediately they say, "No way!" I would stop them, I would punish them, I would..." you get the picture. So then I ask them why it is so different for them, why would they protect their children if what they are doing is not dangerous. At this point few of them can look me in the eye. As they say, "The penny finally fell into the slot." They squirm and try to make some weak case that somehow they are different than their children but in the end I tell them the same thing I am telling you, "Poison doesn't discriminate; one dead ant is the same as any other dead ant. What you do will come home to your children."

Many of the men who I work with in recovery also try to shift the blame off of them by asking me, "Why is God tempting me? Why does he let evil come near me? He knows I am weak yet he still does nothing to stop it from making me do bad things." I always answer them by showing them the next verse:

James 1:13
"When tempted, no one should say, "God is tempting me." For God cannot be tempted by evil, nor does he tempt anyone; but each one is tempted when, by his own evil desire, he is dragged away and enticed. Then, after desire has conceived, it gives birth to sin; and sin, when it is full-grown, gives birth to death."

A Billion Wicked Web Searches

As I am writing this Lesson a headline just came across my news screen; it says "A billion Web searches reveal kinky is the new norm." I read the article and am not surprised to find out that sites featuring granny porn, transsexuals and what gay men prefer to look at are highly frequented by straight men. But the most interesting thing for me is the title of the book this research is being presented in. It is called, "A Billion Wicked Thoughts: What the World's Largest Experiment Reveals about Human Desire."

While it is not a book I'd recommend, the title does have four words that I have discussed in this book: wicked, thoughts, experiment and desire. I have mentioned that our sinful nature is evil or wicked and drives us towards doing wicked things. I have mentioned that the battle for the mind is crucial for winning the war against addictive thinking and acting out. I have even challenged you to take the "big experiment" which is just the opposite of the experiment mentioned in this article. Either way your life is going to be an experiment …I hope you make the right choice. And lastly, this Lesson is all about how human desires can kill you if you choose to follow them rather than obey God.

Right about now your negative inner voice is probably reminding you just how much fun you had the last time you saw something evil on the internet. And the Theater of your Mind is throwing up the images from that thrilling experience so the dopamine will start flowing to your brain, feeding the evil desire inside of you to go repeat this exciting yet deadly habit. And all of your flesh is telling you, "This Christian stuff is boring, it's so dull and worst of all, it is very hard to do."

The Power to "Do Don't"

Being a Christian not only appears hard, it is hard. When we read God's word it is full of don'ts. Don't do this and don't do that…or else! And when we try to obey his commands in our own power we fail miserably. So how can we succeed? The power to "Do Don't" is found in God's Grace. Grace is God's love coming into us with such power that it destroys the evil desires inside of you that want to "mate with evil", have intercourse with the world; and "forn with porn"." It keeps the fire away from the gasoline if you get my drift.

Recovery Truth #57   **I Agree _____ I Disagree _____**
Only with God's Grace can you Stand Firm against your flesh and the world's temptations; Grace is the power that keeps the two separate from each other.

> **Titus 2:11-12**
> *For the grace of God that brings salvation has appeared to all men. It teaches us to say "NO" to ungodliness and worldly passions, and to live self-controlled, upright and godly lives in this present age.*

A. Grace helps you Stand Firm against Your Evil Desires
Ephesians 4:22-24
"You were taught, with regard to your former way of life, to put off your old self, which is being corrupted by its deceitful desires; to be made new in the attitude of your minds; and to put on the new self, created to be like God in true righteousness and holiness."

We often call evil desires the, "I wants!" Our wants and desires are always self-centered, we seldom think of others when we are focusing getting our wants satisfied. Our desires are also almost always based on greed; give me more, give me better, give me bigger! All of this is built into our flesh or what God calls our "old self" or "old nature". When Jesus comes into our lives we receive God's Grace to "put on our new self".

Now most desires do not start out being evil they just unfortunately take us down roads where evil rules. To get what we want we end up selling our souls to feed our compulsions and over time they turn into addictions. And when you live in a country that sells to our wants, desires and "gotta haves" we end up with generations full of self-centered addicts who have lost their ability to make moral decisions. Winning the battle for your mind is crucial because once you surrender your will to anything or anybody you become its slave.

So whose slave are you right now? If God is not in control of your life, who or what is? Are you satisfied with where your life is heading…do you even see what the end result will be if you continue doing what your desires command you to do? Is your mind still saying you are in control and can quit anytime you want to? Problem is …you don't want to quit and you lack the power to change; this is when you must trust in the Lord and He will heal you.

> **Galatians 5:16-18**
> *So I say, live by the Spirit, and you will not gratify the desires of the sinful nature. For the sinful nature desires what is contrary to the Spirit and the Spirit what is contrary to the sinful nature. They are in conflict with each other, so that you do not do what you want. But if you are led by the Spirit, you are not under law.*

Examples of Evil Desires

1. **Lust (sexual passion)**

> **1 Thessalonians 4:3-5**
> *It is God's will that you should be holy; that you should avoid sexual immorality; that each of you should learn to control his own body in a way that is holy and honorable, not in passionate lust like the heathen, who do not know God;...*

2. **Co-dependency (the addiction of control)**

People who put other people before God suffer from Co-dependency, which is the addiction of needing to control someone else because you do not know how to control yourself. Whether you do it with good intentions (you're a pleaser needing acceptance and approval) or with bad intentions (you are a stalker who wants to dominate and destroy) you are still putting your life's focus on a person or group of people rather than God. A key identifier is your interactions are driven by fear and control rather than out of love for the person.

> **1 John 4:18**
> *There is no fear in love. But perfect love drives out fear, because fear has to do with punishment. The man who fears is not made perfect in love.*

3. **Envy/Selfish Ambition**

James 3:14-16
But if you harbor bitter envy and selfish ambition in your hearts, do not boast about it or deny the truth. Such "wisdom" does not come down from heaven but is earthly, unspiritual, of the devil. For where you have envy and selfish ambition, there you find disorder and every evil practice.

4. **Loving wealth and "other things" more than you love God**

Mark 4:19
Still others, like seed sown among thorns, hear the word; but the worries of this life, the deceitfulness of wealth and the desires for other things come in and choke the word, making it unfruitful.

5. **Grace helps you Stand Firm against your Body Parts**

I love it when my wife Denise brings up little children's songs of faith from her childhood. I never learned any of them and I am always amazed at how uplifting they are. I will use the main line from one of my favorites that she sings to make the next couple of points, it goes like this:

Be careful little eyes what you see
Be careful little eyes what you see
For the Father up above is looking down in love
So be careful little eyes what you see

Recovery Truth #58   I Agree _____ I Disagree _____
Not only is your flesh not your friend, it is also your worst enemy.

Every part of our bodies do not want to serve God, they want to serve self. God holds us accountable for what we do with our body parts. It is so important to Him that we surrender each part to Him. God gives us many bible verses identifying how each part misleads us into sin. It is mind blowing to me that all of these verses were written thousands of years ago but still clearly describe human behavior today. Nothing has changed; evil still rules in mankind until we let God take control. Let's check a few of these lifesaving verses out.

1. Your Eyes: Be careful little eyes what you see

Matthew 5:27-28
"You have heard that it was said, "Do not commit adultery." But I tell you that anyone who looks at a woman lustfully has already committed adultery with her in his heart.

This verse is clear as clear can be, thinking lustfully is adultery. But it is important for us not to use our eyes to judge others falsely. God does not judge us by our appearance (what we look

I KID YOU NOT, THEY WILL KILL YOU!

like) but by what is in our hearts and what we actually do. We are not to judge each other any differently.

1 Samuel 16: 7
But the Lord said to Samuel, "Do not consider his appearance or his height, for I have rejected him. The Lord does not look at the things man looks at. Man looks at the outward appearance, but the Lord looks at the heart.

Before I met my wife I went out with a gal who was a knockout from a visual point of view. Stunning in every way but it was one of the worst dates I ever went on. Nothing about her matched with me and by the end of the night she didn't look so great anymore…nor did I to her…thank God!

Our eyes and brains are very misleading and judgmental, leading us into many painful experiences. Remember, just because you think it doesn't make it true. Take the time to find out the "facts" about others before you make decisions about them. Do not be misled by physical (surface) features when God only values what is inside a person's character. Your true character is what you do when no one else is around, what you do when no one sees what you are doing; except God who sees all.

2. Your Mouth/Tongue: Be careful little tongue what you say

Ephesians 4:29
"Do not let any unwholesome talk come out of your mouths, but only what is helpful for building others up according to their needs, that it may benefit those who listen."

I must confess that I am a talker…one who likes to talk and hear others talk so this verse has had much value to me over the years. I have gotten myself into many painful situations simply because I said something I thought was useful, intelligent or funny only to find out that those listening didn't see it that way at all. I hurt many people with things I have said, most of the time without even knowing they were offended by the words I let out of my mouth.

Let's get it clear right here and now, the old saying, "Sticks and stones will break my bones but names will never hurt me" is a lie. Calling people names or making fun of them is very painful. And there have been way too many times that I was the one doing the word attack. I knew immediately I was throwing verbal stones and that they were breaking emotional bones. God does not want me doing this and again it is only by his Grace that I have gained some control over my mouth.

So if any of you reading this book are one of those people I have hurt with my words please forgive me in Jesus name. I must confess I still talk too much but I am way, way better than I use to be …Praise God!

183

James 3:5-6

Likewise the tongue also is a small part of the body, but it makes great boasts. Consider what a great forest is set on fire by a small spark. The tongue also is a fire, a world of evil among the parts of the body. It corrupts the whole person, sets the whole course of his life on fire, and is itself set on fire by hell.

The Bible has so many verses telling us not to use our mouth to blaspheme, boast, gossip, slander, make false accusations, tell rude and crude jokes, argue, complain, inflict pain upon another, lie, steal, cheat, threaten, or give false testimony about others. I am sure I left out at least ten more important "verbal don'ts" but you get the picture on this one. The list is a long one; realize that people talk this way for a reason. All this negativity comes from within our minds, from our store house of recorded phrases and from our "billion wicked thoughts".

3. Your Ears: Be careful little ears what you "listen to"

The key point here goes back to both the negative inner voice and the Theater of the Mind; what we listen to is recorded in our mental sound studio and used by both of these parts of our flesh to hurt us. Lots of poison (Terro for the mind) comes through our ears when we hear things that are not good for us.

One simple example that is very harmful is when children hear adults taking the Lord's name in vain. These "big kids" do it when they get mad, when they are in awe of something, and when they are joking around. The main foundation for standup comedy is often profanity; take away the "rude and crude" and most people today would not laugh. And in many movies, actors use God's name to damn someone, they say it is more "real" if they talk this way because that is what most people would say. Surprising God agrees with them; every word and action any actor does in a movie is considered "real" by God and they will be held accountable for every one of them. God doesn't recognize "acting" or computer generated fantasy to be "entertainment"... you are what you do and what you say. Unfortunately all this "social immorality" ends up in our homes thanks to adults exercising their "free will".

Americans think it is part of our freedom to curse anyone or anything at any time...free expression is not free, it comes with a very high price. And that high price comes when others who are listening (especially little children) repeat what you say. Like ants that eat Terro and then take it back home to their nests to feed death to their young; we allow evil into our minds and then take it home and wonder what is destroying our whole "colony".

We think we are in control of what we think when, in fact, it is our mind that controls us. Words and sounds always penetrate our minds and leave little messages within them. We need to be very discriminating as to what lyrics, words we let into our minds. Advertising and news stations are the same; so many negative things come into our thinking which build up negative thoughts and images, and more importantly stress. Much of this drives you into compulsive patterns of acting out.

4. Your Hands: Be careful little fingers what you touch

Most, if not all, sexual sins involve your hands and fingers to some degree. If you give control of them over to God you will receive the power to never use them to act out sexually. In short, most of the sins you have been committing will stop. The simplest example is masturbation; I know, I know…you never do…but just in case one day you are tempted to try it pray that God will take control of your hands. Imagine Jesus sitting next to you while you are getting ready to do this. As one fella told me, "I tried what you said and it was a real bummer…seeing Jesus there really killed the moment for me." I just nodded my head and said, "Exactly!"

5. Your Legs/Feet: Be careful little feet where you walk and stand

The same is true of your feet and legs. Many men have told me they sinned because they were "in the wrong place at the wrong time." If you don't walk to places you should not be, you will have a "safety zone" between you and that which is tempting you beyond your control. Let God be in control of your movements and the places you go. For example, you can't rent that XXX rated video if your feet and legs don't take you to the adult video store. And you can't go online and watch porn if your feet do not take you into the room where your computer is.

So What Can You Do to Stand Firm against your own Body?

Recovery Truth #59 I Agree _____ I Disagree _____
You will find mercy, grace and freedom when you need God more than anyone or anything else in this world.

1. Cover yourself with Jesus, think pure thoughts

We all need clothes to protect us from outside threats, but we also need Jesus to clothe us from inside threats…are you willing to ask him to do this? Surrender your mind to him. He is more than powerful enough to ruin the billion wicked thoughts that you have been having…grin.

> **Romans 13:14**
> *Rather, clothe yourselves with the Lord Jesus Christ, and do not think about how to gratify the desires of the sinful nature.*

2. Sow Good seed to please the Spirit rather than Bad seed that hurts you

> **Galatians 6: 7-10**
> *Do not be deceived; God cannot be mocked. A man reaps what he sows. The one who sows to please his sinful nature, from that nature will reap destruction; the one who sows to please the Spirit, from the Spirit will reap eternal life.*

Are the seeds you are sowing now leading you into eternal death or eternal life? Do these seeds help or hurt your family? Are you in control of what you currently are planting or do you need God's help to change?

3. Praise and Pray to the Holy Spirit for Help

Do you let the Spirit help you according to God's will...do you realize that the Spirit of God is interceding for you at this very moment? If so, then call on him continually seeking the power that can heal you.

> **John 16:13**
> *But when he, the Spirit of truth, comes, he will guide you into all truth.*

4. Renew your Mind, Get Ready for the Fight, Have Faith

> **1 Peter 1:13-14**
> *Therefore, prepare your minds for action; be self-controlled; set your hope fully on the grace to be given you when Jesus Christ is revealed. As obedient children, do not conform to the evil desires you had when you lived in ignorance.*

The time you spend in God's word will arm you for the fight.

5. See the Big Picture, God's Love for Us Always Rules over Evil

> **Romans 8:38**
> *For I am convinced that neither death nor life, neither angels nor demons, neither the present nor the future, nor any powers, neither height nor depth, nor anything else in all creation, will be able to separate us from the love of God that is in Christ Jesus our Lord.*

In the end, you will live with Jesus in his love if you allow God's love to be in your heart.

6. Expect to Suffer as Jesus Suffered and Praise God for it

> **1 Peter 4:1-2**
> *Therefore, since Christ suffered in his body, arm yourselves also with the same attitude, because he who has suffered in his body is done with sin. As a result, he does not live the rest of his earthly life for evil human desires, but rather for the will of God.*

We have a simple black or white choice; there is no gray area to it. Either we are living for Christ and helping others to find him or we are living for ourselves and leading others away from God. Which are you doing today?

7. Choose God over your desires and pleasures and he will restore you.

James 4:2
What causes fights and quarrels among you? Don't they come from your desires that battle within you? You want something but don't get it. You kill and covet, but you cannot have what you want. You quarrel and fight. You do not have, because you do not ask God. When you ask, you do not receive, because you ask with wrong motives, that you may spend what you get on your pleasures.

When our flesh controls us through our desires it is leading us around with a ring in our nose. We talk stupid, we look stupid and we act stupid. We destroy our lives seeking pleasure that maybe lasts a few minutes and then is gone leaving us with a huge cost to pay. And then we do it all over again putting ourselves into a deep moral liability. Instead of being morally bankrupted, why not accept God's gift which will free you from the overwhelming debt you have built up?

Recovery Truth #60   **I Agree _____ I Disagree _____**
You'll never know what God's gift is if you don't open it, accept it and use it wherever you go.

Have you Received and Opened your gift from God yet?

I am so privileged to teach the Stand Firm class each week to men who are seeking recovery through Jesus. In the classroom there is a very large wooden cross. One night as I was making a point about recovery being part of God's free gift through Jesus I noticed the cross. I asked the men, "How many of you, when you were kids, had a Christmas tree and under it there were presents with your name on it?" Most of the men raised their hands.

Then I asked them to imagine the Cross with many presents, all wrapped with nice paper and ribbons underneath it. And I tell them that there is one present from God under there for each one of them. But to receive the gift they must get up and go to the cross and look for the present with their name on it. I tell them that inside their present is the gift of salvation which includes the inner healing they need to become the person God wants them to be.

Next, I ask them, "So what is keeping you from going to the cross and opening your gift?" At first they just sit there, and then the strongest believers say, "Nothing." Then other voices speak up, "I don't believe there are any presents at the cross." Another voice says, "I don't believe there is a present with my name on it." And lastly, one brother says, "I am afraid if I find my present and open it there will be nothing in it."

I mentioned men who were Spiritually Stubborn in Lesson 11, all of them have been filled with lies that tell them they will never be healed. They live in anxiety that they are not wanted by God and have a great fear (FOG) that others will be saved but not them. Yet Jesus died an extremely brutal death so they might be saved through His sacrifice. And that salvation is a free gift, a present from our Father in Heaven to each of us.

Yet no present is useful if it is never claimed and opened. Men who cannot receive love have great difficulty receiving God's Mercy and Grace. Do not let your flesh cheat you out of getting the greatest gift you will ever be given.

Have you asked God in Jesus name for the gift of eternal life, which he freely gives to all who ask? If not, go back to the end of Lesson 5 and pray the simple prayer that will plug you into God's Grace so you can receive the gift of eternal life. In doing so you will receive the Holy Spirit who will purify your mind and heart giving you Faith to know for certain Christianity is no joke, no cruel trick. God is Real and He is calling you by name to come to the Cross, it is the only power outlet where you can receive power to be truly healed.

A Testimony from a Brother in Recovery

I started taking the recovery class (Stand Firm) that Everett teaches after coming to him with a sexual addiction that was killing me and my marriage. I learned valuable information about the inner workings of who I am, and the major driving forces behind my addiction. I learned that being "plugged in" to God had to be top priority above all else, and I learned various ways this could be done.

I learned that I was the problem, that it was my mind that was causing all this painful stuff to come into my life. I was able to see my "ritual-like" behavior that had got me into trouble every time, and was able to find ways to interrupt it and start new "healthy" rituals. There is so much more I could write about, all of which can be found in the book. Praise the Lord!!

I would recommend this information to anyone who came to me with an inability to control themselves. This has the answers you need about why you just can't seem to stop that terrible stuff you really don't want to do but keep doing. My brother/sister if it helped me I know it can help you!

Zack G.

So What Can You Do to Get Healed?

1. Read with an open mind
2. Complete your inventory honestly
3. Keep turning the pages-keep learning about what is destroying you
4. Exchange your will for God's Will; eternal life for eternal death
5. Plug into God's Holy Spirit and receive forgiveness and power to change
6. Trust in the Lord more than you trust your flesh which is not your friend
7. Control your mind through God's power or it will control you with Satan's power
8. Replace your negative inner voice (lie machine) with God's word
9. Purify your Video Vault by letting God give you a brain bath
10. When you need open heart surgery race to the hospital, don't stroll
11. Don't ever make decisions based on how you feel; pray and ask God first
12. Surrender your desires, "gotta haves" and fears to God and he will bless you

Please complete the Inventory activities for Lesson 12 before reading Lesson 13.

Lesson Twelve Inventory

What were you Thinking when you read Lesson 12?

How are you Feeling after reading Lesson 12?

How is what you are Thinking and Feeling now going to help you with your recovery?

What are you going to change in your behavior after reading Lesson 12?

Plug-in with Prayer - How would you like God to help you right now?
(in the space below please talk directly with God…He is listening.)

What Bible verse in Lesson 12 will you commit to memorizing?

Lesson 12: Activity 1 –
How Much Do You Control Your Body?

Body Parts	I am in Control	I Cannot Control it
Your Left Side Brain		
Your Right Side Brain		
Your Heart/Emotions		
Your Wants/Desires		
Your Eyes		
Your Tongue/Mouth		
Your Ears		
Your Hands, Fingers		
Your Legs/Feet		
Your Sexual Energy		

Lesson 12: Activity 2 – What Does Your Mouth Tell You?

Pray and ask God to give you the answers to the questions below:

What "evil" (negative) things does your mouth say about God?

What "evil" (negative) things does your mouth say about you?

What "evil" (negative) things does your mouth say about your family?

What "evil" (negative) things does your mouth say about Christians?

What "evil" (negative) things does your mouth say about recovery, this book?

What "evil" (negative) things does your mouth say about your future?

Lesson 13 – What You Need Most

The Light of Scripture: Matthew 6:7-8

And when you pray, do not keep on babbling like pagans, for they think they will be heard because of their many words. Do not be like them, for your Father knows what you need before you ask him.

⟋

The Problem: **Your personals needs often lead you away from God and deep into the world.**

The Solution: **Make God your number one need.**

The Procedure: **Humble yourself before the Lord and He will lift you up.**

My Prayer

Thank you Father for meeting all my needs. I praise you for this day. I surrender my mind and problems to you, help me stay focused on you and your goodness. Help me be more like you and less like me today. All I need is in you.

As I sat and listened to the TV with the rest of the nation I heard a voice that I recognized immediately say, "I did not have sex with that woman!" The look on Bill's face was anything but convincing, he was sweating and extremely stressed out. He must have been really upset that he, an American President, would have to justify his moral conduct on national Television not just to America, but to the whole world.

At first I was mad because it was obvious at this point in the story he was lying; and I sarcastically thought to myself, "Sure you didn't."

Then I felt ashamed that I was judging him for sins I had committed. I immediately prayed for forgiveness. And then I prayed for all those involved in this American tragedy; and by that I mean every living American. Even though many Americans honor their marriage we all are still to blame for letting things get so out of control; immorality now rules America because it sells.

Years ago, the famous German actress Marlene Dietrich once said, "In America sex is an obsession, in other parts of the world it is a fact." America has become a sexually immoral culture from one end to the other. Sexual perversion is everywhere and people are becoming more desensitized to it every day. Children are raised with it. America is more obsessed (addicted) with sexual compulsiveness now than ever before. Sexual addiction is, in my mind, the number one addiction in our country today.

It is now what we call "normal" behavior; even the rest of the world shakes its head at us disgusted with our denial. It is ironic that now, years later, Hillary (Bill's wife) is US Secretary of State and is debating with China (a communist dictatorship) about letting its people have "internet freedom". Many internet service companies want to go into China without any limitations, without any restrictions, without any net filters put in place. And what is one of the main points of contention...pornography sales.

China is not more moral than we are but they certainly know human poison when they see it and they do not want the youth of their country infected with this disease. So under the banner of "Human Rights" Hillary is telling them that they cannot restrict their people's freedom (to have their minds poisoned) by installing internet filters. So what's up with that? Why is a "Christian" nation pushing pornography on a communist country? One answer is that it makes billions of dollars every year. Another answer is that America has stopped being a "Christian" nation. God is no longer our greatest love or concern. God is no longer our number one NEED.

So why would an American President, a married man, who seemingly had everything, risk it all; or should I say, throw it all away for sexual contact with women? Why do men (and women) do such immoral and dishonest things every day? It is pretty clear that if most men's spouses were cheating on them they would be screaming about it and expressing their hurt and outrage.

One thing is for certain, until you get rid of your rationalizing, blaming and excuse making, you cannot really comprehend just how much in slavery you are to your own body's demands. You must be careful that your negative inner voice is setting you up to avoid taking responsibility for the real cause of your acting out. It will tell you that if there is something terribly wrong with your marriage; it really is your wife that is causing the difficulties. To help you get to the real problem let's first remove the "smoke screen" your mind is putting up by examining the following false beliefs.

Ten Things Men Who Cheat tend to believe about their Wives

I have heard the following statements repeatedly while working with men who are sexually acting out or thinking about doing so. Whether they are true or not is not the issue; these beliefs <u>do not</u> justify compulsive behavior. While I am sure some men who cheat don't think these lies, every man I have worked with in counseling for sexual addiction have mentioned at least one of them if not more.

1. I married the wrong person and now I am stuck
2. My wife doesn't love me anymore
3. My wife is not interested in sex; it is a very low priority for her
4. My wife only needs to do it once a month to be satisfied
5. My wife is more interested in her hobbies than she is in me
6. My wife cares more about the kids than she does me
7. My wife only cares about how much money I make
8. My wife gets critical of me whenever I ask for sex saying I am self-centered
9. My wife is very shy and doesn't like nudity or sex
10. My wife is in love with another man from her past, not me

Recovery Truth #61   **I Agree _____ I Disagree _____**
Blaming only leads to shaming those God will have you reconcile with later; the less you blame now, the easier and faster your recovery will go.

I realize that women have just as many faults as men do and many of them need to be in recovery for sexual addiction as well. The point here is that you can only be in recovery for one person and that person is you. You have to take responsibility for just you; to take ownership for your "stuff". Each person must choose to work on their recovery or to let it slide; others can listen and encourage but they cannot do it for us. So let's examine another internal human characteristic that causes nothing but trouble if we do not let God have control of it.

History Often Repeats Itself

There is something deep within us driving us to self-destruct; something that we just don't understand and therefore have great difficulty controlling. And it has been around since the beginning of time. Here is a quote from a famous Greek writer that dates back before Jesus was born. This ancient insight points us in the right direction; it illustrates the life and death fight with our flesh to have self-control.

> *It is with our passions, as it is with fire and water; they are good servants but bad masters.* Aesop (A Greek write of fables; 620BC-560 BC)

As you have already read; your thoughts, feelings, passions, desires, fantasies, and past experiences will all mislead you into sexual mistakes. The truth is your flesh is not your friend. It wants what it wants when it wants it; it will nag, threaten, pressure and lie to you until you "feed" it. Most of the book up to now has identified many things in your flesh that sabotage your morality and judgment, leading you into behavior you are later ashamed of. There is still one thing left in you that must be brought out into the open; one thing that must be controlled by God's Spirit every day if you are to be free from addiction; and that is your human needs.

Just like a Barrel of Monkeys

I recently bought the new BBC video series called "Human Planet". It is a typical high quality production by the BBC High Definition teams who search the world for interesting stories about nature, the environment and people. This particular series has videoed over 80 different stories about how humans must adapt to the environment to survive. Survival dictates that these individuals risk their lives to do some pretty amazing things to provide water and food for their existence. But one of the stories shows a situation that is just the opposite. This story is about monkeys.

In a city in India food vendors take their carts of fruit and vegetables out into the streets every day to make a living for their families. Each cart is full of a wonderful array of colors, textures and smells. Fresh produce always looks so appealing that many people stop and examine the contents of each cart. They sometimes even buy some things but they do so very quickly. Fear actually grips each customer as they stand at the cart and decide what they need and can afford. It is not fear of the vendors or the food that grips the potential buyers; it is their fear of the monkeys.

This town and many like it in India worship Monkeys (or snakes, rats, cows, or whatever) as gods and believe that they can't harm them or the gods will be angry with them. Unfortunately for them, the monkeys do not worship human gods so they have no qualms about attacking the vendors, customers and carts to steal anything and everything on it. In the video the woman trying to protect her produce doesn't have a chance as the monkeys show her no respect. Working in teams some quickly distract her on one end of the cart while others take food off the other end. She yells at them but cannot hurt them so they know who is in control and it sure isn't her.

They behave so badly that they destroy her cart and chance for making a profit. And this goes on every day for all the vendors because of what they believe. It is normal for their town, their culture and it has been for many years. They simply do not see how much their internal lies are hurting them externally. And worst of all, the monkeys are not only getting everything they want but are growing in numbers and taking over the whole town. They are bullies in the schoolyard terrorizing the locals who blame them for everything while taking responsibility for nothing. And this all occurs daily because the locals live by a false belief that justifies their enabling behavior. Addicts also live on false beliefs that keep them enabling their weaknesses, beliefs that cause them to feed their internal misbehaving "monkeys".

"I did not give a banana to that monkey!"

Your human needs are like these pesky monkeys, they do not respect what you think or believe. They are driven by being fed; by getting what they "need" to feel satisfied. And just like monkeys, even if they are satisfied one day they will be back the next to continue their attack upon your life. Self-control requires that we master our needs rather than letting them become our masters. But this is not easy to do; in fact, without God's Holy Spirit it's impossible to do.

All humans are born needy and not much changes as we "grow up". A need is simply something we must have to continue living, feeling safe and secure, loved and accepted, and valued for what we do. Our needs can be placed into five categories all which start with the letter "S".

1. **Survival** needs are those things you need to stay alive; which makes them the most important. Things such as: water, oxygen, warmth, shelter from severe conditions, any kind of food supply, protective clothing, reproduction; etc... These kind of needs make daily demands that you must meet if you are to live another day. The goal of these needs is **Physical Survival**.

2. **Safety** needs are also very powerful, besides surviving we must also grow healthier over time. These include things such as: clean water, a regular place to live, regular meals with wholesome food, cleanliness, time to sleep without threats to your person, and protection that keeps harmful others and things from hurting you. The goal of these needs is **Health Survival**.

3. **Social/Love** needs come next; these include: attention, acceptance, belonging, friendship, play time, cooperation, learning, communication, being understood, validation of efforts& achievements, intimacy and interpersonal harmony. The goal of these needs is **Relationship Survival**.

4. **Success** needs would include: achievement, recognition, power, independence, challenge, financial security, respect, having and understanding relevant facts, and creativity. The goal of these needs is **Ego/Self-worth Survival**.

5. **Spiritual** needs would include: salvation for human sins; understanding spiritual realms, trusting God (Faith) to meet all your needs; being one with your Creator so that your needs stop dominating your decision making; seeking and obeying God's laws. The goal of this need is **Eternal/Everlasting Survival**.

Needs often mislead us into going down into the Darkness

If you cannot control your needs it will be very difficult for you to control your morality. In God's word, the Bible, morality is often referred to as Light and immorality as Darkness. God is very clear in his word what is acceptable and what is not acceptable. In our society, we call doing the "right" thing moral and doing the "wrong" thing immoral. For example, if I pay money for food I have ordered I am being moral (an honest man) and if I steal the food without paying for it I am immoral (a thief).

Unfortunately, in our society there are too many different definitions and lists as to what is right and what is wrong. It seems to change every year if not every week. Having rejected God's commandments and spiritual laws we now live by situational ethics or "majority rules" morals. If the majority says something is moral then it is acceptable (i.e. abortion). Of course, when your needs go unmet for a continued period of time your concern for right and wrong goes downhill faster than if your needs are being met.

It only makes sense that being moral is much easier to do when our main needs are being consistently met. For example, if my physical need for food is being met I am less likely to steal than if I am starving and in desperate need of food to survive.

When your needs are not being satisfied on a consistent basis, right and wrong take a back seat to which ever set of needs is being satisfied the least. In short, whenever we are really needy we are most opened to any temptation that promises to meet our needs, even if it is only for a short period of time and comes at a very high price.

Recovery Truth #62   I Agree _____ I Disagree _____
Whatever you need the most is the weakest part of your personality; it is where you are the most vulnerable to be manipulated by your flesh, the world and Satan.

Greed for the Need

It's pretty common knowledge that you can catch monkeys by putting something they really like to eat in a bottle. The food object has to be the right size to just fit through the opening and the bottle has to be tied to a stake in the ground. When the monkey puts his hand into the bottle and grabs the object his fist becomes too big to pull his hand back out. He could be free to run away immediately if he would just let go of the object; but he has decided it is his and will not give it up. And here is where the recovery illustration comes into play. When baited by a temptation that meets one of your biggest needs do you refuse to "let go" and become trapped by your own "greed for the need?"

Compensating for unmet needs starts in our minds (enemy #1), when we get bored with just thinking about it we then go into the world (enemy #2) to see what will satisfy our hunger and soon are faced with Satan's (enemy #3) temptations which are opportunities to act out in ways that meet the need. The best way to win this war is by "mastering" your flesh so it does not respond to the world's baiting and Satan's traps.

For example, most of your "Theater of the Mind Productions" are aimed at meeting the needs you can not get met in reality, through fantasy. Your mind generates all kinds of visions and relationships where you always end up satisfied and successful. In these fantasies you "direct" your mental images (memories) to end up different than what actually happened in reality. You come out a winner rather than a loser. Unfortunately, the more you view these "movies" the less you like reality when you have to come back to it. While you can fool yourself for short periods of time you cannot keep up the "I Love My Life" charade forever.

To try and bring your impure fantasies into reality (the world) you have to start doing immoral things. You get to "act out" (behavior) what you are "acting in" (fantasy). For instance, paying for online sexual images you are not experiencing in reality allows you to bring fantasy into reality. Chatting on line allows some stimulating and suggestive contact with females (or males) you may never meet. The internet is full of sites you can join to meet others with the same fetishes as you have. And from chatting comes phone calls, let's meet for coffee, physical contact and, eventually, self-destruction.

Making dreams come real is not always a bad thing. If you always wanted to fly and dream about doing so for years and then one day pay for a flying lesson where you get to go up and actually fly a plane, that's cool. It is cool because you are not harming you or any others in the process; you are not doing anything immoral. Compulsively acting out, be it with food, sex, alcohol, drugs or whatever else, is always immoral because it is harmful first to you and then to others.

Consequently, whatever I need the most is where I am the most open to being manipulated by immoral people and situations. For instance, if I have a very high need to be secure I may do immoral acts (embezzlement, prostitution, steal cars, etc.) to get money to pay my bills. Or marry someone I do not love who has money and will take care of me even though I hate being with them.

Once the strongest need is met the next strongest one will take over my decision making. For instance, using this last example, if my second highest need is intimacy, I will find someone I am not married to whom I can be intimate with. I would not get a divorce if it will cost me the security I need most but I would cheat to get the intimacy I cannot find with my spouse. Adultery often functions this way and in many societies "flings" are considered moral (socially acceptable, "everybody is doing it", a type of decision making, that we call rationalizing).

And when we have two or three very strong needs in conflict with one another we can end up in some very embarrassing situations. Going back to the opening example in this lesson, we can see that Bill has a very high need for power and achievement so he spends most of his life becoming a very successful politician attempting to satisfy these primary needs. But he also has high needs for affection and intimacy, which lead him into an affair with a much younger woman that almost costs him all that he gained over years of hard work. Basically, his flesh set him up "to fail and to fall"; you might say feeding his monkeys got the better of him.

Needs and Fears: opposite ends of the same Monkey

Needs and fears are reverse ends of the same spectrum. A good illustration is found by examining a coin; one side is "heads" and the other side is "tails". While the two sides are totally different in appearance they still are part of the same coin. If you know what one side of the coin is (your need) you also always know what the opposite side is (your fear).

Needs make human behavior move toward things; they motivate us to attempt to gain something. Fears also motivate us, but not towards people or objects but away from them. The stronger your need is, the stronger the other side of that need (its opposite) will also be. For example, if I have a very high need to be respected I will also have a very high fear of being disrespected by others. So I behave accordingly, doing anything to gain respect of the group or person so my fear does not come true. And avoiding any situation where I might lose respect from others.

Not focusing on basic survival needs such as water, food, etc. let's review some of the more powerful human needs and their related fears that lead us into trouble. Mark any that you know influence your decision making and acting out.

High Need for:	**Opposite Strong Fear for:**
Acceptance	Rejection, ridicule, criticism
Being Understood	Not being listened to, valued
Independence	Being dependent on others
Intimacy	Being alone, living life by yourself
Achievement	No opportunities to accomplish, achieve
Control	Being controlled, dominated
Power	Being powerless in any situation
Harmony	Being in high conflict, anger filled situations
Organization	Being in chaotic, unorganized environments

One really interesting and useful insight is that while everyone has the same needs and fears, not everyone has the same preferences (strength of importance) for those needs. What is really important (a strong need) in one person's life could be totally unimportant (a weak need) to someone else. This is often true in marriage where the statement, "Opposites attract" is often the case. If the husbands needs are very different than the wife's needs there can be extreme stress and conflict in the relationship.

For instance, a very common pattern I have seen in marriage counseling is the wife has a high need for intimacy (fear of being alone) while the husband highest need was for independence (fear of being dependent). These two conflicting needs help explain why she gets very upset at him spending 14 hours a day working in his own company only coming home to eat and sleep, then getting up the next day and returning to work again. She becomes insecure and bitter because he (his behavior) is not meeting her strongest need (companionship, communication, and romance). With him being gone for so long she could end up spending too much time on the internet, where she might find another man who has a high need for intimacy that matches hers. Once she realizes that he is more interested in her than her husband, the immorality door is opened. Even if they "only" talk every night on line as "friends" the marriage has been severely damaged.

He, on the other hand, enjoys work because he can be his own boss. No one is putting demands on him but himself. He works long hours because he wants to be good at what he does, but also because he is afraid of having to go home where he knows his wife is waiting for him. Once there, he is subject to her comments (criticisms, demands, sobs, etc.) which make him feel like she is trying to control him. His fear of being controlled motivates him to go to work early and to stay late. He feels OK about this pattern because he is not involved with any other woman; he doesn't realize he is having an affair with his job, his company.

This is just one of many patterns that break relationships down. And I have worked with couples where it was the woman who was the "workaholic" and the man was the one who needed intimacy. Either way, when needs clash between people there will always be conflict. And the reverse is also true; where there is conflict you can bet there is a clash of primary (strongest) values happening.

Recovery Truth #63   **I Agree _____ I Disagree _____**
Monkey See, Monkey Do; if you don't want to act like a monkey, don't hang out with them.

All of your inappropriate behavior is learned. Somewhere you first saw someone else do what it is you are now doing to hurt yourself. Humans learn new behavior vicariously (through sight, vision) by watching older humans do things. We learn through contact and imitation. This is what makes movies and the internet so powerful; we don't even have to know who the actors are to want to copy their attitudes, movements and actions. The "If they get to do it why can't I?" mentality teaches bad habits to good kids who think it is "normal" to be deviant.

This happens very easily because needs are like underlying magnets within our personalities that lead us to others with similar needs that we tend to copy. For instance, a young boy who loves independence will be drawn towards (and most likely mimic) a male adult who demonstrates how to be independent. The more similar the need preferences are between the actor and the viewer the more likely the "Monkey See, Monkey Do" premise will follow. Advertising uses this approach by hiring superstars at very high prices to hawk their products, young kids all want to be like those superstar so products sell at very high prices. For example, tennis shoes went from around twenty dollars to over two hundred dollars a pair just because some guys name is on them.

So Which One is Your Chunky Monkey?

The more you let your needs dictate your decision making the less happy with reality you will be. Addiction is simply your body telling (demanding) you to get what it wants "or else". Somewhere, somehow, you have to not let your needs control your behavior or else you will sell yourself to the highest bidder. And the biggest bully in the "needs barrel" is what I call the "Chunky Monkey". This need is the strongest one in the pack, the main agitator that insists on being fed the most every day. When you let God take control over this bad boy you will notice a significant decrease in your stress and an instant increase in your joy.

There is an important difference between joy and happiness. Happiness is related to the Greek word for "happening". Happiness is temporary and related to what is occurring in the immediate. Being happy simply means that people get pleasure from what is "happening". So if you call a woman up and ask for a date, and she says yes you are happy; but if she says no, you are unhappy. This feeling leaves you dependent upon the immediate circumstances and behavior of others.

Joy, on the other hand, is long-term contentment that comes from your overall outlook and attitude towards life. It is determined by internal beliefs and values rather than by external people and events. People who have great joy can be unhappy with negative circumstances that are happening to them in the present, but still rejoice in life in general. An excellent example of this is found in Acts 16:16-34 where Paul and Silas are "stripped and beaten", "severely flogged" for casting an evil spirit out of a slave girl. Then they are thrown into prison where the jailer puts them in the "inner cell and fastened their feet in the stocks." Now I would be crying, yelling, screaming and throwing a fit but Paul and Silas are praying and singing hymns to God. I am sure they were not happy about the circumstances but they did not let it rob them of their joy in the Lord. Oh yes, read the rest of the story…the jailer and his whole family end up giving their lives to the Lord.

A good way to remember and apply this spiritual truth is realizing that JOY stands for Jesus, Others and You. Your joy will increase when you put Jesus before others and others before you. When you base your life on happiness you will always be controlled by your needs. So measure your life by how much joy (not happiness) you have in it and then you will know who's in control of your life, God or the "Chunky Monkey".

Now for that inner voice lie. Before I surrendered my life to Jesus, I thought I would never be happy (get my needs met) if I became a Christian. I believed my negative inner voice when it kept telling me that Christians were boring and never had any fun. I also wanted the pictures that were in my theater of the mind, and to get those I needed to do "unchristian" things. My "Chunky Monkey" got fed so much that he turned into King Kong and began dismantling my life big time. Instead of having joy in life I became very stressed, sad, fearful and needier. Feeding your needs makes them bigger, stronger and more demanding. When I finally did surrender them to God they stopped pestering me all day long. So what happened to calm them down?

Philippians 4:19
And my God will meet all your <u>needs</u> according to his glorious riches in Christ Jesus....
All the saints send you greetings, especially those who belong to Caesar's household.

God's Holy Spirit came into me and took control over my flesh and all its weaknesses. God, who understands everything about me, filled me with His love which satisfies all my needs. The "emptiness" inside of me left and now I am not as quick to want to copy other humans who are destroying their lives. I want to copy Jesus.

Recovery Truth #64   I Agree ـــــ I Disagree ـــــ
God can provide abundantly more than what you need. In contrast, the world only offers "smoke and mirrors"; illusions of approval, love, fulfillment and tranquility.

It is sad how many people call themselves "Christians" and have no intentions of ever being like Jesus. They don't study his life or his teachings; they do not intend to surrender their wills to Him or obey his commands yet they still think they are going to be blessed by God regardless of how they live. I challenge you to leave this way of thinking and to take God's offer of help; His free gift of his Holy Spirit and let him meet your needs. In doing so you will be healed and set free of any and all "Monkey Business".

Luke 12:29-31
And do not set your heart on what you will eat or drink; do not worry about it. For the pagan world runs after all such things, and your Father knows that you need them. But seek his kingdom, and these things will be given to you as well.

Your needs make you put things and people before God

To increase your chance of success in recovery it is important to understand that you (and everyone else) create images (fantasies) that are designed to satisfy unmet needs (desires) in your life. This simply means that when reality lets you down you will go to fantasy to get your needs met. There are many ways in which you go about doing this. The three things people choose the most are: entertainment, relationships and work. Let's briefly define and examine each one.

WINNING THE WAR WITH YOUR FLESH!

1. Entertainment   Sports, travel, music, movies, internet, hobbies, reading, etc.

Example

Hollywood creates this dysfunctional situation with most of its movies. What it calls entertainment has become an addiction for anyone who is dissatisfied with his life. Scripts are carefully written to meet unmet needs; to write dialog and show images that will connect with what is missing in your life. Even when people are out of work and can't pay their bills, they always have time and money for being entertained. Movies are just one illustration, there are many others such as: boats, cars, vacations, clothes, eating out, hobbies, sports, video games, etc. When we spend all our human energy being entertained (or entertaining) we lose connection with God.

2.Relationships   Marriage, friendships, team members, work associates, clients, customers, teachers, students, coaches, etc.

Example

People who are needy (and that would be all of us) look most often to other humans to meet their deepest needs. They get involved with others because they hope the relationship will satisfy their needs every day. This seldom occurs as humans are very limited as to how much they can give others. When needs don't get fed quick enough people often grow tired of the relationship and change them like a dirty shirt for something more "fitting". After a while, when that relationship has run its course, we move on again. In sports it's called, "What have you done for me lately?" This reoccurring desertion and abandonment is highly destructive for all involved, especially kids who are left in the dust. In short, God is not impressed.

3. Work   Job related skills and talents, careers, occupations, jobs, schedules, visions, purpose, goals, challenges, resources, training, & rewards

Example

Many people, men in particular, strongly believe that they are what they do for a living. They think their occupations and jobs determine their individual worth in life. Their work becomes their identity and when the job ends, as all jobs will, they have great difficulty living in the now. All their conversations go back to when they were doing this job or winning that award. Their needs are so enmeshed with their work that they lack an identity separate from it. So work demands their attention over their families, their friends and over God. Many Pastors surprisingly fall into this category.

Recovery Truth #65   **I Agree _____ I Disagree _____**
God is Reality and thinking anyone's Flesh will make you happy is fantasy; let Jesus crucify your monkeys (sinful nature, self, needs, fears) before they crucify you.

Galatians 5:24

Those who belong to Christ Jesus have crucified the sinful nature with its passions and desires.

You are either feeding the flesh or feeding the Spirit, you cannot do both at the same time. And if you think you don't feed either you are really feeding the flesh. Laziness, apathy and lack of concern are all signs that your flesh is controlling your life. Most men I meet who are in this state are joyless and totally unhappy; often blaming their emptiness inside on others and events. If this is how you are living your life today it does not have to be that way.

God has all the Love required to meet your needs. His love can fulfill your needs if you let him be in control of your life. He does this through relationships with other Christians; by placing you in situations that best fit your skills and talents; and by placing in you a deep gratitude for all that you have, even if you don't have anything. In God's kingdom Love brings deep contentment and security.

A Testimony from a Brother in Recovery

I am very thankful for Everett's willingness to be used by God thru his materials. I have learned the power of Plugging In!

When I feed the "Good Dog" (my Spirit) by Surrendering, Submitting and Praising God the "Bad Dog" (my flesh) loses power over me. Learning how to starve the flesh and feed my Spirit has given me hope and tools for winning the battle I fight every day. Praising God ten times is so easy to do.

Lord I praise you that you gave your ONLY SON, and LEFT him on the cross to bare my sins.

Lord I praise you that you have saved all the love you have ever had for me that I have not received yet, and are now pouring it into my life.

Lord I praise you and thank you for the grace my wife has shown me and the value you have given her.

Lord I praise you for my wife and the joy she brings me.

Lord I praise you and thank you for all my children and the value you have for each of them.

Lord I praise you and thank you for our business.

Lord I praise you for our employees and the value you have for them also.

Lord I praise you for Everett and how you have used him in my life.

Lord I praise you for the privilege of living in the United States

Lord I praise you for the peace you give me when I surrender and submit and praise you.

John 3:16 taught me that I am a Diamond, I have great value. I am forgiven. Jesus died so I would know this and be free to do His work with the special gifts He has given me.

LORD I PRAISE YOU!!!!!!!!!!!!!!!!!!!!!!!!

Mark d.

So What Can You Do to Get Healed?

1. Read with an open mind
2. Complete your inventory honestly
3. Keep turning the pages-keep learning about what is destroying you
4. Exchange your will for God's Will; eternal life for eternal death
5. Plug into God's Holy Spirit and receive forgiveness and His power to change
6. Trust in the Lord more than you trust your flesh which is not your friend
7. Control your mind through God's power or it will control you with Satan's power
8. Replace your negative inner voice (lie machine) with God's word
9. Purify your Video Vault by letting God give you a brain bath
10. When you need open heart surgery race to the hospital, don't stroll
11. Don't ever make decisions based on how you feel; pray and ask God first
12. Surrender your desires, "gotta haves" and fears to God and he will bless you
13. Need God more than you need anything or anyone in this world

Please complete the Inventory activities for Lesson 13 before reading Lesson 14.

Lesson Thirteen Inventory

What were you Thinking when you read Lesson 13?

How are you Feeling after reading Lesson 13?

How is what you are Thinking and Feeling now going to help you with your recovery?

What are you going to change in your behavior after reading Lesson 13?

Plug-in with Prayer - How would you like God to help you right now?
(in the space below please talk directly with God…He is listening.)

What Bible verse in Lesson 13 will you commit to memorizing?

Lesson 13: Activity 1 –
What Do You Think About Your Wife?

Your Thoughts:	I believe this	I don't believe this
I married the wrong person and now I am stuck with her		
My wife doesn't love me anymore		
My wife is not interested in sex; it is a very low priority for her		
My wife only needs to have sex once a month to be satisfied		
My wife is more interested in her work or hobbies than she is in me		
My wife cares more about the kids than she does me		
My wife only cares about how much money I make		
My wife gets critical of me whenever I ask for sex, she says I am being self-centered		
My wife is very shy and doesn't like nudity or sex		
My wife is in love with another man from her past, not me		
My wife loves to control me and then tells me it is love		
My wife is over-sexed and I can't keep up with her demands		

How does what you believe above help you honor God and love your wife in his Spirit? Surrender in prayer any negative inner voice statements before they ruin your relationship with God and your wife.

Lesson 13: Activity 2 – What are your Strongest needs?

Listed below are 21 primary needs that all of us prefer to one degree or another. You have 10 minutes to circle the five needs (only 5) that are most important to you at this time in your life.

Acceptance   To be accepted for who you are without having to do anything. To be allowed to think, dress and behave as you want to, when you want to. To be liked by many people. To feel like you belong to a group. To have many friendships.

Achievement   To set and reach specific goals within specific timelines. To accomplish difficult tasks. To be able to move into situations requiring more difficult skills. To be allowed to produce quickly and efficiently.

Appreciation   To be acknowledged for being thoughtful and considerate. To be valued for being a hard and reliable worker. To be given this acknowledgment and value without having to ask for it.

Attention   To be able to hold people's attention when speaking. To maintain eye-contact with people. To be in front of crowds for speaking, entertaining and athletic performances.

Challenge   To be pushed to your fullest point of development. To be dared to attempt something that others don't think can be done. To take risks within the environment for profits and/or for thrills.

Creativity   To be allowed to create with ideas and abilities. To be able to express all creativity without rigid structures or timelines. To have variety in what you do and when you do it. To have support for the expression of all creative energies.

Harmony   To live and work in a friendly, safe, and quiet environment. To have emotional stability within personal relationships. To have few conflicts with others. To not have to fight for your rights as an individual.

Honesty   To be told the truth no matter how bad things are. To not be lied to even if it is meant to protect you. To be able to say what is on you mind without fear of retaliation. To not be cheated or deceived by others. To be able to trust someone with all that is important to you

Independence   To be able to do what you want to do when you want to do it. To be allowed to be alone when you choose to be alone. To be able to work without interruption on projects of your choice. To be able to live, work, and play where and when you want to.

Intimacy   To be close to individuals on a very personal level. To be able to trust someone with your inner most thoughts and emotions, and for them to trust you with theirs. To be like "family" with non-family people. To have one-on-one time for introspective discussion.

Organization   To have an orderly environment. To be able to work with systems that are logical and sequential. To be able to provide structure to non-structured situations. To be rational about how things are done.

Play Time   To be able to tell jokes and laugh with others. To organize and enjoy parties with others. To be allowed to create entertainment for others. To have time to play games. To be able to do whatever pleasures you. To be able to relax exactly how you like to unwind.

Power   To be able to control situations and events. To be able to cut through obstacles and adversity which take away from production time. To acquire money, status, and position for influence.

Recognition   To be praised for what you have created or accomplished. To get verbal thanks and credit for work done. To have your name written somewhere that it will be read by many people. To be promoted and/or honored for new ideas and work efforts.

Respect   To be thought of as knowledgeable and competent in a specific area. To be admired for what you think, say and do. To receive the required personal and professional regard and honor due your role and position of authority. To receive credit for the work you do.

Responsibility   To be given accountability for important tasks in important situations. To have the authority to make decisions without having to ask others.

Safety   To have safety guards that protect the individual and loved ones from physical and emotional harm. To work and live in non-threatening environments. To be able to trust others to not be physically aggressive with you.

Security   To have few financial debts. To have few major changes in life. To know that your job is secure. To have a warm home and food in the house. To be able to take care of health needs. To be able to provide for children's necessities.

Spirituality   To have communication with God, a relationship with Him that gives you the power to complete his will for your life, inner peace from being in communion with his Holy Spirit.

To Love   To be able to nurture and care for others in need. To give rather than to receive. To share what one has to help those who have not. To create safe and warm environments for family and friends. To do for others, being thoughtful and considerate of their needs before your own.

Understanding   To know how and why things are the way they are. To be able to get specific answers to questions. To be able to teach others what you know. To comprehend what you are being asked to do before you have to do it. To be allowed to share and use your perceptions of situations and others to make things better.

Lesson 13: Activity 3 -
Needs and Fears are opposite sides of the same coin

Needs are very strong drives within our personalities. We all have strong individual preferences for certain needs while others are less important to us. For example, some individuals have a very high need for **attention** and love people watching them, while others who have a low need for attention feel very uncomfortable when people focus on them. And people who have a very high need for security tend to be low risk takers while others who are big risk takers have a lower need for security and a high need for challenge.

Need Rule #1: You spend more time and energy trying to get what you need the most and way less time and energy pursuing your weaker needs. For instance, if I have a high need for intimacy I will put more effort into trying to obtain that need than if it was very low for me.

Need Rule #2: Whatever you need the most the opposite of it is what you fear the most. For example, if you have a very high need for **acceptance** then you will also have a high fear of rejection. I know that if someone is afraid of rejection it most likely also means they have a strong need for acceptance.

Need Rule #3: Whatever you need the most will be your most vulnerable area. People can manipulate and mislead you easier when they meet your strongest needs. Getting your strongest needs met can lead to addictions that control you; because of this fact your strongest needs are intertwined with "emotional triggers". These triggers (words, behaviors or situations) release powerful emotions (feelings) that cause you to act out. For example, if I have a high need for respect I will get very angry (emotional) when someone is being rude to me (trigger). If they continue I might explode and verbally or physically fight (act out) them to be "respected". By acting out this way I demonstrate that I have become controlled by (dependent) "disrespect".

Needs Activity

Please list down the top five needs you identified in Activity 1, what the opposite fear would be for each need, and what emotional triggers are related to them.

Example: Need/Challenge   Fear/Boredom   Trigger/Routine   Emotion/Depression

<u>Strongest Needs</u> = <u>Biggest Fears</u>   <u>Triggers</u>   <u>Emotions</u>

1.

2.

3.

4.

5.

Lesson 14 – Valuing What's Most Important

The Light of Scripture: John 3:16-17

For God so loved the world that he gave his one and only Son, that whoever believes in him shall not perish but have eternal life. For God did not send his Son into the world to condemn the world, but to save the world through him.

The Problem: **You place way less value on you than God does**

The Solution: **Allow God's love to wash you clean of fear and hate**

The Procedure: **Focus on the diamond rather than on the Pig Poop**

My Prayer

Lord, thank you for your loving touch. I am so grateful you have taught me the value of your sacrifice. Help me to value people as much as you do. Help me to be willing to sacrifice what I need to help others. Thank you for washing off the pig poop and making me useful in your kingdom. May you teach every reader what you would have them know about your mercy and grace.

WINNING THE WAR WITH YOUR FLESH!

I grew up in a small town in Northern California. It was in a valley 3500 hundred feet up in the Sierras with mountains all around it. There were lakes and lots of tall trees; Sugar and Ponderosa Pines that smelled wonderful. I loved running around outside until it got cold, and every winter it got really cold. We had seven feet of pure powder several times while I lived there. It was very beautiful in the winter… but very cold.

The town was located at one end of a big valley where many of my friends lived. So going to see them meant transportation other than my feet. As a young teenager I was still too young to get my driver's license. I often hitched a ride when someone was going the way I was heading. It was no big deal back then as most people knew each other.

One such person was a guy who had been out of school for a couple of years. I was always glad to see him as he was funny and easy going. But I wasn't always glad to see his car. While it ran, it lacked many things that made it desirable to ride in. First of all, several windows did not roll up. Second, the heater never worked. Third, other than the static, the radio didn't work either. Fourth, his tires were bald on bald. Fifth, his chariot never went over 40 miles an hour and smoked more than he did. But worst of all was the battery, which always needed a jump to get it going once it was turned off.

During the summer months these flaws all seemed like minor things and I took them in stride as just another part of the journey. But come winter…then it became hard work. Riding around with the window down brought in lots of cold air through the "pneumonia holes". Having no heat made it the "shiver mobile" and having no tunes back in those days was downright brutal. And of course, having bald tires meant spinning out was a regular event on most every curve… sometimes a thrill a minute, sometimes hair- raising. But having to get out and push the shiver mobile when it would not start was the real killer.

And so it is with you. You have a human battery within you. When it is charged up it runs your personality and when it is drained it leaves you "alongside the road" waiting for a "jumpstart" to get you going again. These jumpstarts often come through toxic relationships, alcohol, drugs, sexual stimulants, erotic encounters, gambling, thrill seeking, overeating…anything that will make you feel "satisfied" (dopamine rush) for a short period of time.

While a car with a dead battery can still have some value, it is considered highly unreliable most of the time. People are the same way. When our human battery is low we lack warmth for others, we are not entertaining, we are often emotionally uncontrollable and we abandon relationships when they are needed the most. And in the end, like many old cars left out in a field or behind the barn, we are abandoned by others who have given up struggling to start us up "one more time".

Recovery Truth #66   Agree _____ I Disagree _____
Recovery (the ultimate human overhaul) is simple; fix it early and pay little, or fix it late and pay with hate.

Like a malfunctioning car, if we fix our "stuff" early we pay little (less work and suffering), but if we fix it late we pay with hate (anger that it is costing way more than we think it should). This concept is so true in recovery. Addicts put off what they need to do over and over again then get mad at everyone for their poor choices. When those who do get help finally surrender their "stinking thinking" they suddenly realize how much refusing help has cost them and others. Unfortunately, sadly …many more brothers and sisters die in their self-destructive unwillingness to get help than those who finally pull in for repair. One of the main reasons for this is Pig Poop.

There's Diamonds in that there Pig Poop!

As I looked out at the men in the recovery class I saw many faces covered with shame and lack of hope. I asked the men, "How many of you feel like you are really nothing more than a big pile of pig poop?" Many of them raised their hands while not making eye contact with me.

I told them, "While growing up, many of you had people throwing pig poop on you so often that you learned how to throw it on yourself. And then you started throwing it on others, even those you cared about. Now you believe, based on what has happened to you in life and what you have done in your life, that there is no hope for you. You think that you are far beyond getting clean, far beyond getting healed. You believe you are worthless and unlovable."

All eyes in the room are now on me. Many are thinking perhaps I will pick certain ones out and tell them to leave, that it is too late for them. Others are afraid I will tell them they are so messed up that even the class cannot help them. As I pause and look around the room I became very aware that what they are thinking would kill them if I did not help them bring the lies in their heads out into the open.

To begin this long process I write John 3:16 on the board leaving spaces where it says the words, "the world".

> *For God so loved _____ that he gave his one and only Son, that whoever believes in him shall not perish but have eternal life. For God did not send his Son into _____ to condemn _____, but to save _____ through him.*

I then ask them to write their full name in the spaces and to read it again. As they do I randomly pick out one name from the class and write it in the spaces in the verse on the board.

> *For God so loved Richard that he gave his one and only Son, that whoever believes in him shall not perish but have eternal life. For God did not send his Son to Richard to condemn Richard, but to save Richard through him.*

Recovery Truth #67   I Agree _____ I Disagree _____
God values you so highly that he sent his Holy Spirit to wash the pig poop off of you so you can have the love and life God intended you to have.

I then tell them the "good news" that while humanity was totally covered with pig poop (sin, hurt, pride, fear, greed, lust, and all the rest of it) God sent Jesus to die in our place…to pay for our sins so that we can be forgiven and healed, washed clean forever. God would only give what he values most, his Son, for us only if he also valued us highly. I add that God is not coming back for anything on earth but our souls…not plants, not animals, not even our bodies…our souls and our spirits are the only thing he values on earth.

Yes, you are still covered in pig poop but Jesus wants to restore you. He wants to clean off everything that is poisoning you (and those you love) if you will let him. Jesus suffered a horrible death and gave his life for you because he values (loves) you. Anyone who says otherwise is a liar, including your own mind. Ah yes, here is where your negative inner voice and theatre of the mind show up again. They tell you and show you why you are nothing but pig poop. They go on and on listing all the bad things that have happened to you and all those bad things that you have done. They show you pictures of you sinning over and over again; and many times you are enjoying every minute of it. A major lie in your head is that you are nothing but a big garbage can of pig poop and that's all you ever will be.

While we all get covered with pig poop (sin) in life God still sees what is deep inside, what he created us to be before the world polluted us, and that is a DIAMOND! Recovery is God pressure washing the pig poop off of (and out of) us. This takes time and is often painful as the poop on us has been there for  a long time. Yet when he is done we are so clean that, just like a diamond, we reflect light… God's light.

Recovery Truth #68   **I Agree _____ I Disagree _____**
The "Pig Poop" from your past is the fertilizer God uses to grow your future.

2 Corinthians 1:3-5
Praise be to the God and Father of our Lord Jesus Christ, the Father of compassion and the God of all comfort, who comforts us in all our troubles, so that we can comfort those in any trouble with the comfort we ourselves have received from God. For just as the sufferings of Christ flow over into our lives, so also through Christ our comfort overflows.

Another miracle is that God not only washes the pig poop off of you but then He uses it in your life to help other men who are just like you. Men who are struggling with their flesh and thinking that they are really alright when in fact they are sinking like a ship. God takes our "lemons" and makes lemonade because that is one of his specialties. It is also how he teaches us to be "Christ like".

As the pig poop is being removed by God we begin to "understand" what it is like to have inner healing. We feel lighter, more hopeful and definitely more loved. We start to see others needs and hurts as more important than our own. We learn to develop a testimony of how God can and does help those who reach out to him, those who accept Jesus as their Savior and Lord. While life is still difficult we no longer feel alone on our Journey and more importantly, we have changed direction and are now traveling towards God rather than away from him.

The journey is life long and doesn't happen quickly for most of us. Some people are healed immediately and I have total faith God can and does do that for certain people according to his will. I believe this occurs so that most of us learn discipline that comes from hard work; once down the trail we become recovery scouts for those who are to follow. To learn our lessons quickly we must surrender all of our minds to God.

Stinkin-Thinkin is Pig Poop in the Brain

A major block to you receiving God's love and healing is self-hatred; you cannot receive his love if you hate yourself (and most addicts do). The roots of self-hatred are lies that are often referred to in recovery as "stink-in think-in". Lies full of hate that tell us every day we are unforgiveable and of no value to anyone. These lies first tell us to sin and then criticize us for doing so.

God will remove the lies that are in our thinking but first we must be willing to give them to him, to surrender what we have believed for years to be our one true friend. You see the biggest lie our brain tells us is that we can only trust our own thinking, when in fact; it is our thinking that is harming us and others the most.

Recovery Truth #69   **I Agree _____ I Disagree _____**
Your relationship with God determines your relationship with yourself; which in turn, determines your relationships with others.

Life is all about Relationships

The relationship that you have with yourself is the oldest, most personal and intimate relationship you will ever have with any human being. You can never escape yourself; even after death you are still with you, just not in your current body. In this life, you spend twenty-four hours of every day with you. Only you will ever live inside your skin. The old saying, "Where ever you go there you are," captures this obvious truth.

So if you do not like who you are, if you do not love who you are, if you mistreat yourself, the time you spend with you will be very unsatisfying. You will be filled with unhappiness, anger and fear. The human way of dealing with this is to find things outside of the body to make up for what's going wrong inside the body. This explains compulsive self-destructive behavior completely; trying to make the internal pain go away by medicating with external stimulants such as alcohol, drugs, sexual acting out, food, shopping, gambling, co-dependency, etc. Of course, these things only make the internal pain disappear for a short period of time at a great cost to your mental, emotional and physical health.

The crucial fact here is that the relationship you have with yourself <u>dictates</u> all the other relationships you will have with all other people. If your relationship with you is negative that negativity will always poison the relationships you have with others. It does this by seeping out of your personality through your speech, your opinions, your insecurities, your anger, your fears, and your uncontrollable need to control the people you say you love.

The relationship you have with yourself is controlled by your brain. Your thinking (positive and negative) starts in the brain creating decisions on how you should act. If you cannot control your thoughts you cannot recover from that which controls your behavior. If your mind says you are pig poop and you believe it, you will devalue yourself and act accordingly. Doing this leads to loss of hope and self-hatred. If your mind says you are valuable because God says so, you will act accordingly. The main challenge is how do you change a negative thinking pattern into a Godly (positive) thinking pattern?

The answer lies in understanding what we often call, "Self-Worth".

<u>Self-Worth</u> (SW) is the measure of the overall evaluation a person makes about themselves. It is the deepest level of relating or intimacy individuals can have with themselves. SW functions like a personality "battery" that provides energy to live life. When it is low there is less energy (pessimism) and when it is high there is more energy (optimism). Our chances of success in life greatly increase when we have higher energy.

At birth our SW battery is empty. Humans are not born with Self-Worth and it is not inherited. It is learned (programmed) by many interactions with family, friends, co-workers, and other significant people that influence us while we are growing up. The key to improving low SW is accepting that what is learned can be unlearned. While self-worth is very tough and hard to humanly change it is very easy for God to change. To better understand how it can be changed let's look at how God created self-worth to be "two sides" of the same coin.

Each side of the "self-worth coin" strongly influences personality and behavior patterns, but in totally different ways. Each one is also equally important in understanding how your personality and behavior are determined and changed. The two sides of the SW coin are called: **self-concept** and **self-esteem.**

A. <u>Self-Concept</u> (SC) is the cognitive relationship you have with yourself.

When you have relationships with others you <u>think</u> about them in many different ways. For example, you constantly are having thoughts, ideas, assumptions, judgments, and perceptions about people you meet. You have made thousands of evaluative thoughts about me just reading this book. The same is true regarding the relationship you have with yourself. You go through these same mental processes when relating with who you are.

Your thought processes about you determines your SC "level" (a measure of how high or low your SC is). High SC is healthy, low SC is unhealthy. As we have read previously, your thinking actually speaks to you inside your head...this is called self-talk. This "inner voice" inside your head can be positive or negative, often it is both. For example, when it tells you to do things that are healthy such as eat good foods, it is positive. But when it tells you it is Ok to do unhealthy things such as shooting heroin, it is extremely negative.

Your inner voice (IV) lies within your self-concept and greatly shapes how you understand things. When your IV is positive you see reality for what it really is; but when it is negative you have a more distorted view of reality. The more negative your IV is: the more lies you believe, the more fear controls you, the more depressed and sick you become, the less you believe you can succeed at anything, and the less hope you have for the future. You actually have your worst enemy living inside your head, telling you things that destroy your body and your relationships.

An example of this would be jealousy. People who suffer from this character flaw always have a strong negative inner voice. It tells them they cannot trust the one they say they love. They cannot trust them because their thinking lies to them telling them the other person is really going to hurt them. Believing this internal lie they become angry, aggressive and often do things to hurt the other person first. Thus destroying the person they say they "love".

Your Identity is who you "Think" you should be

Another important role of self-concept is that it is where your identity comes from. Your mind tells you (through your inner voice) who you are and how you should act accordingly...we call this our identity. Similar to a movie script where you have to play a part in the movie and have to look and talk a certain way to be successful, our identity tells us how to act in life if we want acceptance. Unfortunately, it is often based on lies that are interwoven into our minds by the negative inner voice. And we end up trying to be someone we were never created to be.

Trust God and ask him to "plug you in" so He can begin downloading your true identity and purpose. He will also do this by "washing" your self-hatred away with His Love.

In recovery God reframes our identities to help us understand what our true purpose is in life. Purpose always follows identity; if our identity is flawed then our purpose will also be off course. We will be wasting our time and energy in life trying to be someone we were not meant to be and trying to accomplish things we were not meant to accomplish.

Recovery Truth #70   **I Agree _____ I Disagree _____**
Self-hatred is a major personality weed that is rooted in low self-worth; God must pull it and replace it with His love if you are to have inner healing.

B. <u>Self-Esteem</u> (SE) is the emotional relationship you have with yourself.

Esteem means to "respect" someone, to hold them in high regard or honor. Besides thinking about (analyzing) ourselves we also have feelings about and towards ourselves. The emotional side of your personality (mind) contains your feelings and emotional reactions to self. Just as you emotionally react to other people's personalities and behaviors, you also have the same reactions to your own personality and behavior. (An example would be you have negative feelings towards critical people but you also feel negative about you when you are critical towards others.)

A key component of self-esteem is that it is a measure of the level of love and friendship you "feel" towards yourself. In short, it indicates how much you like who you are and reflects how much you accept yourself. When SE is low a person rejects themselves with disgust and they are not "friendly" towards their existence. This means they make very bad decisions about taking care of their bodies and their lives. And they resist any attempts from others who try to convince them they should treat themselves better. They have no mercy for themselves when they are sick or emotionally down and "heaven help them" if they ever make a mistake because they will not forget or forgive it. They are their own worst enemy.

People with low self-esteem have such lack of regard or honor for who they are that they disrespect their minds, bodies and lives. This is always an indication of deep disgrace and embarrassment of who they are as an individual. This self-devaluation is always driven by deep, painful shame.

Riding the Shame Train is a Pain

One of the biggest chains keeping you bound to your compulsive acting out patterns is shame (another name for pig poop). Shame is the root system for self-hatred; it feeds it and keeps it growing within your personality. You cannot love someone if you hate them. God wants to remove the hate from your heart towards others and yourself so he can use you. God can and will remove your shame for the things you have done, and, the shame for the things that others have done to you if you ask him. Until it is removed you will continue riding "The Shame Train".

The Shame Train's destination is always darkness, anyplace where you can hide from others and hopefully, yourself. It speeds your life into self-destructive relationships, practices and situations. This train runs on pain, your pain. Each car on the train is full of memories, full of hurt, and full of humiliation. Each car is full of pig poop which repulses others. No one wants to ride this train with you. Don't believe you have a one-way ticket and can never get off.

Praise the name of Jesus! Because he died for your sins (shame acts included), you can be taken off this train and never have to get on it again. Does that mean you don't have to be held accountable for all the bad things you have done? No…it doesn't, we must allow God to take us off the train and scrub us clean so we no longer live in the pig poop of our past. And that scrubbing often requires us to make amends for the wrongs that we have committed but in doing so, we not only get off a train full of pain but we also gain freedom to live the life we were created to live.

None of this happens if you do not let God heal both your self-concept (your left-side brain relationship with you) and your self-esteem (your right-side brain relationship with you). In doing so, God heals your mind and fills it with his truth. In short, you start riding the only train that is heading "home".

Having a strong self-concept and self-esteem "in God" is crucial for recovery. SC reflects what you think about yourself and is essential to self-worth development because it directly affects your entire perception of self (identity) and decision making (life choices). A high level of SE is crucial because it influences how well you like and respect yourself (love for self) and the level of friendship you will have with you. God commands us to love our neighbors as we love our self. The more you reject yourself the worse you will treat others. The more you love yourself as Jesus loves you, the more you will love others, even when they don't deserve such love.

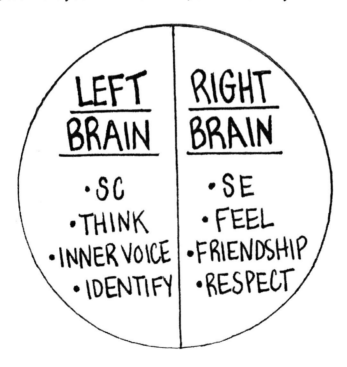

Steps for Increasing Your Self-Concept (Left-side Brain Healing)

1. Surrender your mind (will, thoughts, mental images) to God daily. Nothing powers up our human battery (our spirit) quicker than giving God our will which is an act of plugging into his Spirit. When we do this his Grace strengths us and gives us the wisdom we need to get through life's challenges.

2. Accept God's identity for you rather than the one the world gave you. God created you for a purpose; your identity in Christ and your spiritual gifts are to be used to help others so God is glorified.

3. Identify and Confront what your Negative Inner Voice is telling you. Listen to your inner voice and decide on what is not honoring to God; these thoughts will harm you and others if you continue letting them influence your decisions. Confront them using God's scripture.

4. Praise God especially when you feel worried, depressed or angry. Thanking God (Praise) is another way to plug in and drive negativity out of your head. God is light and when we plug into him his light comes into us.

5. Protect your relationships by checking your thoughts before you speak. Your behavior always follows what you think and then decide. Your thoughts often set you up for failure and you don't even know it. Making decisions based on lies will mess up your relationships. Protect them by letting God heal your mind.

6. Value yourself and others based on what Jesus says and did for you, not on what you (or someone else) can do in this world. Individual worth should never be based on appearance or performance levels, only on what God says about us. We are never worthy of God's love, but our spirit and souls (not our flesh) are still highly valued by him.

Steps for Increasing Your Self-Esteem (Right-side Brain Healing)

1. **Praise God daily, thanking him for everything you have really feels good.** This time of praise pleases God and he in turn will bless and energize you.

2. **Pray and ask God to give you strength and a clear memory.** Ask and you shall receive, seek and you will find…God is reaching out for your hand to help you up from your misery and despair. When you accept his help your mind will be healed and you will remember what you need to give to him

3. **Don't Trust Your Emotions.** Our emotions and feelings are part of our flesh and often mislead us. Remember, God is real no matter how we feel. Do not let emotions make decisions for you or you will be sorry.

4. **Forgive yourself and others as God forgives you.** Once God forgives you of something

that you have confessed then it is a sin to keep hating yourself for it. Make amends to those you have harmed as he directs you.

5. **Improve your level of friendship with you Self-esteem** is a direct measure of how much we like ourselves. Knowing who you are now, would you pick yourself as a best friend? If not, identify why not and change it.

6. **Understand the difference between your Guilt and Shame.** Guilt (left-side conviction) says you deserve punishment for doing something wrong. Shame (right-side damnation) says you are unforgivable, unworthy and unlovable for having committed that wrong. Guilt says you deserve to go to jail while Shame says you should never get out of jail. Shame leads to self-hatred and loss of hope.

When you bring your Shame to GOD he washes you spiritually clean, restoring your ability to receive love from God and others. When you don't, you continue to sin (relapse) knowing it is wrong and more guilt and shame grows within you.

7. **List down all shameful things you have done; or that were done to you.** Pray and ask God what he would have you write down; list things in time zones such as: 0-5 years old, 6-10 years old, right up to your present age. Do not leave this list out where others can find it, protect yourself by protecting it.

8. **Confess these shameful things to someone trustworthy that will pray with you and keep them confidential.** Have an accountability partner (or partners); sharing with others who can keep what you say confidential helps drain the pain that comes from shame. Do not confess to those who will reinforce your shame or try to harm you in other ways with your confession. Ask God for wisdom in whom to share with.

9. **Sing songs of praise; listen to Christian music that lifts up the name of the Lord.** Turn off music and movies that poison your relationship with God.

10. **Don't be in the wrong place, with the wrong people, doing the wrong thing,** just because it's fun and the people with you like you better for doing it.

A Testimony from a Brother in Recovery

I was a mess. It wasn't apparent on the exterior, but inside I was falling apart. My life had been dedicated to academics, something I thought would allow me to boost my confidence, but it didn't help. My low self-worth persisted. In addition to that, I was struggling with unwanted same sex attraction. For years, this attraction had shamed me so much that I had never dared speak of it. I was so confused and felt so alone. I tried to change, but I seemed stuck. When I felt like I had hit bottom, I sought help. I joined a group of guys at my church who were also facing the broken realities of their own lives. We all signed up for a class called Stand Firm. Little by little, we began a series of steps aimed to bring us out of denial to reality. This book identifies these steps.

Through the work of the Spirit, I have learned that my low self-worth and same sex attraction stem from prior childhood and adolescence wounds. I had coped with this pain in broken ways, so part of the healing process has required me to walk back through the pain. It's been a dark road at times, but I have clung to verses like Psalm 23:4, "Even though I walk through the valley of the shadow of death, I will fear no evil, for you are with me; your rod and your staff, they comfort me."

I believe that my healing is directly connected to my relationship with God. The more I am filled with truth and delight in his ways, the more my old ways become less and less desirable. In fact, my heavenly Father sets out a banquet table for me every day for me to feast on truth. In Isaiah 55:2 it says, "Why do you spend your money for that which is not bread, and your labor for that which does not satisfy? Listen diligently to me, and eat what is good, and delight yourselves in rich food."

Even still, I continue to fight to be fully confident as a man and claim my identity in Jesus, knowing that my enemy cannot prevail against me and that the Lord is my deliverer.

Dietrich B.

So What Can You Do to Get Healed?

1. Read with an open mind
2. Complete your inventory honestly
3. Keep turning the pages-keep learning about what is destroying you
4. Exchange your will for God's Will; eternal life for eternal death
5. Plug into God's Holy Spirit and receive forgiveness and power to change
6. Trust in the Lord more than you trust your flesh which is not your friend
7. Control your mind through God's power or it will control you with Satan's power
8. Replace your negative inner voice (lie machine) with God's word
9. Purify your Video Vault by letting God give you a brain bath
10. When you need open heart surgery race to the hospital, don't stroll
11. Don't ever make decisions based on how you feel; pray and ask God first
12. Surrender your desires, "gotta haves" and fears to God and he will bless you
13. Need God more than you need anything or anyone in this world
14. Go to the Cross every day and receive your free gift from God; plug into His Grace and you will have the power to crucify your flesh.

Please complete the Inventory activities for Lesson 13 before reading Lesson 14.

Lesson Fourteen Inventory

What were you Thinking when you read Lesson 14?

How are you Feeling after reading Lesson 14?

How is what you are Thinking and Feeling now going to help you with your recovery?

What are you going to change in your behavior after reading Lesson 14?

Plug-in with Prayer - How would you like God to help you right now?
(in the space below please talk directly with God...He is listening.)

What Bible verse in Lesson 14 will you commit to memorizing?

Lesson 14: Activity 1 – What's the Difference?

In the spaces below write out what you think the differences are between the terms Guilt and Shame:

Guilt is

_____

_____

_____

_____

_____

_____

Shame is

_____

_____

_____

_____

_____

_____

When you have finished writing out your definitions go back and reread the Lesson and see how close it comes to what was written.

Lesson 14: Activity 2 - The Five Trails of Shame

Shame = Overwhelming feelings of disgrace, dishonor, disgust and self-hatred.

Do NOT do this activity until you have lots of time and privacy to complete it then follow the steps below:

Steps to Remove the Shame (poison) in your mind.

1. Pray for God's guidance and protection as you go down each trail.

2. Turn off negative inner voice; do not let it convict/stop you from getting healed by you believing its lies. It's time to take care of your business with God.

3. List down all offenses in each category (trail), divide them according to age categories: 0-5, 6-10, 11-15, etc. Identify who was harmed and what each offense was.

4. Ask God to forgive you and to "wash your spirit clean of Shame" in each offense in each category. Take each one to the cross and leave it there.

5. As you pray over each act ask God to heal all people involved where ever they are. Remember Jesus said, "Father, forgive them, for they know not what they do." Luke 23:34

6. Burn your lists when done, do not re-read them giving the negative inner voice power to attack you again with the same old lies. Reading them just puts them back into your mind. Repeat this process as often as you need to.

Trail 1: Self-Abuse

List up to 3 Shame related actions (negative, harmful, and self-destructive behaviors) you committed towards yourself during your life. Do this in point form, be brief...God already knows all the details.

Examples: lying, masturbation, reading/looking at pornography, intentionally cutting yourself, suicide attempts, all addictive behavior patterns, self-destructive behavior, not letting others help you, etc.

	Action 1	Action 2	Action 3
Ages 0-10:			
Ages 11-15:			
Ages 16-20:			
Ages 21-25:			
Ages 26-30:			
Ages 31-35:			
Ages 36-40:			
Ages 41-45:			
Ages 50-above:			

Trail 2: Abuse by Others with Your Permission

List up to 3 Shame related actions (negative, harmful, and destructive behaviors) that were committed by others against you <u>WITH</u> your permission.

Examples: Letting others (you giving in to peer pressure, fear) make you do things you knew were wrong, harmful, and shameful.

	<u>Action 1</u>	<u>Action 2</u>	<u>Action 3</u>
Ages 0-10:			
Ages 11-15:			
Ages 16-20:			
Ages 21-25:			
Ages 26-30:			
Ages 31-35:			
Ages 36-40:			
Ages 41-45:			
Ages 50-above:			

Trail 3: Abuse by Others without your permission

List up to 3 Shame related actions (negative, harmful, and destructive behaviors) that were committed by others against you <u>WITHOUT</u> your permission.

Examples: theft, acts of violence, rape, fraud, ID theft, gossip, false accusations, injustices, spouse/parent/family member/friend suicide, etc.

	<u>Action 1</u>	<u>Action 2</u>	<u>Action 3</u>
Ages 0-10:			
Ages 11-15:			
Ages 16-20:			
Ages 21-25:			
Ages 26-30:			
Ages 31-35:			
Ages 36-40:			
Ages 41-45:			
Ages 50-above:			

Trail 4: Abuse you did to others with their permission

List up to 3 Shame related actions (negative, harmful, and destructive behaviors) that were committed by you against others <u>WITH</u> their permission.

Examples: Anything where you manipulated others to take advantage of them; convinced them it was OK to sin (with or without your involvement).

	<u>Action 1</u>	<u>Action 2</u>	<u>Action 3</u>
Ages 0-10:			
Ages 11-15:			
Ages 16-20:			
Ages 21-25:			
Ages 26-30:			
Ages 31-35:			
Ages 36-40:			
Ages 41-45:			
Ages 50-above:			

Trail 5: Abuse You did to others without their permission

List up to 3 Shame related actions (negative, harmful, and destructive behaviors) that were committed by you against others <u>WITHOUT</u> their permission.

Examples: here you are the offender, the one who victimizes, overriding others wills and safety. Acts of harm you did to others because you wanted to or had to. Violence, stealing, sexual assault, murder, lying about them so they are injured, etc.

	<u>Action 1</u>	<u>Action 2</u>	<u>Action 3</u>
Ages 0-10:			
Ages 11-15:			
Ages 16-20:			
Ages 21-25:			
Ages 26-30:			
Ages 31-35:			
Ages 36-40:			
Ages 41-45:			
Ages 50-above:			

Section Three:
Plan to Work Then Work the Plan

Lesson 15 – The Skill of Protecting Yourself

The Light of Scripture: John 17:11-12

I will remain in the world no longer, but they are still in the world, and I am coming to you, Holy Father, protect them by the power of your name—the name you gave me—so that they may be one as we are one. While I was with them, I protected them and kept them safe by that name you gave me.

The Problem: **Without God you have absolutely no protection against your flesh, the world or Satan.**

The Solution: **Enter into God's Kingdom and the Holy Spirit will protect you in Jesus name.**

The Procedure: **Come near to God and He will come near to You**

My Prayer

Lord, I thank you for your protection. Every day you watch over all your saints and I am so grateful for your mercy and grace. I need your help today to explain assertiveness in such a way that it makes sense; that it will motivate men in recovery to want to let you protect them from themselves. Give me the right words Father God; let me not be a stumbling block to my brothers.

Long, long time ago when there were large castles in small kingdoms, peasants called serfs, lived outside the castle gates. As farm-workers they tended gardens, animals and large fields of crops for the land owner whom they called "Lord". The Lord owned the serfs as well as the land and they worked to provide him with the food they grew on his property. They also chopped wood from his trees and delivered it to the castle for heating and cooking. And they most likely spun wool from his sheep to provide clothes for his family. In return the Lord let them keep part of the "fruits" from their labor and provided them with protection.

Inside the castle the Lord lived with his family, servants and soldiers. They obviously lived much better than the peasants. They had better shelter, more food, better clothes, faster horses and everything else needed to run the kingdom. The soldier's main purpose was to protect the kingdom which included the serfs. This was easy for them to do when everyone remained behind the strong, high walls of the castle and the draw bridge was raised.

When bandits or raiders did arrive in the kingdom threatening to "kill, steal and destroy" most of the serfs would flee into the castle for security. Unfortunately there were always some who wouldn't or couldn't make it in. The serfs that made it inside the walls were safe from the enemy; while those outside with the barbarians were considered "dead ducks".

When the kingdom was severely threatened by hostiles several things made the difference between life and death. These key things were: the value of the walls, the effectiveness of the defense plan, the training of the soldiers, the obedience of the serfs, and the benevolence of the Lord. Let's examine each one as it relates to your recovery:

1. Boundaries Built by God are your Castle Walls

It makes sense that Castles back then needed high walls all the way around to keep barbarians out. If a castle had high walls in the front and short walls in the back, the hordes would simply go around to the weakest part of the wall and attack there. It is the same with you in recovery; you need boundaries that are strong enough to keep your invaders (porn, alcohol, drugs, greed, etc.) out. Your boundaries need to cover all of your life, not just certain parts of your Castle (life) leaving critical areas open for invasion. To do this you must gain self-control which means control over your flesh, your sinful nature, your body.

Proverbs 25:28
Like a city whose walls are broken down is a man who lacks self-control.

2. A Recovery Plan is required for a Successful Defense of Your Life

Defending Castles always required a plan of action. Everyone from the Lord, his knights and soldiers, right down to the serfs had jobs to do and do well if they were to survive the attack. Each person went to their battle station and did what was required to survive the onslaught. Your recovery is no different, to protect your life you must have a plan (Lessons 17-18 will help you develop this).

Having an effective plan is only half the battle; you must also execute the plan competently whenever it is needed. Any plan of defense that is ignored (or implemented slowly) quickly becomes useless. Plans that keep you safe are proactive, future focused so that no one can sneak up on you. They also are designed to maximize your strengths and to eliminate your weaknesses before the barbarians are at the gate.

The enemy is relentless, strong and very shrewd. He does not just attack when you are expecting him. He is a 24-7 invader, looking for any advantage he can get to destroy you and your family. This is especially true when the enemy, more often than not, is the weaknesses in your own flesh. When your weaknesses connect with the world's temptations you fall into wickedness; even if it feels good you are sliding down into darkness without a way back out.

> **Mark 14:38**
> *Watch and pray so that you will not fall into temptation. The spirit is willing, but the body is weak.*

3. Your Personality and Body Parts are the Soldiers you must train to Stand Firm

Besides Castle walls protecting the serfs there were also soldiers who had been trained to defend the Lord's property. They were well equipped and knew their opponents well enough to be ready at all times. In your recovery these soldiers are those parts of your flesh that you control. Your will, mind, heart, feelings, needs, etc. all must be working with the plan rather than against it.

In history, many great battles and kingdoms were lost because of sabotage. When soldiers (who were trusted to fight for one side) suddenly turn and betrayed their side by providing crucial information that led to the enemy's success sabotage had occurred. As we have learned in previous Lessons, our flesh is often sabotaging our recovery and health. You think your personality and body parts are on your side but in reality they often are not, causing you to fail repeatedly in your attempt to gain freedom from compulsive, self-destruction behavior patterns.

You must learn to control yourself (flesh, body parts) if you are to win the fight. There is only one way you can succeed, and that is to teach (command) your flesh to Stand Firm under attack and to not give in to temptation. This requires you to be plugged into God's power and Grace so you can stand firm against the adversary. Wearing God's armor always keeps you safe from the enemy's fiery arrows.

Ephesians 6:10-11
Finally, be strong in the Lord and in his mighty power. Put on the full armor of God so that you can take your stand against the devil's schemes.

4. Obedience to Your Lord's Will and Commands will save your Life

Timing is everything in an emergency. Minutes even seconds can make the difference from you being "almost harmed" or you going to the hospital, jail or ending up in the morgue. When the Lord calls you come running and don't look back. Leave everything that hinders you getting behind safe walls. Hesitation has sent many a man into years of suffering due to his wanting to stay outside the Lord's will just a little bit longer. When the Lord calls; run, don't stroll.

Proverbs 8:10
The name of the Lord is a strong tower; the righteous run into it and are safe.

So what keeps serfs (addicts) from coming into safety?

Many people want to obey God; they want to please him…but not just yet. They believe they can "have their cake and eat it too" which is an old saying meaning they want to keep living in sin and be blessed at the same time. God doesn't play that game. Here are a few reasons many men never make it back to safety:

A. Pride; thinking they can do whatever they want whenever they want
B. Stupidity; they do not know the true danger of their choices and actions
C. Too busy being self-indulgent to pay attention to obvious warning signs
D. Do not want to leave their "stuff" (acting out) behind
E. They have wandered too far away from the castle (Lord's will) to make it back on time
F. Betraying the Lord and negotiating with the enemy to gain pleasure and payoffs
G. Believing Satan's lie, "It will never happen to you!"

All these choices leave men outside of God's protection and, in the end; they become "dead ducks".

A Recipe for Dead Duck Soup

1. Add one cup each of pride and stupidity to hot boiling water, along with a large dash of "I can take care of myself"; then bring it to a slow "I have all the time in the world" boil.

2. Add salt and pepper to taste plus throw in a bay leaf if you choose and let it simmer in its own juices.

3. Of course, you will need to add one dead duck; for this to happen just wait till the serf outside the wall tells the enemy he doesn't bow down to anyone and then bring the fowl to a full boil.

4. Finally, let it cool for ten minutes and serve with "quackers".

Speaking of Dead Ducks

A woman brought a very limp duck into a veterinary clinic. As she laid her pet on the table, the vet pulled out his stethoscope and listened to the bird's chest.

After a moment or two, the vet shook his head and sadly said, "I'm sorry, your duck, Cuddles, has passed away."

The distressed woman wailed, "Are you sure?"

"Yes, I am sure. Your duck is dead," replied the vet.

"How can you be so sure?" she protested. "I mean you haven't done any testing on him or anything. He might just be in a coma or something."

The vet rolled his eyes, turned around and left the room. He returned a few minutes later with a black Labrador retriever. As the duck's owner looked on in amazement, the dog stood on his hind legs, put his front paws on the examination table and sniffed the duck from top to bottom. He then looked up at the vet with sad eyes and shook his head.

The vet patted the dog on the head and took it out of the room. A few minutes later he returned with a cat. The cat jumped on the table and also delicately sniffed the bird from head to foot. The cat sat back on its haunches, shook its head, meowed softly and strolled out of the room.

The vet looked at the woman and said, "I'm sorry, but as I said, this is most definitely, 100% certifiably, a dead duck."

The vet turned to his computer terminal, hit a few keys and produced a bill, which he handed to the woman.

The duck's owner, still in shock, took the bill. "$150!" she cried, "$150 just to tell me my duck is dead!"

The vet shrugged, "I'm sorry. If you had just taken my word for it, the bill would only have been $20, but with the Lab Report and the CAT scan it's now $150." (Internet humor – anonymous)

5. The Lord's Mercy lets you inside the Kingdom

The best part of the Castle analogy is that the Lord values his serfs and wants all of them to come into safety. God wants you to receive his mercy and protection but first you must let him become Lord of your life. For me it was the best gift I ever received in life. I just regret taking so long to let it happen. One of the main reasons I rejected the gift for so long was that I did not value myself enough to protect myself. By not protecting myself I let my body be abused by the sinful things I did outside of protection. Many times I was the "dead duck" in the pot.

1 Corinthians 6:18-20
Flee from sexual immorality. All other sins a man commits are outside his body, but he who sins sexually sins against his own body. Do you not know that your body is a temple of the Holy Spirit, who is in you, whom you have received from God? You are not your own; you were bought at a price. Therefore honor God with your body.

Recovery Truth #71   **I Agree _____ I Disagree _____**
Self-abuse is never approved by God and therefore, it can never be Healthy, Helpful or Holy.

Hurting Your Body and Destroying Your Life Really Upsets God
God wants us to value our bodies (our Castles if you will) and not let the enemy take control of them. He values us so much that he wants to put his Holy Spirit into us to live so we have the power to overcome the world and all its temptations. Satan on the other hand wants to keep that from happening so he tricks us with lies, deception and temptation to surrender our bodies to sinful things such as alcohol, drugs, sexual immorality, gluttony, dishonesty, greed, hatred, fear, revenge, and the list goes on and on. These things destroy our bodies, lives and relationships.

God has more than enough forgiveness, healing, love and discipline to restore us even though we have failed over and over again for years; but we must accept his invitation to come inside his walls of protection. To do this we must value our lives enough to receive his gifts. For addicts one of the main roots to repeating self-destructive behavior is self-hatred; not valuing who we are keeps us from entering into the Kingdom leaving us outside for the enemy to use and abuse.

Recovery Truth #72   I Agree _____ I Disagree _____
We don't protect what we don't value.

People with addictive behavior patterns do not realize or will not admit (denial) that they are destroying their bodies and lives; that they need protection from themselves! To recover you must be able to make the shift from not valuing yourself to protecting yourself out of love. Many family members and friends just do not understand why we do not just stop doing whatever it is that is destroying our world; the answer is, "We don't Protect what we don't value!"

As we learned in the Self-Worth section (C. 13) individuals with low self-worth place little if any value on who they are. Their very strong negative inner voices keep telling them they are losers, worthless, incompetent and will never accomplish anything so why would they "think" they are valuable enough to protect, to fight for? If the negative inner voice is not transformed into a loving, positive inner voice then no individual can learn how to protect themselves. No boundaries (walls of safety) will ever work because they refuse to enforce them.

Here's a simple example; let's say I own a nice house that is not very old and I have a very expensive alarm system in it. If I never turn it on when I leave it would indicate that I don't value anything in the house enough to protect it. In short, I don't care if someone comes and destroys it. Your body is the "nice house" God has given you to live in here on earth. If you are not protecting it (and addicts don't) then you have low self-worth, a negative inner voice, and are so nonassertive (passive or aggressive) that you will not fight to protect yourself and those you love.

As you read in Lesson 13, low self-esteem means you are not a friend to yourself. You do not like who you are and hate being alone. You have no love for yourself so you let yourself be abused and continue to put your body in harmful situations and relationships. Yet, if your best friend came to you for help you would treat them better than you treat yourself because you value them (their house) more.

When your best friend comes to you for help, do you help them or tell them they deserve to suffer? I would hope that you would care for them. So why should it be any different when you turn to yourself for caring and help? Many times others are not immediately available and you need to help yourself immediately. So treat yourself as you would treat your best friend if they came to you with the problem. See yourself as valuable like Jesus sees you; holding yourself accountable for your recovery is love not hate.

So What is Love?

1 Corinthians 13:4-7
Love is patient, love is kind. It does not envy, it does not boast, it is not proud. It is not rude, it is not self-seeking, it is not easily angered, it keeps no record of wrongs. Love does not delight in evil but rejoices with the truth. It always protects, always trusts, always hopes, always perseveres.

As I started my recovery God brought me to this verse often and it was very hard to admit that I was just the opposite, especially towards me. I wasn't patient or kind. I was envious, boastful and prideful. I was rude, self-absorbed, and had a bad temper with a long memory of those who had harmed me. I found way too much pleasure in worldly things and very little in learning.

Yet, as I started to trust God with my recovery, I found that the truth Jesus speaks in his word was protecting me, giving me hope and strength to keep going when I wanted to quit, which was almost daily. God's love for me slowly changed me back into the person He created me to be, and with His love I started to love myself as well as others.

Your recovery needs fuel to drive it through all the mud and tough roads you have to travel. This fuel is Love. As you let God fill up your tank you will find amazing power to get up and get it done. You will feel successful over areas of your life that you long thought would never be conquered. You will have hope that your future life will not be a repeat of your past life. You will also become assertive ("Stand Firm") in front of the enemy; you will not run away, give-in or give up, and let your flesh help the enemy to destroy your life.

To Stand Firm you have to have a Firm Place to stand

The bible has many verses in it commanding you to Stand Firm; I recommend you read all of them. One of my favorites is:

Exodus 14:13-14

Moses answered the people, "Do not be afraid. Stand firm and you see the deliverance the Lord will bring you today. The Egyptians you see today you will never see again. The Lord will fight for you; you need only to be still.

This is an excellent picture of God loving his children. As you know, the Israelites were held in bondage for over 400 years by the Egyptians who were cruel masters over them. As they attempted to leave captivity the Egyptians sent their own army out to kill them all or to bring them back into slavery. They were very afraid as they had no weapons but Moses called upon the name of the Lord and he fought for them. The rest you might say is "history".

This verse fits your recovery perfectly in that deliverance means freedom from anything that would destroy you. For the Israelites it was not just the Egyptians, God also delivered them from their lack of faith (lack of trust) in Him. You are just like the Israelites in that you not only need deliverance from your acting out (additions) but also, and more importantly, from your acting-in (being controlled by your flesh). God liberates those who surrender to Him and seek to serve Him. He protects and fights for those who Stand Firm in His Spirit, His Word and His Will.

Psalm 40:2
He lifted me out of the slimy pit, out of the mud and mire; he set my feet on a rock and gave me a firm place to stand.

Even if we are standing on the rock (Jesus) we must also learn how to stand firm against our enemies, or in modern day terms, learn how to be assertive in an unassertive world.

Assertiveness is the Skill of Protecting Yourself and the Helpless

I find that many people just do not understand what assertiveness is because they cannot identify what the behavior actually looks like. And it can be confusing depending upon circumstances. To best describe it you need to understand how it relates to two other interpersonal style categories: passive and aggressive. There are some key concepts that separate the three behavioral styles; they are outlined in the **Understanding Assertiveness Chart** below:

	Aggressive	Passive	Assertive
Relationship Attitude & Approach	Win-Lose Thinker Competitive	Lose-Win Thinker Unhappy Servant	Win-Win Thinker Teammate, Partner
Proactive-Reactive Thinking	Externally Reactive, "Greedy" thinkers	Internally Reactive, "Fearful" thinkers	Internally/Externally Proactive - Optimistic thinkers
Self-Worth Level	Low	Low	High
Protection Focus	On Self only, harms others	None	Self and the helpless
Rights	Want Theirs & Yours	Believe they have none	Believe people have God-given rights
Responsibilities	Refuse them, reject accountability	Feel obligated for theirs & yours	Accept responsibility for their behavior only
Emotional Triggers	Anger, jealousy, loss	Fear, pain, hurt	Injustice, dishonesty
Situational Triggers	People telling them no, having their aggressiveness challenged	Conflict, treats, demands made upon them, being yelled at, Seeing others suffer	Innocent being hurt, Criminal behavior, the helpless being taken Advantage of.
Boundaries	Boundary busters	No Boundaries	Boundary setters
Roles played	Takers, Dominators, Controllers, Blamers, Bullies, Abusers	Marks, Floor mats, Victims, Martyrs, Nurses, "Mothers"	Protectors, Providers Planners, Leaders, Problem solvers

As you review the chart you can see that aggressive people want all their rights and yours as well, which is why they are perceived as "Takers". They "fake people out" by acting secure, but underneath all their bluster they really are very insecure and have low self-worth. They are competitive in all that they do, believing that they either win or they will lose. This leads to them being controllers. Aggressive people also do not accept responsibility for their errors in life and blame their mistakes on others. They are fear driven and are very reactive to worldly pressures. They operate by using intimidation to scare others (passives) into giving them what they want. They are often perceived as: abusers, bullies, villains, dominators, criminals and selfish.

Passive people have low self-worth. They don't believe they are worthy of any rights. To feel useful and to keep relationships at home and at work they take on others responsibilities as well as their own. They are perceived as martyrs, targets and "floor mats" by aggressive people. Passive people live under a heavy stress load as they let aggressive people walk all over them. It doesn't take too much thinking to figure out that aggressive people "mark" passive people for abuse. The passive person gives in because they hate "conflict" and believe (negative inner voice lie) that if they give the aggressor what they want they will stop hurting them. It actually works the opposite way, once the aggressive person gets something they always come back for more.

Assertive people take responsibility for what they are responsible for and nothing else. They stand up for their rights and refuse to take rights away from others. This style does not match the aggressive person who gets very frustrated (angry) when they meet assertive people who will not give in to their demands. Assertive people are way too much work and too big a threat to aggressive people so they try to stay away from them. Passive (Marks) people are much easier to use and abuse. A key difference between Assertive people and the other two types of interpersonal styles is Assertive people will do what it take to protect themselves because they have high self-worth; they value their lives enough to protect themselves from anything (including their own flesh) that would destroy them.

Assertiveness can be described as "the skill of protecting yourself" from you, others, and from the world. For instance, if you repeatedly put yourself in dangerous situations that can bring extreme harm to your body and to your life you are not assertive. As we have read previously, your body is the temple of the Holy Spirit and God takes exception to any negative treatment of it.

Recovery Truth # 73   I Agree _____ I Disagree _____
The success of your Recovery all depends upon how solid your spiritual foundation is.

The world of architecture and its achievements has always amazed me. I love looking at huge buildings and bridges, covering very large areas of ground and space, all built by man's brains and hard labor. One of my absolute favorite modern day examples is the St. Louis Arch. If you have not seen the History channels video on the making of the St. Louis Arch I highly recommend it. Stunning pictures of all the challenges while it was being built, all overcome with human resourcefulness, are provided. Watching tiny men build a structure out of stainless steel that is 630 feet high (tallest manmade monument in the United States) is fascinating.

A basic building principle in creating any architectural structure is that the foundation or base must be much broader (larger) than the rest of the structure if it is going to be able to carry the load or weight for a long period of time. The bridge, arch and pyramid are all prime examples of this principle. In recovery finding forgiveness, healing, and restoration all require a large base from which to build upon if your recovery is to last the test of time. You must learn how to "Stand Firm" in God's power...and to do this you must have faith.

The following Stand Firm (Assertiveness) Pyramid illustrates this principle.

The Assertiveness Pyramid

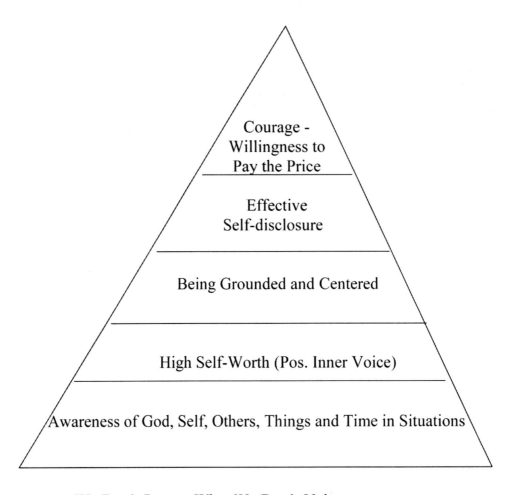

Courage -
Willingness to
Pay the Price

Effective
Self-disclosure

Being Grounded and Centered

High Self-Worth (Pos. Inner Voice)

Awareness of God, Self, Others, Things and Time in Situations

- We Don't Protect What We Don't Value
- If You Don't Protect Yourself Who Else Will?
- Personal Freedom Comes at a High Price

Recovery Truth # 74   **I Agree _____ I Disagree _____**
Healthy change requires learning how to replace negative habits with healthy behaviors; therefore, the foundation of recovery is learning God's Word.

Romans 10:17
Consequently, faith comes from hearing the message, and the message is heard through the word of Christ.

Starting at the foundation of the pyramid let's examine each section.

1. Awareness of God's Truth vs. Self, Others, Things and Time
    Knowledge needs to start with God (his truths) and work down towards earth and humans; not the other way around. It also clarifies who God is and who you are. It defines your relationship with God, others and "things". It provides answers to life's questions and helps us learn how to live life. This knowledge comes from God's word first through the Holy Spirit; and from other sources second. Increased awareness (truth) clarifies what is from God and what is evil; and helps you know how valuable you are to God.

2. High Self-Worth (Christian Inner Voice)
    You cannot change if your mind is full of lies that say you are useless and can never be saved (reconciled and changed) by God. You need to accept and believe that you are highly valuable to God, so much so that he sent his Son Jesus to die for you. Then let God reprogram your computer (brain) to believe what he says is truth. To change you need Love, and those with low self-worth cannot receive love from God or anyone else because they are stuck in the lie that they do not deserve it. When you value you (and others) as God values you your mind becomes clearer and you will become more grounded and centered.

3. Being Grounded and Centered
    Being "Grounded" is the skill of living in the now. Learning to focus on what you need to be doing in the present rather than worrying about the past or the future. Jesus talks about focusing only on "today" in Matthew 6:34 because we have no guarantees of what tomorrow will bring. We only learn in the "now", when we are completely focused on what we are trying to learn. If you cannot stay grounded you will have great difficulty being centered.

    Being "Centered" is the skill of "knowing who you are". This involves understanding what you believe, think, feel, value, desire, need, what your strengths and weaknesses are, etc. When you know these things, you can surrender them to God easier than if you do not know that they are operating inside of you in negative, ungodly ways. When you are centered you know what your "identity" really is; you know who God created you to be rather than who the world says you should be. Memorizing God's word (bible verses) grounds and centers you in the truth, exposing evil (lies) for what they really are, messages from Satan.

    People who are not grounded and centered have great difficulty self-disclosing in healthy ways. They often are "not sure" of who they are or what they are responsible for. Denial is a key indicator of people who struggle with these two skills. Often when you ask them direct questions about their internal experiences they answer, "I don't know" or tell you something someone else says about them because they do not know.

In this condition they are easily misled into darkness.

4. Healthy Self-disclosure/Transparency
    Healthy self-disclosure can only occur if you are being controlled by the Holy Spirit because only God knows what is healthy and what is not. His words in Scripture are HOLY and unholy; righteous and sinful. In recovery we must take responsibility for our mistakes and character flaws. We must be able to articulate internal things within our personality that are harming us and misleading us into sinful behaviors, relationships, and situations. We call this skill in recovery "Transparency" or being transparent.

    Transparency is being honest about yourself with others in an appropriate manner. Appropriate means sharing "in the right way, to the right person, at the right time". This usually occurs with your accountability partner or in a support group or with a professional helper. It does not mean you go and tell your "story" to anyone and everyone such as family members, co-workers or neighbors…all who may mean well but who lack the helping knowledge you require. And once you share to the wrong person it is out there and is impossible to get back. So using Social Media sites to be transparent can be very risky; think twice before you hit the send button

5. Courage/Willingness to pay the Price
    Standing Firm (being assertive) takes great courage. It is hard to stand for righteousness when the majority around you wants to be immoral. It is very unpopular and as Jesus has warned us in Matthew 10:22 "all men will hate you because of me" and John 3:20, "Everyone who does evil hates the light." You have to be willing to pay the price, like Paul and Silas did in Acts preaching the truth about Jesus. Sadly, I have worked with many men in recovery who could not (would not) quit their acting out because of what "friends" said about them being Christians. They cared more about what people said than what Jesus said.

Recovery Truth #75   **I Agree _____ I Disagree _____**
You are commanded to dedicate yourself to preaching and teaching God's truth, but you can't teach what you haven't learned.

> **1 Timothy 4:13**
> *Until I come, devote yourself to the public reading of Scripture, to preaching and to teaching.*

Giving testimony about what God has done in your life, preaching His Holy Word to the lost and teaching God's truths to the spiritually immature all require the skill of assertiveness. They all require you to Stand Firm upon the rock (Jesus). We are commanded to do this in the power of the Holy Spirit until Jesus comes again.

A Testimony from a Brother in Recovery

The Stand Firm class and book helped me to understand who I am and the forces behind my behavior. It was helpful to learn that listening to negative thoughts from my inner voice could cause me to act out hurtfully against others. I learned how to listen to the positive inner voice from God to change my behavior and avoid making the same mistakes my father made. The most important thing we can do is stay plugged in to the cross to allow the power of Jesus Christ to work in us and help us to become the men He created us to be. This book contained tools that helped me along my journey. Praise the Lord for His teaching and refinement!

Joe W.

So What Can You Do to Get Healed?

1. Read with an open mind
2. Complete your inventory honestly
3. Keep turning the pages-keep learning about what is destroying you
4. Exchange your will for God's Will; eternal life for eternal death
5. Plug into God's Holy Spirit and receive forgiveness and power to change
6. Trust in the Lord more than you trust your flesh which is not your friend
7. Control your mind through God's power or it will control you with Satan's power
8. Replace your negative inner voice (lie machine) with God's word
9. Purify your Video Vault by letting God give you a brain bath
10. When you need open heart surgery race to the hospital, don't stroll
11. Don't ever make decisions based on how you feel; pray and ask God first
12. Surrender your desires, "gotta haves" and fears to God and he will bless you
13. Need God more than you need anything or anyone in this world
14. Go to the Cross every day and receive your free gift from God; plug into His Grace and you will have the power to crucify your flesh.
15. Stand Firm in Jesus (God's Love) so He can protect you from self-destruction

Please complete the Inventory activities for Lesson 15 before reading Lesson 16.

Lesson Fifteen Inventory

What were you Thinking when you read Lesson 15?

How are you Feeling after reading Lesson 15?

How is what you are Thinking and Feeling now going to help you with your recovery?

What are you going to change in your behavior after reading Lesson 15?

Plug-in with Prayer - How would you like God to help you right now?
(in the space below please talk directly with God…He is listening.)

What Bible verse in Lesson 15 will you commit to memorizing?

Lesson 15: Activity 1 – How Well do You Stand Firm?

Stand Firm/Assertiveness Characteristics	I Seldom do this	I do this about half the time	I do this over 80% of the time
Communicate your beliefs, needs & feelings clearly			
Refuse to let bitterness/ anger to ruin relationships			
Refuse to excuse others non-assertive behavior			
Take full responsibility for your speech, behavior			
Are loving, kind, respectful towards self and others			
Protect yourself financially; handle money wisely			
Protect yourself mentally, emotionally, physically and Spiritually.			
Ask God and others for help when you need it			
Apologize when you make mistakes, are wrong			
Reward self for your effort as well as for success			
Let God turn negatives into positives			
Surround yourself with believers who are positive			
Set and protect boundaries in all areas of your life			
Respect other's assertive behavior, boundaries			
Live by Faith in God not fear of man, situations			
Forgive others whether they ask for it or not			
Say yes when you mean yes and no when it is no			
Keep your promises and commitments if possible			
Fellowship with believers, friends and family			
Stand Firm against manipulation, demands, threats			
Call for help before you fall into temptation, sin			
Play, laugh and enjoy life as well as work hard			
Proactively live following your recovery plan			

Lesson 16 – Skiing in Bounds

The Light of Scripture: Titus 2:11-12

For the grace of God that brings salvation has appeared to all men. It teaches us to say "No" to ungodliness and worldly passions and to live self-controlled, upright and godly lives in this present age..."

The Problem: You are not strong enough to just say no to ungodly choices and behaviors; you need a recovery plan that creates boundaries for protection.

The Solution: Ask God to identify your preferences, patterns, rituals and payoffs; and let him remove them from your life.

The Procedure: Develop and use a recovery plan that has God established boundaries in it.

My Prayer

Dear Lord, I am grateful for your boundaries. I am thankful that you reinforce them. I know that you love me and that is why you provide such protection for me. I ask that you will open the minds of the readers to your precious gift. Help them Lord to know how important it is to live within your blessings instead of outside of them. Amen

One of the saddest counseling sessions I ever had was with a young man who came to me because he was depressed. As I listened to his story I too started to feel depressed. His Father taught him how to ski and together they skied often in the mountains above Vancouver, British Columbia. Some of his greatest memories with his Father were skiing together.

The last time they skied together his Dad challenged him to race down the mountain to see who would come in first. He had never beaten his Dad but he was now big enough and strong enough to do it so he eagerly accepted the challenge. As they flew down the slope at top speed he could see his Dad out of the corner of his eyes but then he was gone. Figuring he was behind him he pushed harder and made it down to the bottom of the run. When he stopped and looked back up the hill he couldn't see his Dad.

He waited for about ten minutes and realized something must have happened. He went up the hill calling for his Dad but there was no answer. After searching he skied down to the aid station and asked for help. Immediately rescue skiers arrived and the search continued. Sadly, they found his Dad face down in a deep hole in the snow, he had died from suffocation.

What made this story so tragic is that his Dad had always taught him to never ski out of bounds and on this particular day Dad did just that. Trying to beat his boy down the hill to win the contest Dad took a "short-cut" that looked so inviting, perfect snow with no observable hazards. Hitting a hazard underneath the snow flipped him over causing him to land head first into a very deep drift. He could not get out by himself and no one was there to help him.

The only comfort from this sad experience was that the son ended up being a ski instructor who taught young skiers to never ski out of bounds. But he did so in a unique way, by sharing his grief he helped them understand why not skiing out of bounds is so important. He helped them to understand the consequences of breaking boundaries.

It can happen in a moment or it can occur over a long period of time. We push our boundaries, testing them to see if we are stronger than what they are protecting us from...only to find out when we want to turn around and come back to safety, it is too late.

Are you skiing within your boundaries...or are you taking high risks by crossing over to what appears safe but is really destruction waiting to claim you ...causing overwhelming pain to you and those who love you? Do you currently have boundaries? Do you really understand what they are?

Setting Boundaries protects yourself and others

Traditionally, a boundary was a mark that divides something into two. Every nation has boundaries, what we often call borders indicating where each nation begins and ends. These markers let people know when they are in one country or another. Boundaries are only valuable if they clearly indicate when you are inside and outside the boundary.

There are many other kinds of boundaries besides physical ones. In Exodus 20 God gives Moses the Ten Commandments which are moral boundaries for all people to follow if you want to please God. The 10 commandments were also designed to keep us safe; when we go outside of them we are always in harm's way. God gave us these limitations to protect us from the consequences which lie outside of them.

Recovery Truth #76   **I Agree _____ I Disagree _____**
A boundary is anything that protects you from a harmful person, event or situation; boundaries protect you from your flesh, the world and Satan.

A boundary provides a buffer with enough personal space for you to maneuver away from harm and back to safety. For example, my house provides me with a safe place to rest, rejoice and relax from the everyday work pressures that are stressful. It also gives me protection from bad weather, extreme heat or cold, and from people who want to take what I own. When I go outside my house my protection from its boundaries disappears.

For our purposes, think of a boundary as each of the following three things:

1. **A Protection Plan**
   Unfortunately, to survive and succeed in life we need many boundaries, not just one. Each one acts like a protection plan helping you to avoid negative situations and thrive in positive ones.

2. **A Protection Tool**
   Boundaries are protective devices or tools that keep you safe. They are similar to brakes, lights, seatbelts and airbags in your automobile. Most of the time you don't need them so you don't pay much attention to them. Yet once a serious accident takes place you are glad they are there. While these safety devices may not completely protect you in an auto accident, you are much better with them than without them.

3. **A Protective Force Field**
   Lastly, visualize boundaries as Force Fields that surround you with a layer of defenses from which you can make healthy decisions. If you have a solid plan and the tools necessary you can create a field or zone of protection. To keep any force field or boundary functional requires power, maintenance, and revision. Therefore, the main threat to your boundaries is You. If you lack energy you cannot have boundaries. No energy, no shield - no shield, no protection. God's Holy Spirit provides that energy if we surrender our wills to him daily and ask for his force to protect us.

Make No Mistake About It! Boundaries without the Holy Spirit may help you a little in this life, but they will not help you at all in the next life.

In life there are Many Areas that Need Boundaries

Your cravings, compulsions, and habitual ways of responding all point to areas that need removal. It is your responsibility to make sure you do not let your sinful nature connect to the evil in the world. That connection will only lead to addiction and a loss of safety for you and your family; that connection will lead you to ski out of bounds into danger every time.

And this presents a very big problem as there are so many areas that require boundaries. Here are just a few examples:

- Your Body - what you do with and/or what happens to your body parts
- Honesty- frequency for Telling the Truth, not stealing
- Emotional Distance - intimacy and closeness vs. isolation & depression
- Geographical Distance - how close you let toxic people get close to you
- Time - who controls it in your life, you or something or someone else?
- Relationships – choosing healthy vs. toxic interactions with people
- Consequences - taking ownership for your mistakes vs. blaming others
- Your Finances – how you use money to act out.
- Your Mind – not letting your mind think of sinful thoughts

Recovery Truth #82   **I Agree _____ I Disagree _____**
A major part of stopping addiction is you planning, establishing and maintaining boundaries against your preferences, patterns, rituals and payoffs.

A. Preferences determine Patterns (Stage 1 of Addiction)

A preference is your favorite or first choice out of many. When Denise and I go to get ice cream at Baskin Robbins we have many choices. While we both ooh and ah over the many choices we almost always go for our favorites: for D its Jamocha Almond Fudge and for me it's Peanut Butter and Chocolate. Those are our preferences and when we are actually paying for something we'd rather go with our preferred choice.

The same is true with addiction. When we have to commit our money and time; when we have to choose something that involves risk we go with our number one preference. If that is not available then we go to our number two preference. Most addicts have more than one thing that they are addicted to and there is always a preferred choice list. For me, sexually acting out was at the top of my list compared to getting drunk on alcohol which was on the bottom of my list.

When people consistently go after their top one or two preferences they create what are called "patterns" or predictable behavior in specific situations. All my family knows that I will go for the peanut butter and chocolate every time because it is my pattern. Now it is important to point out here that some people have a high need for variety, so their pattern is to make a different choice instead of the one they made previously. By doing this they think they are not predictable but in fact, not being predictable becomes their pattern. In the ice cream store, for example, they go around tasting many different kinds before getting one of their top three choices. When patterns turn into Rituals, the need for variety disappears and the top preference will demand satisfaction every time.

B. Patterns can turn into Rituals (Stage 2 of Addiction)

In recovery a pattern is a repeated step by step approach to a person, event or substance for the purpose of getting high. A ritual is a pattern that you have repeated so many times that it is now a major part of your everyday life. It has become the priority of daily existence, even when you are not doing it you are constantly thinking about it. It is in control of all your choices, so much so that you plan all your daily activities around it.

A pattern becomes a ritual when it is so strong that it becomes a "Plan of Addictive Acquisition". In short, Rituals are super strong patterns. Rituals are the Tsunamis in your life that destroy you and others around you. They totally control all of your logic, reason, emotion and need for safety.

C. Rituals are fueled by Payoffs (Stage 3 of Addiction)

In the world of addiction a "Payoff "is the one thing you will trade everything in your life to get. It becomes your ultimate goal for living, even though it is killing you. It is what drives you to do whatever it is you are doing. It is the "prize" you seek even though it is painful to get it.

The Payoff is often referred to as the "high" but for our purpose it is much more than that. The most important thing is realizing that the payoff is never the "medication" or source of addiction. For the heroin user, who sells everything they have to get the next fix, the payoff is not the drug. For the person who loses job after job and marriage after marriage to get the next drink, the payoff is not alcohol. And for the sexually addicted person who risks everything to get more "touch" the payoff is not sexual contact. The payoff is what happens internally (i.e., detachment from reality, euphoria, peaceful rushes of bodily sensations, etc.) after the medication is administered.

Have I mentioned your flesh is not your friend? Inside of us is a deep emptiness, hopelessness and loneliness that drives addicts crazy. So much so that they have to medicate to make it stop bothering them. Your flesh tells you that certain things make the best payoffs; things like power, security, companionship, erotic indulgence, revenge, and excitement. These things are all false substitutes for the real thing, they are counterfeit payoffs that God didn't put in your life but Satan did. They are just copies of the real thing because all these things only bring temporary relief. And with them the cost of getting them is always deep regret and shame.

I believe the real payoff found in God's will for your life is: inner peace, a sense of unconditional love, hope for your future and a faith that drives out fear. If you want to stop your ritual (what you do to use and abuse your body) you must know what it is and allow God to replace it with his will for your life. God's will is his plan for your life. It is so valuable because it leads towards life and away from death.

Rituals and Payoffs bring you short-term pleasure and long-term pain; while Boundaries bring you short term pain and long term (eternal) gain.

Recovery Truth #83   **I Agree _____ I Disagree _____**
Recovery is all about being here (inside God's protection) and not there (outside of God's protection).

There are Two Types of Boundaries You Will Need to Create.

There are two main kinds of boundaries or areas where you need protection from something or someone who will harm you. These two areas contain Internal and External threats. You need to set boundaries for each area. If you do not have internal boundaries you cannot maintain external boundaries; and, if you do not have external boundaries you will not be able to retain your internal boundaries.

A. Internal Boundaries (protection from your flesh, sinful nature)

We have identified many things inside of your personality and flesh that require strong management. Each one can lead you into self-destructive behavior patterns if you let them control you. In fact, self-control is self-management. Your will, for instance, is very strong and can mislead you if you don't have a way of controlling it. Feelings and emotions are other "things" inside of us that get us into trouble all the time. It is good to have them but we must not let them control us.

Other internal areas requiring boundaries are the left and right brain. You must have power and a plan to keep the inner voice positive and the theatre of the mind playing healthy "movies" and images rather than unhealthy ones. And determining what enters your brain in the first place is a very good place to place a very solid boundary; if you do it with your children why not protect your mind as well?

And the internal list goes on and on: pride, fear, greed, desires, gluttony, hatred, bitterness, lust, criticalness, slander, dishonesty to name a few.

B. External Boundaries (protection from the World and Satan)

Anything outside of your skin and your behavior (actions) that threatens to hurt you falls into the external boundary area. The porn shop you pass on the way home from work every day. The woman's house you have been to several times "just as a friend", without your wife knowing of course. The friend you have who always has the extra "smoke" you don't need. Maybe the work environment that abuses you mentally and emotionally, creating high levels of stress in you. That special restaurant or drive-by fast food joint that serves up the "high-Cal" diet that is slowly killing you.

I think you get my point on this one. There are lots and lots of things and places in the world we must avoid and not partake of if we are to stay healthy. To do this we need a plan that not only keeps us from these things but also rewards us for doing so. The results can be devastating if we fail to set internal and external boundaries, I believe this section of Luke clearly speaks to the consequences:

Luke 8:11-15

v. 11 – 12 "This is the meaning of the parable: The seed is the word of God. Those along the path are the ones who hear, and then the devil comes and takes away the word from their hearts, so that they cannot believe and be saved. (These people have no internal or external boundaries)

v. 13 – Those among the rock are the ones who receive the word with joy when they hear it, but they have no root. They believe for a while, but in time of testing they fall away. (These people have no internal or external boundaries)

v. 14 – The seed that fell among thorns stands for those who hear, but as they go on their way they are choked by life's worries, riches and pleasures, and they do not mature. (These people have no internal or external boundaries)

v. 15 – But the seed on good soil stands for those with a noble and good heart, who hear the word, retain it, and by persevering produce a crop. (These people have both internal and external boundaries)

Recovery Truth #84   I Agree _____ I Disagree _____
Creating Boundaries is where the tires of recovery finally turn onto the road to healing.

To recover back to sanity and health you need to stop the force and direction of your acting out and turn your life around to start driving it back in the opposite direction. The "assassins" (your flesh, the World and Satan) fully intend to destroy you if you do not put a protective force between you and them. It is easier to figure out how to put a protective barrier between you and something external to you, but internal boundaries often confuses people. So how is that actually done?

Every Recovery Target (RT) Requires a Boundary

Establishing boundaries requires identifying those things you are doing to hurt others and yourself. These things become your Recovery Targets (RTs). RTs include the secrets we don't want others to know about us. It is our shame list if you will. Jesus said that the "Truth will set you free!" By creating a complete list of our destructive behavior patterns, and sharing with a few trustworthy people, we can begin the process of being held accountable. This process is only helpful if we then eliminate those preferences, patterns, and if need be, rituals. You can do this by creating boundaries for each one.

Each RT consists of a series of negative behavioral steps that take you to the target. When you identify those steps and put boundaries at each step it protects you from making it to the Target which is the purpose of having boundaries. You need to identify the steps that lead up to your acting out which includes a weekly frequency count of how many times you broke your boundary by taking that particular step. Writing your score down will give you a visual aid to help you not lie to yourself about how well you are doing in your recovery.

Example:

Recovery Target	Steps leading to the Acting Out	Times Committed
Renting	**1. Took money to rent movies**	**5**
XXX movies	**2. Drove by video store with money**	**4**
	Parked car by video store	2
	Went in store and looked for movie	2
	Paid for movie	1
	Went home and watched movie	1

Simply stopping destructive behavior is not enough; for boundaries to be effective you must also **replace** all destructive behaviors (RT) with healthy behaviors (RG).

Recovery Goal	Steps Stopping the Acting Out	Times Completed
Stop Renting	**1. Prayed to Jesus and asked for strength**	**20**
XXX movies	**2. Recite 1 verse that brings strength**	**15**
	3. Called a support person <u>before</u> you fell	10
	4. Took 1 Christian Brother to xxx store and prayed with them in the parking lot.	5
	5. Left cash/credit cards at home	**2**

Recovery Truth #85   **I Agree _____ I Disagree _____**
Those who plan to work, work the plan; and those who fail to plan, plan to fail.

The main strategy in a recovery plan is to replace every unhealthy behavior pattern with a **much stronger healthy behavior pattern**. In short, you: "Blow up the pathway to your next fix" by creating a new pathway with God's power. If the new, healthy behavior pattern is not powered by God it will leave you weak and unsatisfied and you will return (relapse) to your self-destructive patterns.

To build boundaries that work requires knowing and applying everything you have learned up to this Lesson. Making a recovery plan is hard work but maintaining it is extremely difficult. The activities in the workbook will help you create one that is tailored to your situation. Take the time to complete them and you will find out just how helpful a recovery plan is to staying sober. The choice is yours, I pray you choose life.

A Testimony from a Brother in Recovery

For me, recovery was not just about stopping a behavior, but realizing and understanding the root cause of the behavior so that not only could I stop it but prevent it from recurring and relapsing into the same old patterns. Everett's recovery class taught me concepts about human behavior (left brain vs. right brain wiring) and God's love and plan for my life. The first concept is to understand that I am highly valuable to God. I must value myself because Jesus died for me and God didn't send his Son to die for me because I'm worthless.

I have no right to self-criticism and self-accusations since the Holy Spirit is in me. I'm more valuable than diamonds because Jesus died for me. I must not treat myself as anything less. Nor does anyone else have a right to treat me as anything less. The concept of "we don't protect what we don't value" is critical to understand so that healthy boundaries can be established. No one else will protect me, my new boundaries enforce how I treat myself and behave as well as how I will let other people treat me.

As boundaries were implemented and I "plugged in" with daily prayer, praise, and surrendering my will to God, I had fewer negative thoughts and my "self-worth" increased. So did my health, optimism, and hope for the future. My negative inner voice had allowed fear and worry to control me and I was critical of myself and others. It allowed me to dwell in blame, bitterness, regret over the past, and unforgiveness. This was a sin that required confession. Forgiving myself and others heals me. I learned that "if you blame you stay the same." I now understand that without forgiveness for myself and others I cannot grow in the Lord.

I also learned that needs and desires make me selfish when they are not under God's control. I am responsible for ensuring my needs are met, but I now do so through God's Holy Spirit. No human can do that for me. Standing Firm (assertiveness) sometimes requires stepping out of my comfort zone, which can be a challenge for someone who was raised as the classic nice guy to always be polite, kind, and well mannered. I always wanted to please people rather than please God. I have learned to put God first and by doing so am now treating others better than I was before. I look forward to reading the book when it is finished as I have much more to learn if I am to serve God by serving others.

Lance C

So What Can You Do to Get Healed?

1. Read with an open mind
2. Complete your inventory honestly
3. Keep turning the pages-keep learning about what is destroying you
4. Exchange your will for God's Will; eternal life for eternal death
5. Plug into God's Holy Spirit and receive forgiveness and power to change
6. Trust in the Lord more than you trust your flesh which is not your friend
7. Control your mind through God's power or it will control you with Satan's power
8. Replace your negative inner voice (lie machine) with God's word
9. Purify your Video Vault by letting God give you a brain bath
10. When you need open heart surgery race to the hospital, don't stroll
11. Don't ever make decisions based on how you feel; pray and ask God first
12. Surrender your desires, "gotta haves" and fears to God and he will bless you
13. Need God more than you need anything or anyone in this world
14. Go to the Cross every day and receive your free gift from God; plug into His Grace and you will have the power to crucify your flesh.
15. Stand Firm in Jesus (God's Love) so He can protect you from self-destruction
16. Create a recovery plan by developing boundaries that protect you and your family on a daily basis.

Please complete the Inventory activities for Lesson 16.

Lesson Sixteen Inventory

What were you Thinking when you read Lesson 16?

How are you Feeling after reading Lesson 16?

How is what you are Thinking and Feeling now going to help you with your recovery?

What are you going to change in your behavior after reading Lesson 16?

Plug-in with Prayer - How would you like God to help you right now?
(in the space below please talk directly with God…He is listening.)

What Bible verse in Lesson 16 will you commit to memorizing?

Lesson 16: Activity 1: - Are you Ready and Willing?

This means: are you ready and willing to share the plan with a recovery partner who will hold you accountable in love? Check the level you are currently at for each Recovery Plan prerequisite/goal:

A. Readiness Check:	Don't Do	Do 50/50	Do Daily
1. Surrender your will and the battle with your flesh to God daily	_____	_____	_____
2. Confess Your Sins – Keep short accounts, confessing to God quickly	_____	_____	_____
3. Convert Your Lifestyle – Renewing your mind, heart, values; changing your behavior.	_____	_____	_____
4. Committed to God's Purpose (not yours) for your life - setting new goals to serve others	_____	_____	_____
5. Eliminate Isolation and your "Secret" Life (all other acting out)	_____	_____	_____
6. Identifying clear "Boundaries" that protect you and others	_____	_____	_____
7. Create a Support Network – work only with those who build you up both Spiritually and Emotionally	_____	_____	_____
8. Plan to work and work the Plan – on a hourly, daily, weekly basis – recovery takes time	_____	_____	_____
9. Have Mercy on yourself as Jesus has Mercy on you	_____	_____	_____
10. Praise God for everything, his discipline as well as his mercies and blessings.	_____	_____	_____

Circle the steps you marked "Don't Do" and "50/50"...you must complete these on a daily basis to have a plan that will lead you out of insanity and into Sobriety.

B. Willingness Check: Mark below how willing you are to recover from darkness.

Not Very Willing ....Sort of Willing...Totally Willing

Anything less than total willingness will sabotage your recovery plan.

Lesson 16: Activity 2: -
Targeting Threats to You and Others

A. Identify Recovery Plan Targets

A recovery target is anything that needs a boundary put between it and you to protect yourself and others. Recovery targets are your addiction's "demands and commands" for your life. Recovery targets are anything that leads you into relapse; anything that breaks your promise, commitment, and focus on God. For instance, a financial target could be you misusing your credit card to sin; or, a neighborhood target could be your neighbor's bedroom window that you watch way too often.

Target Categories (circle the ones you need to create boundaries for):

- Emotions (yours or others) – Anger, fear, loneliness, sadness, grief, excitement, bitterness, envy,
- Family – Any reaction to (or by) a family member that sets you up to fail morally; such as incest, criticalness, rejection, domination, disrespect.
- Financial – A spending habit you have that pays for sinful behavior or creates debt stress that drives you into acting out.
- Internet – Going to XXX web sites, chat rooms, internet sex lines, cybersex, erotic stories, etc.
- Home – Things at home that cause you to sin: TV, home videos, alcohol, computers, drugs of any kind,
- Mental – Thoughts that set you up to fail; sexual thoughts, coveting things others have, judgmentalness, fantasies, worries, fears.
- Neighborhood – Anything in a one-mile radius of your house you need to stay away from: stores, people, places, massage parlors, etc.
- People – Anyone away from home who leads you into sinful thinking and/or behavior: co-workers, co-students, fellow addicts, etc.
- Phone – Using your phone to talk or text people about immoral things.
- Physical – Immoral things you need to stop doing with your body parts: talking, winking, touching, walking/driving places you should not be.

B. Prioritize Target Categories (rank most serious ones first)

1.

2.

3.

4.

5.

6.

7.

8.

9.

C. Set Boundaries (turning negatives into positives)

Definitions:

Target – Behavior you want to stop

Goal – Behavior you want to start

Boundary – What you promise God you will do to change targets into goals.

Examples:

Target (STOP)	Goal (START)	Boundary (protection from evil) (a commitment, promise to God; a request for protection)
1. Using Credit Cards to Sin	Use cards as God wills	1. Show all credit card statements to accountability partner 2. Hand cards over to someone to keep till you can keep Your Boundary Plan
2. Looking in neighbor's window	Read God's word instead	1. Read Bible far away from window 2. get counseling, confess...find out "why" you are looking 3. If need be, completely board up your window 4. Call a brother who can pray with you

Lesson 16: Activity 3 - Boundaries Protect You from Your Rituals

Freedom comes when you replace unhealthy behavior patterns with healthy ones. This occurs when you target behavior patterns (your rituals) that keep taking you into sinful behavior. A Ritual is a series of behavior steps that you take on a regular basis. It is your "pattern" for reaching the high (medication) you are seeking. After reviewing the example please list four acting-out Rituals that you want to change and identify Healthy steps to replace them.

1. EXAMPLE	Steps that keep "it" happening (behaviors to stop doing)	Steps that make "it" change (behaviors to start doing)
Buying/renting porn movies	1. Porn itch begins	1. Get on knees & pray, Praise God for ten things
	2. Get money for movies	2. Give all money, credit cards & check books to someone
	3. Drive by Porn store	3. Drive to a friend's house or have a friend over
	4. Go in and get movie, Go home and watch it	4. Read all of John in Bible, Talk to Jesus as you do

The easiest step to win the battle is on step one, then two, then three…it is very hard to succeed if you wait until step 4…by then you are committed to do the act. Have a plan in place and follow the plan before getting to steps 3 and 4.

1. Recovery Target	Steps that keep it happening (behaviors to stop doing)	Steps that make it change (behaviors to start doing)
	1.	1.
	2.	2.
	3.	3.
	4.	4.

2. Recovery Target

Steps that keep it happening
(behaviors to stop doing)
1.

2.

3.

4.

Steps that make it change
(behaviors to start doing)
1.

2.

3.

4.

3. Recovery Target

Steps that keep it happening
(behaviors to stop doing)
1.

2.

3.

4.

Steps that make it change
(behaviors to start doing)
1.

2.

3.

4.

4. Recovery Target

Steps that keep it happening
(behaviors to stop doing)
1.

2.

3.

4.

Steps that make it change
(behaviors to start doing)
1.

2.

3.

4.

Lesson 16: Activity 4 - How to Set Internal/External Boundaries

Let's consider how you can establish boundaries for your recovery. These targets are divided into Internal and External Threat categories. Identify the threats you are targeting on the left side and then list the behavioral steps that you need to stop and start to get healthier.

A. Internal Threats	Current Recovery Targets (behavior to stop doing)	Protection Plan/Steps (behavior to start doing)
Boundaries that Protect You from:	1.	1.
A. Your "Neg. Self-Talk": (Left brain)	2. 3. 4.	2. 3. 4.
B. Your Fantasies : (Right brain)	1. 2. 3. 4.	1. 2. 3. 4.
C. Your Needs (i.e., respect, security, independence, safety, acceptance, etc.):		
Need #1:	1. 2. 3. 4.	1. 2. 3. 4.
Need #2:	1. 2. 3. 4.	1. 2. 3. 4.
Need #3:	1. 2. 3. 4.	1. 2. 3. 4.

D. Your Wants (i.e., new car, electronics, clothes, house, promotion, etc.):

Want #1:
1.   1.
2.   2.
3.   3.
4.   4.

Want #2:
1.   1.
2.   2.
3.   3.
4.   4.

Want #3:
1.   1.
2.   2.
3.   3.
4.   4.

E. Your Fears (i.e., rejection, violence, failure, being unloved, etc.):

Fear #1:
1.   1.
2.   2.
3.   3.
4.   4.

Fear #2:
1.   1.
2.   2.
3.   3.
4.   4.

Fear #3:
1.   1.
2.   2.
3.   3.
4.   4.

F. Your Emotions (i.e., anger, loneliness, bitterness, unforgiveness, etc.):

Emotion #1:
1.   1.
2.   2.
3.   3.
4.   4.

Emotion #2:
1.   1.

	2.	2.
	3.	3.
	4.	4.
Emotion #3:	1.	1.
	2.	2.
	3.	3.
	4.	4.

B. External Boundaries
(people, places, things, time,
money issues)

External Threats	Current Recovery Targets (behavior to stop doing)	Protection Plan/Steps (behavior to start doing)
Boundaries that Protect You from:		
Your Addictive Rituals (acting out, self-destructive Patterns that control you)	1. 2. 3. 4.	1. 2. 3. 4.
Dominating People (demanding, controlling)	1. 2. 3. 4.	1. 2. 3. 4.
Spiritual Threats (spiritual protection)	1. 2. 3. 4.	1. 2. 3. 4.
Financial Threats (spending your money)	1. 2. 3. 4.	1. 2. 3. 4.
Health Threats (health decisions)	1. 2. 3. 4.	1. 2. 3. 4.
Interpersonal Threats (toxic relationships)	1. 2. 3. 4.	1. 2. 3. 4.

Work Threats	1.	1.
(Co-workers, boss, work load)	2.	2.
	3.	3.
	4.	4.
Time/Schedule Craziness	1.	1.
(Things you put before God)	2.	2.
	3.	3.
	4.	4.

The Journey Goes On...the Race must continue

Well this book has to end somewhere (Thank God!) but your journey in recovery will never end until Jesus comes back for you. Keep working on all the key components from this book so you can control your flesh rather than letting it controlling you.

There are many sections of the Bible that support what has been presented in this book. In closing and in summary, let me offer several sections that clearly state how you can find inner healing and learn how to walk as Jesus did.

Ephesians 4:17-24; 5: 3-14

(4:17-24)

So I tell you this, and insist on it in the Lord, that you must no longer live as the Gentiles do, in the futility of their thinking. They are darkened in their understanding and separated from the life of God because of the ignorance that is in them due to the hardening of their hearts. Having lost all sensitivity they have given themselves over to sensuality so as to indulge in every kind of impurity, with a continual lust for more.

You, however, did not come to know Christ that way. Surely you heard of him and were taught in him in accordance with the truth that is in Jesus. You were taught, with regard to your former way of life, to put off your old self, which is being corrupted by its deceitful desires; to be made new in the attitude of your minds; and to put on the new self, created to be like God in true righteousness and holiness.

(5:3-14)

But among you there must not be even a hint of sexual immorality, or of any kind of impurity, or of greed, because these are improper for God's holy people. Nor should there be obscenity, foolish talk or coarse joking, which are out of place, but rather thanksgiving. For of this you can be sure: No immoral, impure or greedy person—such a man is an idolater—has any inheritance in the kingdom of Christ and of God. Let no one deceive you with empty words, for because of such things God's wrath comes on those who are disobedient. Therefore do not be partners with them.

For you were once darkness, but now you are light in the Lord. Live as children of light (for the fruit of the light consists in all goodness, righteousness and truth) and find out what pleases the Lord. Have nothing to do with the fruitless deeds of darkness, but rather expose them. For it is shameful even to mention what the disobedient do in secret. But everything exposed by the light becomes visible, for it is light that makes everything visible. This is why it is said:

"Wake up, O sleeper, rise from the dead, and Christ will shine on you."

WINNING THE WAR WITH YOUR FLESH!

Plugging into Jesus' power (the Holy Spirit) gives you a chance to stand firm against your flesh, the world, and Satan. God has given you steps to follow, they are:

1. Surrender   Agree with God that Jesus died for your sins, washing them away with his loving sacrifice on the cross, so that your soul and spirit might be washed clean. Take up your cross daily by "plugging into" his Holy Spirit through Praise, Prayer, Reading and Memorizing His Word.

2. Submit   Surrender your will to God for His will for your life. Obey his commands so you are trained for the good works he has already created for you to do. Participate in God's "Boot Camp" so you will be strong enough to make the sacrifices that He will ask of you.

3. Sacrifice   Let God strip away all of the character flaws, relationships, plans, goals, things and commitments that get between you and the purpose He has created you to accomplish.

4. Serve   Fulfill your Christian ministry by putting others Spiritual (eternal) welfare before your safety and comfort.

5. Stand Firm   Focusing on the first four steps daily so that when evil comes against you it does not prevail or sidetrack you from God's purpose for your life. Be ready to always give your testimony for Jesus no matter what the forces against you might be. Learn to work and rest in God's Grace.

Everett Robinson has a Master's in Counseling Psychology and is the founder of Armor of Light Online ministries (www.armoroflightonling.com). He works with men who seek freedom from self-destructive sexual preferences, patterns and payoffs. In addition to providing men with Biblical Spiritual Coaching, he also teaches "Stand Firm" (an intensive recovery class for men struggling with addictive personalities) at Christ the King Community Church in Bellingham, Washington.

Everett is available by phone if you should wish personal coaching. Please email him at www. armoroflightonline.com if you wish to communicate with him.

CPSIA information can be obtained at www.ICGtesting.com
Printed in the USA
BVOW051955050812

297042BV00001B/47/P